PRAISE FOR "CAST A GIANT SHADOW"

Ted White is the real deal. He was kind of like a father figure to me but now is more like a brother. He was the king of television in the mid-60s. He was the man, by golly. He had shows going all the time.

> *Terry Leonard*
> *Legendary stuntman, stunt coordinator, actor, director*

Larry Meredith explores many of the high points of Ted White's extraordinary career in the movie industry. Ted has worked with ALL the film giants. He's generous of spirit and a downright nice guy. We've listened to many of those tales firsthand, and this book now offers readers the opportunity to enjoy his many astonishing Hollywood experiences.

> *Kym O'Connell-Todd and Mark Todd*
> *Authors of the* Silverville Saga *series*

Ted is one of the great men in the motion picture business. The man is a rock, a great teacher and a wonderful friend.

> *Dean Smith*
> *Former Olympic athlete, great stuntman, actor*

A book on the life and times of the great Ted White is long overdue. And who better to write it than Larry Meredith - a long-time friend of Ted's and a man with a satchel full of writing credentials. Ted White is a striking, imposing, and talented individual while at the same time remaining humble, composed, and gentlemanly. He remains one of the most significant behind-the-scenes participants in the history of American film. It's about time the rest of the world learned about him.

> *W. C. Jameson*
> *Author of* Amelia Earhart: Beyond the Grave

ALSO BY THE AUTHOR

This Cursed Valley

Cast a Giant

SHADOW

Hollywood Movie Great
Ted White
And the Evolution of American Movies
And TV in the 20th Century

LARRY K. MEREDITH

RASPBERRY
CREEK

BOOKS

For those legions of movie fans
whose lives have been enriched
by the films they've seen and enjoyed
that were made memorable by
individuals like Ted White

CAST A GIANT SHADOW

Copyright © 2017 by Larry K. Meredith

Raspberry Creek Books, Ltd.
www.raspberrycreekbooks.com

First edition: 2017

ISBN: 978-0-9851352-7-0

Library of Congress Control Number: 2017937584

Printed in the United States of America

www.raspberrycreekbooks.com

Raspberry Creek Books
Gunnison, Colorado and Tulsa, Oklahoma

Unless otherwise noted, all photos are from Ted White's personal collection

COVER DESIGN BY KYM O'CONNELL-TODD

INTRODUCTION

If you don't believe life can take strange turns, ask Ted White.

While growing up on a west-Texas ranch the strapping youngster watched the latest B Western movies when he could get to the small theatre in nearby Snyder, never dreaming that he might one day appear on that same silver screen. He saw some war movies, too, but had no idea that he would one terrible day be wounded by Japanese soldiers on a Pacific island called Iwo Jima.

In fact, as a youth Ted White had no specific plans about life as an adult. He might well have been satisfied with his job selling used cars at a Los Angeles Lincoln-Mercury dealership but fate intervened and his life changed drastically. That's what this book is about. Ted has combined an innate talent with an entrepreneurial spirit and has taken advantage of every opportunity to become a valuable and sought-after member of the film and television community.

Ted White in an early publicity photo

As movies changed and television was introduced into nearly every home in America, Ted White changed as well. He learned what people wanted and he tutored himself in new technology and the techniques of directing and camera work. Through hard work and a desire to make himself useful in this creative word, he carved out places for himself as a stuntman, actor and director.

His life has been like a movie itself. It unfolded in bits and pieces until one day he found himself appearing in a John Wayne movie and his career was set. He got started in the industry during Hollywood's heyday and in the early days of television. He was, indeed, in the right place at the right time. He fit the genre. Tall, handsome, outgoing and willing to do what needed to be done to "get the shot," he quickly became in demand and soon was travelling the world for roles in one film after another.

The man has appeared in literally hundreds of films and television shows, sometimes in roles that are uncredited. Frequently, he is listed as part of the crew under "stunts." Often, his name appears as a character in the production or as Second Unit Director. What movie-goers almost never know is that their film hero or heroine is, in most cases, not the one performing the dangerous, death-defying, exciting action they are witnessing. In almost every situation it's a stuntman or stuntwoman. Very often it has been Ted White.

Ted White has lived a life that many men can only dream about. A Texas native who grew up on a ranch, he became a Marine and fought his way across the Pacific in World War II, being wounded twice in his legs on Iwo Jima. He played college football for Bud Wilkinson at the University of Oklahoma, was a boxing champion and a professional rodeo roper who married a one-time Miss Oklahoma before finding his way into the world of movies.

He has worked with, and often was a stunt double for, such stars as John Wayne, Clark Gable, James Garner, Charlton Heston, Lee Marvin, Fess Parker, Jeff Bridges, Walter Matthau, Gregory Peck, Anthony Quinn, Rock Hudson, Andy Griffith, William Holden, Dean Martin, Kirk Douglas, Gary Cooper, Sidney Pottier and many others.

He worked alongside Marilyn Monroe, Jane Fonda, Constance Towers, Kim Baysinger, and Lana Turner, to name just a few leading ladies.

He has taken orders from the world's great directors including such notables as Howard Hawks and John Ford.

He has won a Taurus Award (the top award to stuntmen and akin to an Oscar), is a member of the Hollywood Stuntmen's Hall of Fame and is a co-founder of the Stuntmen's Association of Motion Pictures. In 2011 he received the "Reel Cowboys Silver Spur Award" and joined other well-known honorees such as Glenn Ford, Ernest Borgnine, James Garner, John Ford, and dozens of others.

Ted White says he can't count the times he's been shot and killed in films or television productions. He has (in the movies) gone into space, fought alongside Spartacus, fenced with King Arthur, stood side-by-side with Custer on the Little Big Horn, served as a Texas Ranger and robbed trains with Jesse James. He has ridden in the Oklahoma Land Rush, been shot by Danny Glover, joined Robin Hood and his band as they saved Maid Marian, helped establish the nation of Israel and knocked Jeff Bridges out cold. He's played one of the world's great "slashers," been an American Indian, shot and killed himself (in two different roles) from the walls of the Alamo, set the Lone Ranger on his path of doing good and righting wrongs, and helped capture King Kong.

He has turned down roles that would have made him millions of dollars.

He's been battered, bruised and broken.

He's travelled the world and he's had more fun than most groups of a dozen men all together.

"I wouldn't have missed it for the world," he says.

The author has known Ted White for nearly 20 years. When first approached about publishing his biography Ted was reluctant to consider it. "I'm not that interesting," he said. As readers of this book are soon to discover, he was wrong.

Fortunately, he ultimately agreed and eventually, after countless days of listening to his fascinating stories, his reminiscences about good times with old friends, his sadness at the loss of many of them, his lessons in movie-making and his tales about good directors and bad, we had accumulated many hours of recorded interviews. There were additional hours of taped conversations with his wife Jeri and his sons and some fellow actors who were more than happy to talk about "ol' Ted."

For days we sat in his Colorado living room with the Gunnison River rushing by outside the patio doors as he talked about his life. All the author had to do was to suggest a topic, push the "record" button and listen to him tell stories that were hilarious, sad, exciting and always interesting.

Ted White has "Cast a Giant Shadow" over Hollywood and the television studios and his career has been an exemplary one of hard work, strong beliefs and dedication to doing a good job that reflects well on "his" industry.

Following is his story.

Larry K. Meredith
Gunnison, CO

1

FADE IN

A PLUME OF dense dust rises wildly behind a weathered Jeep as it speeds across the broad Serengeti Plain in southeastern Africa. Looming ominously in the distance is Mt. Meru, at 15,000 feet an active volcano that erupted most recently in 1910. Clear blue sky dotted with specks of tiny white clouds wraps the savanna in choking heat.

Seated precariously in the passenger side of the Jeep, screen star Bruce Cabot is unconcerned with the scenery or the heat. His only thought is to avoid the deadly sharp protruding horn of a giant rhinoceros which runs furiously alongside the vehicle with murderous intent in its angry eyes. The rhino races between the Jeep and a modified flatbed vehicle bearing three huge movie cameras and a dozen nervous crew members. Suddenly the crazed animal lowers his head and bores his single sabre-like horn into the side of Cabot's leg. Blood spurts into the dusty air and the Jeep veers away from the animal as Cabot tries to stop the crimson flow and stay conscious.

The sequence is to become part of the now-legendary movie, *Hatari*.

Ted about to be gored in Hatari

In another scene John Wayne, the film's lead character, rides a specially made seat on the front bumper of a large truck holding a long pole with a noose on the end. As the truck chases a giraffe Wayne attempts to slip the noose over the animal's head and down its slender neck. The truck races barely behind the giraffe's long legs and tries desperately to keep up with its twists and turns.

But that's not Cabot being gored by the rhino. And that's not Wayne attempting to loop the noose around that giraffe.

In an iconic horror movie called *Friday the 13th: The Final Chapter* the hockey-mask-wearing Jason Vorhees slashes his way through horrifying scenes of blood and gore. However, the movie's credits don't list the individual who many say is the most believable and frightening Jason ever.

Why the actor isn't credited will become clear later on. Despite not being credited, thousands of people flock to his table at autograph signings (once he even autographed a woman's breast above a tattoo of his face in his role as Jason).

In *The Misfits* starring Clark Gable, Marilyn Monroe and Montgomery Clift, the trio head for the Nevada desert to capture wild mustangs to be sold for dog meat. In a scene that has become famous, Gable tries frantically to keep one of the horses from escaping by grabbing it by its ears and holding on as he is lifted off the ground and tossed about like a rag doll by the terrified animal.

Except that it's not Gable doing the wrestling.

James Garner, playing an aging Wyatt Earp, sits in the front seat of an open cockpit bi-plane piloted by Bruce Willis who is portraying Tom Mix. The movie is *Sunset* and Earp (Garner) has journeyed to Hollywood to provide technical advice to one of Mix's (Willis) movies. As the plane careens wildly through the air, Earp is panic stricken. It suddenly goes into a terrifying dive toward the ground far below and finally levels out just in time to avoid crashing through a barn. Garner, as Earp, is terrified throughout the flight, thinking he is going to die.

But of course it wasn't Garner in that plane at all.

The actor in all those films, and many others, might well be one of the most famous movie stars you've never heard of.

His name is Ted White. At least that's his screen name.

2

TED WHITE'S CAREER has bookended an era of movies and television that saw enormous changes in the quality of the productions, the popular subjects and in public tastes and expectations. In the fifties he played an important part in the early days of television viewing when the networks were feeling their ways into how best to utilize the new medium and when Westerns were all the rage. He was (and is) a big man among big men who became heroes to a movie-going and TV-watching public that equated the successes of their heroes with American might and right.

As America's tastes changed and Westerns waned, Ted changed with them. The public continued to crave "Action" films but, in addition to riding fast horses and getting shot off of roofs while cattle stampeded below, Ted drove fast cars and leapt out of windows in pursuit of the bad guys.

The production quality of movies and television shows was getting better and better and Ted found ways to become ever more valuable to studios and independent producers. He devoted himself to learning film techniques, proper lenses and directing skills. His multi-faceted talents earned respect throughout the industry.

The improvements in the entertainment world occurred, in large part, thanks to those unheralded individuals like Ted White who did the work deemed far too dangerous for the stars, devised ways to make action scenes more realistic and exciting, and who labored behind the scenes in many other ways that resulted in wonderful visual scenes, better acting by the stars and happier and more efficient crew members.

Ted leaping from a 2nd story window in an episode of Murder She Wrote

The second half of the 20th Century saw an evolution in the quality, scope, subject matter and world-wide appeal of Hollywood movies and TV productions. At the same time, Ted White and many of his brothers and sisters who toiled in the background of those we remember as the great stars of the era, reinvented themselves and found ways to participate in that evolution and to contribute meaningfully to the industry of which they are a part.

Ted White comes across as a serious man who is not to be messed with.

When Rock Hudson once asked him to get him a cup of coffee he told the actor to "get your own damn coffee." Yet he called famous film directors "Mr." Hawks and "Mr." Ford out of respect for their work and their professionalism.

On the other hand, he has told directors they were wrong in what they wanted to do and that, if they persisted, he'd walk off the set and turn them in to the Director's Guild. He's a rough cut of a larger-than-life man, hewn from the toughest timber in the forest.

But he can be as gracious and pleasant as the most charming gentlemen in polite society.

In his film roles he has played good men but also mean, tough hombres, hoodlums, one of the greatest "slashers" in horror film history, and dirty, filthy, rotten scoundrels. But when he goes before the public he dresses nicely in sports coat and slacks, shunning the bluejeans and ragged dress of many others, saying he wants to represent "his" industry positively.

He loves to laugh and play practical jokes on his friends. But he is quick-tempered and opinionated.

He can sit for hours and read books on many subjects and remember the important points.

But he's a man of action who would just as soon be fishing or hunting or driving his truck somewhere new and exciting.

He's proud of being a World War II Marine but is reluctant to talk about his experiences in some of the bloodiest fighting in the Pacific.

Ted White is at his best when he is in the company of old friends, laughing with them and glorying in their shared history and in the knowledge that they believe he is an interesting man who has carved a fulfilling life out of a willingness to take chances, take advice and pay attention to the things that matter.

Behind the masculinity and the outward appearance of total bravado, there is an ever-present twinkle in Ted White's eyes that betrays a wonderful sense of humor and enjoyment of life that has endeared him to many of the industry's top stars, other stuntmen and stuntwomen and to crew members for whom he would stick up at every opportunity.

He's done that during a film career of more than half a century.

This is his story. Most of it came from Ted himself as he reminisced and laughed about the good times or shook his head and pondered the sadness that resulted from accidents, betrayals and sometimes just outright stupidity. Some of the story came from his family, and some of it from friends he's known for decades and who aren't shy about speaking up.

It begins with a name-change.

Another of Ted's early publicity photos

2

What can you do?

TED WHITE IS NOT his real name, of course. Few stars of the silver screen keep their given names when they enter the movies. Ted's wasn't even "Ted." Nor was it "White." He began life as Alex Bayouth but a secretary in the Screen Actors' Guild told him, when he went by to join, that nobody would remember Alex Bayouth. A college coach had begun calling him "Ted" years ago so he said how about that? "You look like a Ted Knight," she said. But after checking her list she found that "Knight" was already taken. So she changed it to Ted White and that was that.

Pretty soon "Ted White" was getting shot, falling off of speeding horses, swimming with killer whales, getting gored by rhinos, climbing fences with Spartacus, jumping out of windows, threatening pretty ladies, slashing college kids and cracking up with Dom DeLuise – all in the process of making one great movie after another.

It began when Ted was selling cars in the Los Angeles area in the early 1950s. By then he was married to Miss Oklahoma and had two small boys. Shorty Johnson, a friend he'd met in Oklahoma City during his college years and then living in Los Angeles, was home visiting his parents in Oklahoma and urged Ted to move to L.A. where he could get a job. Ted packed up and moved his family to the west coast with a desire to get into aeronautics. At Douglas Aircraft he worked in a group correcting malfunctions in older planes and earned about $125.00 per week. Discouraged, he dropped by Frost Lincoln-Mercury where Johnson worked. His friend told him he could make $150 by selling only one car.

"That's more than I make in a week," Ted said. Before long he was a car salesman and soon became the manager of the used car department.

He later sold a new Mercury to Roydon Clark, who was an extra in the motion picture business (later to become a great stuntman). Clark told Ted, who was big and good-looking, that he ought to get into pictures. Ted said no thanks. He felt settled down in the car dealership. But Clark began stopping by the dealership now and then and formed a friendship with Ted. One day he called and said "we're making a picture at Warner Brothers. Come on over and watch. I'll leave a pass for you at the gate."

Warner Brothers' studios were not far from the car dealership. Curious, Ted went and stood quietly on the sidelines. "It was a Western starring Mamie Van Doren," he said. Ted wore a sports coat, a tie and dress slacks and watched the filming of a scene where a cowboy tried to rope a man standing on a porch but continually failed.

"Why hell," Ted said to Roy Clark who stood beside him. "I could do that."

"You can?" Clark answered.

Ted shrugged a "yes."

Clark walked to the director and said "see that guy over there? He says he can rope." Howard Koch, the director, beckoned Ted over and asked if he could ride horseback. "I've been doing it since I was a kid," Ted replied.

Ted shook out a loop and roped whatever was nearby. Koch was impressed and told Ted he'd do well in the business. He offered to get him into the Screen Extras' Guild and when Ted went to the office to get signed up the man there asked "What can you do?"

"Well, nothin', really," Ted replied. Despite that, he said, on the recommendation of Howard Koch, "they let me in."

"Letting him in" was a decision that would prove beneficial to not only Ted White but also to the movie industry as a whole. Here was a tall, muscular man who would be willing to carry out incredibly dangerous stunts that would make even a mediocre motion picture better. Also, he was willing to take advantage of every opportunity to learn the finer points of the film world.

Now that he had his Screen Extra's Guild card, Alex Bayouth (aka Ted White) was embarking on an adventure that was to last a lifetime and that would eclipse an already storied life that had been full of exuberance, recklessness and life-threatening experiences in the bloodiest battles of World War II.

8

3

It still haunts me today

IN 1943 TED was barely 17 when he told his father he wanted to enlist in the Marine Corps. Ted, a brother and four sisters lived with their widowed father on a ranch near Snyder, Texas, southeast of Lubbock. "Why the Marines?" his dad asked. Ted, who had not yet grown nearly to his eventual 6' 4" height and was a skinny 150 pounds to boot, took a stand and said he and two buddies had definitely decided on the Marines.

Grudgingly, his father drove the boys to Dallas where Ted was the only one who passed the Marine's physical and mental tests. His two buddies ended up in the Army and within three days Ted was on a train to San Diego for Marine boot camp. After several months of training he eventually was assigned to the newly formed 4th Marine Division that would become famous for its involvement in some of the fiercest fighting of the war.

Ted as a 17-year-old Marine in 1943

The stories of his wartime experiences are difficult for Ted to recount. "I'll have to take a sleeping pill tonight after I talk about this," he told the author. This tough man, often reluctant to show his emotions, paused for a long several seconds. Like many veterans of his age he tried not to think too often or in too much detail about the horror of war and of the many friends who died on Pacific beaches. "For many years I haven't been able to talk about it. In fact, in many instances I've not been able to sit through a war movie because it brought back too many bad memories."

According to 4th Division records, it became the first to go directly into combat from the states, landing on the island of Roi-Namur in the Kwajalein Atoll on February 1, 1944, and it was the first to capture Japanese territory in the Pacific. And then things got worse.

In June the 4th landed on Saipan and suffered 2,000 casualties in the first two days of battle. Finally, 25 days later, the U.S. flag was raised on the island but only after the Division sustained 5,181 casualties killed, wounded and missing.

A month later, Ted and his division stormed ashore on Tinian. There they faced more than 9,000 Japanese troops in a battle that lasted nine days and earned the Division the Presidential Unit Citation.

Then came Iwo Jima.

"We'd been at sea for six or seven days when we were told that Iwo was our destination," Ted said. "Our officers said the Japanese soldiers had been there for years and were solidly entrenched but they would be bombed and strafed for days before the landing. "

Ted, a corporal by then, had no idea how bad it would be.

Iwo Jima was a small volcanic island of little more than eight square miles but it was supremely important. Its strategic location half way between Tokyo and Saipan reduced the distance for B-29 bombers to reach Tokyo from 1,400 miles flying out of Tinian to only 660 miles from Iwo.

Nearly 23,000 Japanese manned the most elaborate fortified defenses of World War Two. In the end, the Marines turned the battle into a literal blood bath for the Japanese with only 216 Japanese troops surviving. In addition to the 22,000 Japanese killed, the Marines suffered 25,000 total causalities of killed, wounded and missing.

Ted was in the first wave ashore and by the time his squad of 12 men had advanced 50 yards seven of them were dead, including the squad's lieutenant and sergeant.

"We dug in as best we could," he said. "It's tough to talk about . . ."

Learning that the squad was without leadership, a sergeant from another group told Ted that he was now in charge. Within the next two hours two more men were hit and the three who were left were still pinned down. Finally, Ted's group was reinforced with half a dozen men who had landed in the second wave. Following orders, they began to move to another location but were pinned down again by heavy machine gun fire from a blockhouse 150 yards away. A lieutenant crept to the squad's location and told Ted to "take charge of these guys. You're now a second lieutenant."

"I'll do what I have to do," Ted replied.

He was barely 19 years old.

"We got through that day but lost two more men," he said. "Three others were wounded as we got to within 30 or 40 yards of the blockhouse." The squad received an order to move forward and suddenly Ted was hit in both legs. He went down as the squad continued to move toward the blockhouse.

"I passed out and when I woke up I was on the beach," he recalled. He lay there for nearly seven hours before medics began moving men to a hospital ship, the *USS Comfort*. "Men were lying in the aisles and medical personnel were frantically trying to take care of the most seriously hurt."

Ted doesn't remember much about the trip back to Pearl Harbor as he faded in and out of consciousness. The seas were too rough for the surgeons to operate during the trip and he would spend nearly five months undergoing surgery and healing up in a hospital. He was later shipped back to Division headquarters on limited duty but kept his battlefield commission as an officer.

After an assignment in Japan following that country's surrender Ted was back in San Diego during the filming of *The Sands of Iwo Jima* starring John Wayne. He and another Marine were assigned as "technical advisors" to the film. "A lot of motion picture making is just standing around and my legs were hurting badly by then," he said. After two weeks of involvement with the film, Ted had had enough.

When he later saw the completed film Ted said it was "nothing like the real thing. It's impossible to show 7,000 men dead," he said, "impossible to show the blood, the pieces of men..."

Even Clint Eastwood's films made in the 21st Century "didn't scratch the surface," he said.

After his stint as a movie technical advisor, Ted was asked to return to Camp Lejeune but decided instead to resign his commission.

"Those war experiences still haunt me today," he said. In fact, after attending half a dozen reunions of the unit, he quit going. "It was a very important part of my life," he says, "but most of my friends from there are now gone. Guys you hit the beach with, who you went through training with…we'd been together a long time. There are very few of us left. I would have sleepless nights for weeks afterward."

Years later, in 2010, Ted was invited by a Marine Sergeant Major to be his guest on the reviewing platform of a Marine graduation ceremony from boot camp. Reluctant to show up in civilian clothes and stand before thousands of Marines wearing dress blues and greens, Ted graciously turned down the invitation. "I felt like I'd be disgracing the Marine Corps," he said. His wife and sons disagreed but, as usual, Ted stuck to his guns and stayed away.

World War II was an incredibly important part of his life and its impact upon him had been significant. But, by the late 1940s, Ted had put the war behind him and began another phase of life that would take him in more unexpected directions.

4

Swimming with Killer Whales

WITH THE WAR OVER and his small exposure to the motion picture business behind him, Ted returned home and enrolled at the University of Oklahoma.

"When I got home my dad had to look twice to make sure it was me," Ted recalls. He had grown to his full height of 6' 4" and weighed more than 200 pounds. Grown up and full of the confidence that his wartime experiences had ingrained in him, he accepted a scholarship to play football for OU's famous coach Bud Wilkinson. "As I recall," Ted said, "we won 27 straight games in those years until Army finally beat us with Glenn Davis and Doc Blanchard, two of the greatest football players ever."

While at OU Ted got interested in boxing after he met the boxing coach who was a former heavyweight contender. Pretty soon he was playing football and boxing at the same time. He was in great shape and claimed he could go three rounds "standing on my head." In those days boxing was an intercollegiate sport and he also fought Golden Gloves and AAU. With no money for travel he couldn't compete in the national AAU championships in New York. However, in a fight in Kansas City he met the AAU winner and knocked him out in the second round. He never lost in 88 fights.

Ted had thought he might go into coaching but California beckoned and he headed for the land of opportunity where he found his way into the motion picture business.

Even after being a star athlete at a famous football school like Oklahoma, after earning a Purple Heart on Iwo Jima, after marrying, fathering two boys and becoming a successful salesman, Ted began at the bottom in the movies. Even though he started at that low rung on the ladder, Ted's entry into the motion picture business in the 1950s actually couldn't have come at a better time. Despite the onslaught of television, audiences were drawn to movie theatres to see such epics as *The Robe, The Ten Commandments,* and *Ben Hur.* The science fiction genre began its own "golden age" with such notable films as *The Day the Earth Stood Still, The Thing from Another World, The War of the Worlds* and *Creature from the Black Lagoon,* among many others.

Highly noted actors such as James Stewart, John Wayne and Marlon Brando were at the peak of their popularity. Cary Grant and Deborah Kerr teamed up for one of the most famous tear-jerkers in movie history – *An Affair to Remember.* James Dean and Paul Newman initiated the rise of the anti-hero. Elvis Presley jumped from driving trucks to the *Ed Sullivan Show* and then to the movies.

It was also a decade of changing technology. Cinemascope, VistaVision and Cinerama, as well as the introduction of 3-D film, drew more and more people – especially young people – away from television sets.

Ted White was in on the ground floor, even if it meant taking on a smelly job.

"My first real job in the movies was on a Western," he said, "and all I did was to lead a billygoat around in the streets. I did that for two weeks."

In those days extras weren't provided a wardrobe. He wore Levis and an old shirt and Western boots. At night he came home smelling like that billygoat, took off his clothes on the back porch and hurried into the shower. He was making $12.50 a day.

Another early publicity photo of Ted

One day, Ted said, the crew brought in a number of stuntmen. There was a big gun battle in the middle of the town. Men rode horses wildly through the street, horses were falling, riders were falling, a man was shot off the roof and fell to the ground.

Ted was wowed! He edged up to Chuck Roberson, the man who had done the fall. He was the same size as Ted and the two looked very much alike. "How much do you guys make?" Ted asked.

Roberson replied that he normally made $54.00 a day but by doing that fall he had earned $275.00. Ted's eyes widened and he said "I just quit working as an extra."

With the help of director Howard Koch, Ted was able to get into the Screen Actors' Guild and suddenly became "Ted White."

Soon after that, attempting to become known and get work, Ted found various ways to get onto the studio grounds. Often, he'd wait until the stunt guys came in and he would walk in with the group as though he belonged. He also frequented the casting offices, saying "my name is Ted White and I'm a stuntman. Do you have something for me to do today?"

Finally, he received a call from a woman in casting – he remembers her name was Dorothy – who asked if he could swim. Ted told her he could. "Then be here at 3 o'clock tomorrow morning."

"Three in the morning?" he asked. Before she could say yes, Ted told her he'd be there.

"What should I bring?" he asked. She said the studio would furnish what he needed.

At three the next morning Ted and others were driven to the coast and put aboard a naval mine destroyer. On the ship were Andy Griffith and Claude Akins.

By 10 a.m. the ship was about 40 miles out to sea. "Do you have any idea what we have to do?" asked Tom Hennesy, another stuntman. Ted shook his head no.

Finally the first assistant director approached the two new stuntmen. "Here's the shot," he said. He explained that one man would be out in a small boat which capsizes, the man is not able to swim and the current would take the boat away. "That'll be you," he said, pointing to Hennesy. Turning to Ted, he said "you'll dive off the bow of the boat and swim out and get him. You bring him back to the boat and start up a rope ladder hanging over the side. At that point we'll cut and insert the real actors."

"That's it?" Ted asked. The man nodded.

They waited while the crew set up the shot and looked for the right light. Lunchtime came and the crew threw the garbage overboard.

The garbage attracted a group of killer whales.

Nevertheless, the director shouted to put the men in the water and "let's shoot it."

Hennesy whispered to Ted: "are they talking about us getting in the water with those whales?"

"I think they are," Ted replied.

Thinking quickly, Ted recalled that when he had watched other stuntmen work they had often talked to the assistant directors about how much money they wanted for doing a certain kind of stunt. He told Hennesy they needed to bring up the subject.

After they'd dressed in clothes that matched those worn by Griffith and Akins, Ted approached the assistant. "This is pretty dangerous with those killer whales out there," he said. "What do you intend to pay us?

The assistant had no idea and asked what Ted had in mind. Ted didn't know either, but blurted out "one thousand dollars for each of us."

The assistant shrugged and said okay.

With Hennesy in the water, Ted dove off the bow, swam to the supposed drowning man and started swimming back as several killer whales zigzagged back and forth around the two. Back at the ship, they were halfway up the rope ladder when the director called "cut." The camera was shooting down and showing only the tops of their heads. Griffith and Akins were inserted into the scene and Ted and his friend were through for the day.

"We got back around 5 p.m. and with overtime, we each made about $3,000 for the day's work," Ted said.

Ted's photo soon appeared among those in an album in the casting office. Actors and stuntmen were pictured with their height and weight and their skills listed – horseback ride, fight, swim, box, high fall, etc.

Ted was soon in demand and working steadily.

5

Bouncing off the Barn Door

As TED BECAME known, he found himself being called frequently to do stunts in various films, play small roles or double for a number of stars.

In *Lone Star*, for example, he doubled both Clark Gable and Broderick Crawford. He appeared with Lucille Ball and Desi Arnaz in *The Long, Long Trailer*; in *Giant* with James Dean, Rock Hudson and Elizabeth Taylor; in *Friendly Persuasion* and *Man of the West* with Gary Cooper; in *The Big Country* with Gregory Peck and Charlton Heston; and in many others.

One day, though, in the late 1950s, he got a call from Warner Brothers Studios that would lead to a long and wonderful association with a major star and one of the world's great directors.

A woman called from the studio and asked, innocently enough, if Ted was busy. When he said he wasn't, she said "we have a job for you. Pack some things up. You're going to be gone for a while."

She then told him to go to "Western costume" and to the green room.

"When you go to Western costume, the green room is where the stars get dressed," Ted said. "It's a large room and very private. Extras have little cubby holes about eight feet square."

In the green room the wardrobe people brought out some Western clothes and Ted tried them on. They fit and that was it.

The next day Ted and others were flown to Tucson, Arizona, where the film would be shot at Old Tucson Studios, a long-time movie set. Among those on the plane was Chuck Roberson, the stuntman whom Ted had asked about what stuntmen made on that first set years ago. Also there were two stuntmen who would become lifelong friends – Jack Williams and Bobby

17

Herron. On the first day of shooting Ted and the others were picked up at their hotel at 5:30 a.m. and driven to the set where he was dressed in the clothes he'd tried on in the green room back in Burbank. Ted walked onto the set and immediately came face-to-face with John Wayne. Wayne was wearing clothes identical to what Ted was wearing. Ted says he literally froze. Wayne looked Ted up and down and said "what's your name, son?"

Ted managed to stammer out "Ted White."

Wayne smiled and said "Well, Ted, it's nice to have you on the set. Do you play chess?"

"Yessir."

"When we get a little time we'll play chess," Wayne said.

Ted recalls that he was shaking like a leaf. "I went over and sat down and a couple of other stuntmen came over. I said 'Jesus Christ, do you know I'm doubling John Wayne?'"

The two said "sure, didn't you know?"

Ted said "Hell no, I didn't know."

The movie was *Rio Bravo* and featured, along with Wayne, Dean Martin, Ricky Nelson, Ward Bond, Angie Dickinson and Walter Brennan. The film's director was Howard Hawks.

The main cast and crew of Rio Bravo. Standing, left, Walter Brennan: seated, Dean Martin, director Howard Hawks and John Wayne. Far right, Ricky Nelson.
(Photo courtesy of Boyd Magers, www.westernclippings.com)

18

Soon the wardrobe man came to Ted with a long white coat called a duster. He told Ted that some important people were to shortly be on the set and that Mr. Wayne didn't like people to know he was being doubled. Ted put on the duster, walked onto the set and immediately met them all – Martin, Nelson, Dickinson and Brennan.

"Nice to meet you Ted," Martin said. "Are you one of the actors on the show?"

"No," Ted replied proudly. "I'm a stuntman and I'm doubling John Wayne."

The first opportunity to double Wayne, who plays Sheriff John T. Chance, came in a scene where one of the "bad guys" shoots Ward Bond, but thinks he has missed and runs into a barn.

The film's assistant director Paul Helmick gave Ted the setup. "The barn doors are closed," he said. "You're back about 35 yards with a rifle in your hand. You run and hit the barn doors any way you want and they'll burst open. You land inside the door and flip over a bale of hay and come up with the rifle. That's a cut and we'll put Duke in." It seemed simple enough to Ted who was more and more nervous about doubling Wayne for the first time. "I was pumped and when they hollered 'action!' I ran as hard as I could and hit those barn doors."

And bounced off!

"I couldn't believe it," Ted says. "There was supposed to be a balsa wood bar across the inside that would break easily."

Ted heard the Director Howard Hawks call out asking if he was okay. Ted said "yessir" but his knee was hurting, along with his shoulder and the side of his head.

In the background he heard Wayne and Ward Bond laughing loudly. Ted walked behind the barn doors and saw that the balsa wood had been replaced with a large 2" X 8" timber.

Director Hawks called the prop man over and said "what's this doing here? Where's the balsa wood?"

The prop man sheepishly replied that "Mr. Wayne and Mr. Bond replaced it. They said they wanted to test him."

Other stuntmen joined the group and told Ted that this was Wayne's regular way of testing new people. Later Wayne asked if Ted was okay. He said he was fine and laughed it off. Wayne patted his sore shoulder and said "good."

There were other stunts in the movie but that was the first and it earned respect for Ted from among the entire crew.

Ted would later be involved in four other major films with Wayne. He did *The Horse Soldiers*, *The Alamo* and the one he is most proud of, *Hatari*. He also doubled Jim Hutton and drove a bulldozer into a raging oilfield fire in *Hellfighters*, starring Wayne and directed by Andrew V. McLaglen. The story is about a group of oil well firefighters and is based loosely on the life of Red Adair (played by Wayne).

He had other opportunities to work with Duke but was always involved in other projects and was unable to get away.

Ted was actually taller than Wayne by an inch and when pictured with the man was always standing downhill from him. "Wayne was a proud man," Ted says, "and rightfully so. He started as a prop man and finally got in those early Westerns that were made in two or three days. As everyone knows, his big break came from John Ford in the movie *Stagecoach*."

Ted posing with John Wayne
on the set of The Horse Soldiers

6

The Duke and *Rio Bravo*

TED'S INABILITY TO accept offers to appear in several John Wayne films was often due to the fact that he was tied up with a television series. He appeared in numerous episodes of more than 40 series for TV and once was often working for several major productions at the same time. Among them were such favorites as *Daniel Boone, Sheriff of Cochise, Man Without a Gun, Maverick, Cheyenne, Lawman* and others.

He was working five days a week, jumping from one set to another, but was able to be at home with his family at the same time.

When he worked with Wayne it meant being gone for long periods of time. The work was exciting and the locales were often exotic but Ted missed his family. Still, doubling John Wayne and playing roles opposite him was an incredible boost to his career, and it was good money at the same time.

When shooting *Rio Bravo*, for example, he was gone for more than three weeks. But the experience was worth it, Ted says. The film was well-received but many of the cast members had no idea at the time that director Howard Hawks saw it as a spirited response to Gary Cooper's *High Noon* which Wayne felt was "un-American."

"Although it's a classic Western, not unlike *High Noon*," Movieguide reports, "in *Rio Bravo* Hawks actually wanted to make a riposte to what he saw as that film's highly immoral premise. Unlike that film's sheriff, who pleads for help from his town's civilians, Chance is constantly turning down help, reasoning that having armed amateurs around would simply give the [bad guys] 'more targets to shoot at.' Better to leave it to the professionals."

The movie is referred to as "one of the great Westerns" in the 1990 _Overlook Film Encyclopedia: The Westerns_, edited by Phil Hardy.

"The majesty (and humor) of _Rio Bravo_...is that it shows that independence, self-respect and dignity are essential but mustn't get in the way of relationships," the book states. "Hence, in a shift that would be intensified in _El Dorado_ (1966) and _Rio Lobo_ (1970) which, with _Rio Bravo_ form a loose trilogy, the film sees Hawks treating his characters less as a group and more as a family."

Terry Teachout agrees. Writing in _American Cowboy Magazine_ he calls _Rio Bravo_ "one of those supremely rare works of art that has the power to take you out of yourself and set you down again in a parallel universe of pleasure, one in which nothing matters but the experience of watching a group of gifted men and women doing something as well as it can possibly be done."

He calls _Rio Bravo_ "a string of pearls, an anthology of perfect lines delivered perfectly, most of them by Wayne," and says "it is a sexy comedy, a good old-fashioned shoot-'em-up and meditation of masculine friendship, all rolled into one gloriously unhurried package."

In _Rio Bravo_, John T. Chance (Wayne) is surrounded by friends. Among them are Dean Martin (Dude), a recovering alcoholic; a young gunfighter called Colorado (Ricky Nelson); a crippled "Stumpy" played by Walter Brennan; and a young woman named Feathers (Dickinson in an early featured role). Chance repeatedly turns down aid from anyone he doesn't think is capable of helping him, though in the final shootout they come to help him anyway.

Director Howard Hawks goes over a scene with John Wayne, Dean Martin and Ricky Nelson. (Photo courtesy of Boyd Magers, www.westernclippings.com)

Reports of the time say Wayne was anxious to do another Western. It had been at least three years since *The Searchers*. Hawks was also looking for a vehicle that would restore his once proud Hollywood name. *The Big Sleep* directed by Hawks several years earlier, and which starred Humphrey Bogart and Lauren Bacall, had been his last successful endeavor. It was the first film version of Raymond Chandler's 1939 novel of the same name.

"What a gentleman," Ted said of Hawks. "He was one of the finest directors I ever worked with." A good director, he said, knows his story, his script and his actors. "With Howard Hawks, there was seldom a loud word with anyone."

Stars John Wayne and Angie Dickinson
visit with director Howard Hawks
(Photo courtesy of Boyd Magers, www.westernclippings.com)

When he wanted filming to begin, Ted said, Hawks never shouted "action!" Instead he said "camera." He felt the word "action" indicated that something physical was to happen and that was not always the case.

The simple word "camera" told the actors the camera was rolling and it was time for them to start doing their parts.

Hawks had other peculiarities which were respected by the cast and crew. Usually, when a scene is finished and the director calls "cut" the crew begins talking and moving about. "But when Hawks finished a scene he would stand by the camera, think about it, check what lens had been used and when he was satisfied he'd turn around and ask which scene was next," Ted said. "The crew, out of respect for Hawks, remained quiet until he was ready. Then they would begin talking and getting ready for the next shot."

Ted said Hawks cared for all his actors. He used the same crew over and over again and they learned to trust his decisions and, after working with him, were able to anticipate how he might want a scene set up.

"All the big name directors had something magic within them that came out when they got behind a camera and started putting shots together," Ted said. "They knew how to put actors in the right position to make their moves and say their lines. It made you want to do it like they wanted. They were telling you what they knew and you knew you should take advantage of it."

Roger Ebert, the film critic for the *Chicago Sun-Times* from 1967 until his death in April of 2013, agrees with Ted about the importance of a film's director.

"You see that some movies are made by individuals and others by committees," Ebert wrote. "Some movies are simply about the personalities they capture (the Marx Brothers and Astaire and Rogers). Others are about the mastery of genre, from *Star Wars*, which attempts to transcend swashbuckling, to *Detour*, which attempts to hide in the shadows of *noir*. Most good movies are about the style, tone and vision of their makers. A director will strike a chord in your imagination, and you will be compelled to seek out the other works."

Fittingly, in her book *How Hollywood Invented the Wild West* Holly George-Warren calls *Red River* and *Rio Bravo*, both starring John Wayne "at his most testosterone-fueled," Hawks' most famous films. Upon its release in 1948, some critics hailed *Red River*, the John Wayne-Montgomery Clift picture, as the milestone Western of the decade.

Ten years later Hawks made *Rio Bravo*, a completely different type of Western, though the emphasis again is on character development.

24

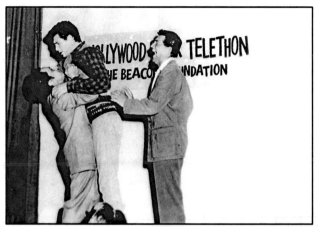

Two photos from the Rio
Bravo *telethon. In top
photo Gonzales Gonzales
(one of the film's main
characters), pretends to get
rough with Ted*

WHATEVER THE POLITICAL implications, and however it contrasted with *High Noon, Rio Bravo* was a breakthrough for Ted White. Not only was he getting paid as a stuntman but also as an actor when he had a brief speaking role.

In the film, Joe Burdette, played by Claude Akins, is being held in jail for murder while Chance (Wayne) waits for the U.S. Marshall to show up and take him off his hands. Burdette's brother and his gunhands hang around waiting for a chance to break him out of jail.

At one point in the film Wayne and Martin come out of the jail to patrol the main street at night. "You take that side of the street and I'll take this one," Wayne says.

Director Hawks placed Ted on a street corner leaning against a porch support. "Now Wayne's gonna come by and say a few things and all you say to him is 'yes sir'," Hawks told Ted.

Wayne saunters by and says "beautiful night, isn't it?"

"Yessir," Ted replies. It's his first speaking part in a film and it's with John Wayne!

Rio Bravo was tough on Ted physically. In addition to the sore shoulder, knee and head resulting from the joke Wayne and Bond played on him with the barn door, Ted did some rugged horse falls and was ultimately required to do a fall down a staircase in the film's hotel.

In the scene Burdette's men are on the hotel's main floor and know that John T. Chance (Wayne) is upstairs. They tie ropes on the stairs to trip him and then lure him down. Ted doubled Wayne, of course, and as he started down off a landing he tripped before he got to the ropes. He fell upside down, landed on his shoulder and broke it. Hawks wanted more takes so Ted hustled to the Warner Brothers dispensary and told them to "tie this thing up and I don't give a damn how you do it. And give me a shot."

Back on the set Hawks shot the fall from another angle and it worked. Paul Helmick, the assistant director, then came to Ted and asked how badly he was hurt. Told Ted had broken his shoulder, Helmick said "why the devil did you do it again?"

With a characteristic bravado that would last his entire film career, Ted said "I came here to work and I got it done. Anything else?" That was the final scene for Ted and he headed home where he found the break was much worse than he had thought. The doctor told him it would do no good to operate. The flesh was very thin over the top of the bone which was pushed up and nearly protruding. "You're going to have to live with it," the doctor said. Ted still has a knot on his shoulder and says he can no longer throw a football. "There's lots I can't do anymore," he says. "But that's just part of the business, as I found out very early."

In the film's final version, viewers see Ted tumble down the stairs to the point of impact and then Wayne falls into the picture.

But that was far from the most dangerous stunt Ted ever did. That came in *Hatari*. Before that, however, there were two other Wayne films — *The Horse Soldiers* and *The Alamo*.

7

Working with John Ford

IN *THE HORSE SOLDIERS* directed by John Ford, Ted again did double duty. He doubled Wayne and is often seen carrying the American flag at the head of the column of Civil War Union cavalry.

Ted, in character for The Horse Soldiers

In addition to Wayne, the film starred William Holden and Constance Towers. The movie is based on the true story of a troop of Union cavalry led by Colonel Benjamin Grierson (Wayne). Grierson led 1700 soldiers from northern Mississippi several hundred miles behind enemy lines in 1863 where they cut the railroad between Newton's Station and Vicksburg, Mississippi. *The Horse Soldiers* was filmed on location in Natchitoches Parish Louisiana along the banks of Cane River Lake and in and around Natchez, Mississippi.

The story of the making of the film is interesting on several levels. The first is the relationship between director Ford, Wayne and Holden. The second is how Wayne and Holden were actually punished by Ford for too much drinking. And finally, a death near the end of filming deeply affected Ford (and the rest of the cast and crew) and caused an early end to location shooting.

"No one contributed as much to the Western as director John Ford," wrote George-Warren. "He started his career as Westerns began and retired just as the genre was embarking on a radical new direction. As its poetic mythmaker, he has been called the Great Romanticist of the West."

John Ford (center) talks over a scene in The Horse Soldiers
with John Wayne, Constance Towers and William Holden
(Photo courtesy of Boyd Magers www. westernclippings.com)

"What a character Ford was," Ted said. "He was one of the most unforgettable men I ever met. He was so completely different in his mannerisms, speech and stature."

During the production of *The Horse Soldiers*, Ford came to work in the mornings in a limousine. Ted recalled that Ford brought with him an accordion player named Danny Borzage. When Ford arrived all the cast and crew would line up to greet him – Wayne and Holden included. As Ford emerged from the limo and trooped the line, saying "good morning" to everyone, Borzage played *Bringing in the Sheaves*.

Scott W. Smith, author of the award-winning blog *Screenwriting from Iowa*, says Ford had a long tradition of having an accordion player on his movie sets. He quotes William C. Dowling who says Borzage would greet the arrival on the set of each principal player with a theme drawn from a film they had done with Ford – "Red River Valley" for Henry Fonda, "Wagons West" for Ward Bond and "Marquita" for John Wayne. Dowling said "Borzage's presence on every Ford set for over forty years has a great deal to do with the emotional quality of Ford's films."

"Upon arriving on the set," Dowling quotes Harry Carey, Jr. as saying, "you would feel right away that something special was going to happen. You would feel spiritually awakened all of a sudden. . . This feeling has never happened to me again on any set."

Smith says Borzage was also a bit player on some Hollywood classics – *Stagecoach, Citizen Kane, Mister Roberts, The Man Who Shot Liberty Valance*, and most fittingly, is the accordionist at a funeral scene in Ford's *The Searchers*.

"FORD HAD ONE eye that was weaker than the other so he wore a black patch on the good eye believing that helped strengthen the weaker one" Ted said. "He had a bit of a drool so he kept a handkerchief in the corner of his mouth. He also wore a hooded cape."

When he first saw Ford like that Ted thought "oh, my God. It looks like God Himself walking in here." Because both Wayne and Holden enjoyed their liquor, Ford made each of them take a pledge that, during the production of *The Horse Soldiers* they wouldn't drink. But one night they slipped away and got drunk, Ted said.

The next morning, as Ford arrived he walked the line as usual, greeting each and every member of the cast and crew. "When he got to Wayne and Holden," Ted said, "he got right up under their noses and when they replied with a 'good morning' he could smell the whiskey on their breath."

As punishment, Ford decided there would be no stand-ins for the two stars. Instead, Wayne stood in for Holden as shots were prepared, and Holden stood in for Wayne.

"They put those hot lights on them and you could just see the booze boiling out of them," Ted said.

In this scene from The Horse Soldiers *with Holden and Wayne, Ted is second from left with beard*

Every afternoon, as often as possible – "I think it was around three o'clock," Ted said – "the crew set up a tent for Ford and he hosted the main actors at a tea. But you had to be invited to join the group."

In the film, actor Bing Russell has a good part as Dunker, a Yankee soldier who must have his leg amputated by Holden who is playing a doctor. But Russell wasn't aware of Ford's rules about who attended the afternoon tea.

"So, the first afternoon he innocently went into the tent and sat down with the group," Ted said. "But he wasn't served. Finally, somebody whispered to him that this party was by invitation only and he meekly got up and left."

When Ford set up a shot there was never any argument or discussion about how it was to be done, Ted said. Everyone respected the man and knew he had good reason for whatever steps he was taking to shoot a scene.

At one point they were to shoot a sequence by a barn. The cavalry was to ride into the area and, as shots rang out from the Confederates, Ted and others would need to do some horse falls in the space between the barn and a house.

"All of us got off our horses to check out the area," Ted said, "and there was a big rock in the area that I picked up and threw off to one side."

Later, Ted saw Ford walking around the area and he called to the cameraman. "Have you seen the rock that was right here?" he asked. "Get those stuntmen up here!"

When everyone was assembled Ford said: "there was a rock right here. Did anybody move that rock?"

Ted swallowed hard. "I thought I'm gonna go home or they're gonna line me up and have a firing squad," he said. "So I walked over and picked up the rock and had it in my hand ready to take it back."

"What are you doing with that rock?" Ford yelled. "Put it back."

Then he started laughing, Ted said. The rock had marked the spot where he wanted to place the camera.

There were other light moments during the filming.

Borzage, the accordion player, was a small man with gray hair and a bit of a beard. "Once, we were in a swamp and the horses were up to their bellies and we were all pretty miserable," Ted said, "but Ford put Borzage up to his stomach in the swamp and had him playing *Bringing in the Sheaves*. We couldn't help but laugh and it made us all feel better."

In the cavalry scenes Ted is carrying the American flag in the front rank just behind Wayne who had a favorite horse called Dollar. "That horse was furnished by the studio to begin with," Ted said, "but after five or six movies Wayne wouldn't do one without him. He used Dollar in a dozen or so pictures."

Later, fellow stuntman Chuck Roberson owned a horse Wayne rode

31

for several years. When Wayne got sick Roberson sold the horse. "Word got around," Ted said, "and somebody from the east called and wanted to know how much money he wanted for that horse. He wanted a horse that Wayne rode. Chuck told him he had recently sold the horse for $600.00. The guy said he'd have given $600,000 for him."

A still photo from the scene in the swamp

THE PRODUCTION of *The Horse Soldiers* ended on a sad note when an older stuntman who was a longtime friend of Ted's was killed in a freak accident.

Fred Kennedy was a veteran stuntman but was getting older and Ford brought him on *The Horse Soldiers* as a kind of tribute to his career. Ford had also assigned Kennedy and another stuntman to stay close to Constance Towers throughout the film to make sure she didn't get hurt. Now and then she would try to kiss Kennedy who was shy and would not allow it to happen.

It was one of the film's final shots and the crew was anxious to get home as it was only four days before Christmas. The scene was to be simple. Ted would lead half a dozen riders in a light gallop in front of a row of cannon. In the scene there would be fires beside each of the cannon for lighting the fuses. As the group rehearsed the scene, the fires were not lighted. At a certain point there would be a gunshot and Kennedy would fall from his horse.

32

The shot was set and the horses were out of sight of the cannon. The fires were lit and the riders began the gallop in front of the cameras. Near one of the cannons the fire flared as the gunshot went off. Kennedy's horse lurched to the right and Kennedy fell off the left side and went straight down, breaking his neck.

Ted recalls that Connie Towers ran to Fred, grabbed him and was about to kiss him and then screamed: "My God, he's dying!" The cast and crew ran to him but he died within a few minutes of the fall.

Kennedy's brother had also been working on the film as a wrangler. He put Kennedy's body in the bed of a pickup truck and drove him to the hospital but it was too late.

"The next day," Ted said, "we boarded a plane and flew home." He paused. "That's not what you want to hear about, but it's the kind of thing that happens."

Reviewers of the film report that Ford was so upset he closed the set and had to film the rest of the scene later in the San Fernando Valley.

On a more lighthearted note, Ted recalled that on a rare day off from the filming, he and some others were walking past a small bar in a nearby town. They heard a voice singing, went in and discovered the voice belonged to long-time cowboy star Tex Ritter.

The next day Ted told Wayne and Holden about it and that night Wayne, Holden, John Ford and about 100 or so cast members and crew showed up at the bar. "Ritter came out and got all choked up," Ted said. "He could hardly talk." He went into the audience and shook hands with everyone and put on a great show. The next time Ted and others visited the bar the owner said the drinks were on him. He'd never had better business.

Coincidentally, another old-time Western star also worked on the production. Hoot Gibson is seen as a horseshoer.

Some reports say *The Horse Soldiers* marked the beginning of mega-deals for Hollywood stars. John Wayne and William Holden reportedly received $775,000 each, plus 20% of the overall profits, an unheard-of sum for that time. Unfortunately, the movie did not do well at the box office and, in the end, never made a profit.

Ted's next film with Wayne would be *The Alamo*.

*Ted, center, prepares for a scene in another western
even though he had broken his arm when he hit a
railing during a high fall*

34

8

Remember the Alamo

IN THE LATE 1950s John Wayne was nearly broke, the result of bad investments by a man he had trusted with his money. In their 1995 book *John Wayne: American,* Randy Roberts and James S. Olson say "the financial catastrophe could not have come at a worse time" because Wayne needed big money to make *The Alamo.* Duke had dreamed for years of making a film about the Texas freedom fighters.

It certainly wouldn't be the first to chronicle the 186 men who gave their lives trying to delay General Antonio Lopez de Santa Anna during the war for independence from Mexico. In fact, dozens of novels and several films had made a stab at portraying the heroic stand in the old adobe mission. But Wayne's vision was of a magnificent film that would literally dwarf all other attempts and, in the process, become, in his eyes, one of the greatest pictures ever made.

This would be John Wayne's picture. He would produce it, direct it and star in it. For months, his every waking moment would be spent finding locations, planning shots, assembling the cast, trying to raise money and dealing with one problem after another. It was enough to make a strong man ill. And it did.

At union rates Wayne estimated the film would cost $70,000 to $90,000 a day if it were filmed in Texas. If, however, he could film it in Mexico he could cut the cost down to perhaps $35,000 a day. But the thought of filming their beloved story of the Alamo in Mexico infuriated most Texans. To them, the Alamo was hallowed ground, a shrine. That problem was solved when Wayne met a man named Happy Shahan who suggested that Duke build the set on his ranch – about 22,000 acres – outside the

Southwest Texas town of Brackettsville, where Republic Pictures had filmed another Alamo movie, *The Last Command*, in 1956.

Wayne finally estimated his film's budget at about $7.5 million. That settled, he began putting together the cast.

Working on The Alamo,
*John Wayne is pictured with
famous bullfighter Carlos
Aruzzo*

Duke originally wanted Clark Gable to play William Travis but Gable had a prior commitment to do *The Misfits* which would be his last film. Laurence Harvey was the eventual choice for the role. Likewise, Wayne hoped Burt Lancaster would take the role of Jim Bowie. Lancaster, however, was under contract to star in *Elmer Gantry* and the part went to Richard Widmark. Richard Boone, star of the TV series *Have Gun, Will Travel*, signed on as Sam Houston. Sammy Davis, Jr. wanted the role of Jethro, Jim Bowie's slave, but (possibly because of his association with the famous "rat pack" -- Frank Sinatra, Peter Lawford, etc.) he was passed over in favor of Jester Hairston. In a nod to the youth market (ala Ricky Nelson in *Rio Bravo*) Wayne assigned the part of Smitty to Frankie Avalon whose song "Venus" was on top of the hit parade.

He also brought in Ted White to play a Tennessean.

In addition, he gathered more than 300 Texas Longhorn steers from throughout the state, leased 1,600 horses, housed the "permanent" cast and crew of 342 people in Brackettsville, prepared costumes for 6,000 extras, and planned to serve more than 190,000 meals to cast, crew and extras during the filming.

Ted was on location for nearly three months – and not everything went smoothly, although there were light moments.

"I shot myself," he recalls. "I was playing a Tennessean and was on the Alamo's ramparts shooting at the advancing Mexicans. Then, later when they filmed Santa Anna's army, I was playing a Mexican. The edited version shows me firing from the Alamo and then cuts to me as a Mexican soldier getting shot. So I shot myself."

Some of The Alamo *cast. Ted is second from left, in hat*

During the filming, Wayne was constantly on edge. "We had an excellent group," Ted says. "We had top stars, top stuntmen, top everything. But Wayne was producer, director and money man. Having to wear all those hats drove him to a point where it was difficult for him to get along with a lot of people."

As a result, Ted said, he had a good stream of people coming and going. Among them was John Ford who began to show up uninvited and provided constant advice to Wayne, who felt he owned Ford for much of his success and wouldn't ask the man to leave. Finally, he got Ford to direct some second unit scenes.

Roberts and Olson in their definitive Wayne biography, report that Dean Smith, a fellow stuntman who became a close lifelong friend of Ted's, said Duke was a good director but "at times he didn't have a lot of patience."

Ted saw it firsthand. At one point Denver Pyle walked up to Wayne and suggested a different way of doing a particular scene. Wayne bristled and said "if I wanted your goddamned advice I'd have called you and asked for it." Pyle went back to his business and didn't say any more.

During the filming Chill Wills, playing the role of "Beekeeper," occasionally used an old trick to try and steal a scene. Ted said Wills bought a large bag of pecans and when standing behind or near the principal actors in a scene, would crack and eat the pecans. Finally, Wayne blew up and told him "if you crack another of those pecans I'm going to fire you." The trick is used often, Ted said, as a means to attract attention. Any kind of movement in a scene will draw a viewer's eye. He recalled Steve McQueen's actions in *The Magnificent Seven* when he would take off his hat or make some other move to attract attention away from Yul Brynner.

At one point in the filming Wayne barely averted disaster when he became angry with fellow star Richard Widmark.

"It was a thing about acting," Ted said, "a way of doing a scene that drew Widmark's objection."

Ted said he didn't remember Wayne's choice of words exactly but Widmark packed up and headed for the airport. "We were halfway through the production," Ted said "and losing one of the main stars would have required costly re-shooting."

Ted said Widmark was a solid actor who knew his dialogue and also knew his character, Jim Bowie. In the scene being shot, Widmark didn't do it exactly as Wayne had perceived it.

"You've got to remember that Wayne is the executive producer, he's the owner, he's the star and he's got lots of his own money involved in the picture," Ted said. "He's wearing a lot of hats. He's behind the camera directing, then he has to get out in front of the camera and act."

At any rate, Wayne got into it with Widmark and called him a few names.

"Now Widmark is no baby," Ted said. "He'd been around the block and this wasn't his first rodeo. He said 'F… you' to Wayne and walked off the set." Wayne had to have him so he chased Widmark to the airport and apologized. Widmark relented and rejoined the set but things were tense between the two throughout the remainder of the filming.

Wayne directing The Alamo
(Photo courtesy of Boyd Magers www.westernclippings.com)

On top of everything else the film's all-important script book was lost in a fire.

"The script book is without a doubt one of the most important aspects of film making," Ted said. "Everything is in there. When the script clerk comes on the set he or she starts writing." He said pictures are taken of the cast in the costumes they wear in specific scenes and those photos are clipped to the book. The clerk is constantly making notes about individuals – "he is standing next to a cabin, has salt & pepper hair, wears glasses, his right hand on cheek, brown socks, brown pants." This is done so, at a future date during a possible reshoot, the clerk can say here's what he wore and here's a photo of him. In addition, the book contains such information as the timing of each shot so the film cutter knows what goes with what and in what order.

On *The Alamo* the script clerk was a man who was very experienced and quite efficient, Ted recalls. One evening he took the book home with him and it was lost in a house fire. "We were halfway through the filming," Ted said, "but the clerk began rewriting the book from memory and that would have saved hundreds of thousands of dollars if we needed to reshoot important scenes. So it's no wonder Wayne's nerves were on edge so much of the time."

Ted, left, doubling Hank Warden, right. Warden's daughters are in the center

Wayne's edginess apparently wore off on others in the cast and crew – including Ted.

Ted roomed with two other stuntmen during the filming – John "Bear" Hudkins and Bob Morgan. Hudkins, a long-time stuntman, appeared in dozens of films including *The Quick and the Dead, Dick Tracey, Young Guns, The Outlaw Josey Wales, High Plains Drifter* and *Rio Lobo*, among many others.

Morgan was married to screen star Yvonne DeCarlo and had a similar long list of movies to his credit. They included *How the West was Won, The Man Who Shot Liberty Valance, The Comancheros, North to Alaska, Spartacus* and many others.

Hudkins died in 1997 and Morgan in 1999.

"About the second day of filming on *The Alamo* I had to ride a horse in a jump over a wall," Ted said. Morgan made a comment in front of everyone – "Hey, we've got a great jumping horse rider in a new guy" – that didn't "set well" with Ted.

That evening, after filming had ended for the day, Ted was at the house when Morgan came in. "Let's go out in the back," Ted said. "I'm gonna teach you a lesson."

Morgan was surprised. "What are you talking about?"

Ted told him it was about the comment he made when he jumped the wall.

"I'm not gonna fight you over that," Morgan said.

"I was floored," Ted said. "Completely floored."

"It didn't mean anything," Morgan said. "It was so trivial."

"It meant a lot to me," Ted said. "From this day forward don't you utter my name in a way that pertains to stunt work. You leave me out of your conversation."

Morgan said "believe me, I will."

Ted didn't speak to Morgan again until the man was in the hospital. He had been doubling George Peppard in *How the West Was Won* and lost a leg in an accident as they filmed the gunfight on the moving train near the end of the film.

"Bear Hudkins and I called him long distance just to ask if there was anything we could do," Ted said.

He was dumfounded when Morgan said "now you can get all my jobs."

THE ALAMO WAS one of the most expensive films to produce up to that time, with an estimated $17.5 million invested by the time it was released. It earned $2 million in its first three months – not bad by 1960s standards. But even after some re-editing and being re-released several times, the film did not recoup the total cost of production.

That year *The Alamo* earned six Oscar nomination – Best Sound, Best Song, Best Cinematography, Best Score, Best Supporting Actor (Chill Wills) and Best Movie. But it was up against *Elmer Gantry* with Burt Lancaster, *The Apartment* starring Jack Lemon, *Sons and Lovers* based on a D. H. Lawrence novel and *The Sundowners* with Robert Mitchum.

Finally, *The Apartment* won Best Picture, Peter Ustinov of *Spartacus* won Best Supporting Actor (beating out Chill Wills) and *The Alamo* won its only Oscar for Dmitri Tiomkin's score.

Roberts and Olson quote Wayne as saying to a friend: "Sonofabitch. After all this work I thought we'd win something."

Wayne was worn out, physically and mentally, and in no shape to begin work on his next major project – *Hatari*.

Ted takes a break between scenes of Hatari

9

Hatari means "Danger!"

IN THE LATE 1950s, about three years before work began on *Hatari* and just as *Rio Bravo* was wrapping up its shooting schedule, Ted was leaving the set when Director Howard Hawks called to him and asked if he had a minute.

"Do you like animals?" Hawks asked Ted.

"Yessir."

"What about wild animals?"

"Sure," Ted replied. "I do a lot of hunting."

"Well," Hawks said, "I think we're going to Africa before long and we're going to take you with us."

Three years later Ted was on the back lot at Warner Brothers filming a Western television series show when a limousine drove onto the set and the driver asked for Ted White. "He's wanted in Jack Warner's office," the man said.

"Oh, Lord," Ted thought. "What have I done now?"

Ted hadn't met Warner and, in his office, the studio head said "an old friend of mine wants to see you." When Ted told Warner that he was busy working on a series show, Warner laughed and said "I think I can take care of that."

Ted was driven to Paramount Studios and Howard Hawks welcomed him. "Are you working on anything?" he asked.

"Just a two or three-day television shoot," Ted replied.

Hawks told him to come in Monday morning to get ready to go to Africa. "We're not going to leave for a month," Hawks said, "but I'll keep you busy checking on things we'll need and making sure we're equipped with the right stuff."

Ted had heard Wayne was involved in the picture and was excited about the opportunity.

At the conclusion of filming *The Alamo* Wayne was involved in another film, *North to Alaska,* directed by Henry Hathaway as part of a three-picture deal he had made a few years earlier with Twentieth Century Fox. When not needed on Hathaway's set, Wayne spent his time in his Batjack editing room in Beverly Hills finalizing *The Alamo*. He was exhausted from the work on that film but managed to do good enough work on *North to Alaska* that it got decent reviews and earned a profit for Twentieth Century Fox.

He was doing double duty editing *The Alamo* and getting ready to head for Africa when another kind of bad news brought on more despondency.

His good friend from college and his co-star in many pictures, Ward Bond, died of a massive heart attack on November 5, 1960. He was only 57 years old. Wayne was heartbroken but bravely delivered the eulogy at Bond's funeral and was among those who took a boat into the Catalina Channel where Bond's ashes were ceremoniously spilled into the ocean.

Soon after Bond's funeral Wayne left for Tanganyika in East Africa where Howard Hawks, Ted White and the rest of the cast and crew awaited him. His wife Pilar and their children went with him. Wayne had readily accepted Hawks' invitation to star in the film even though the script was unfinished and was quite short on plot. Hawks had directed *Red River,* after all, and Wayne knew the man would make a good film.

The story involved African game hunters who captured wild animals for zoos throughout the world. Simply put, Wayne (playing Sean Mercer) heads a crew that includes Bruce Cabot, Red Buttons and Kurt Mueller. The female lead, Elsa Martinelli, lends a love interest to the film.

Ted and others had flown to Africa far ahead of Wayne to shoot scenes in which Ted would double the star and others in some rather perilous scenes in the Serengeti Plain of the Great Rift Valley in Kenya and Tanganyika.

But first, Ted and others had to get there.

TED SITS IN AN aisle seat of a DC9 propeller-driven plane reading the draft of the script for *Hatari*. Beside him is a boy who is perhaps three years old.

44

The boy's mother sits next to the window. "I was chewing tobacco in those days," Ted says, "and a couple of hours out of New York the stewardess came by and told us to put down our trays for dinner."

Ted dutifully complies, sets the cup he was spitting tobacco into on the tray and reaches down to place the script he was reading beneath the seat. As he does so, the little boy picks up the cup of tobacco juice and drinks it. Immediately he is throwing up.

"Well, that woman went bananas," Ted says. "She called me everything you can think of. I can't imagine a name she didn't call me."

The stewardess shows up with a doctor who asks what the boy drank. "I said it's chewing tobacco," Ted said. They get the boy settled down and move Ted to an empty seat near the front of the cabin. Later the mother walks past on the way to the restroom and, looking at Ted with a snarl, says loudly "you assassin! You mother f......!'"

"She was horrible," he said.

After being detoured to Geneva, Switzerland, the plane finally reached its original destination – Paris. "We got to spend two days in the Hotel George Cinq," Ted said. This is a famous luxury five-star hotel set just off the Champs Elysees. It is named, like the street in which it is situated, after King George V.

Rooming with Ted was Carey Loftin, "one of Hollywood's greatest stunt drivers ever," he said. The man's amazing driving and stunt skills were utilized in dozens of Hollywood productions over a period of nearly half a century. Ted said Loftin's expertise with motor vehicles including cars, trucks & motorcycles saw him involved in contributing his skills to numerous cult films of the 1960s and 1970s that featured thrilling car chase sequences including *The Love Bug* (1968), *Bullitt* (1968), *Vanishing Point* (1971)*Diamonds Are Forever* (1971), *The French Connection* (1971), *Duel* (1971) (TV), *Thunderbolt and Lightfoot* (1974) and *White Line Fever* (1975). Loftin was to be the principal driver in *Hatari's* spectacular scenes of the hunters capturing wild animals.

"So we're in this enormous, beautiful room in one of the world's great hotels," Ted says, and Loftin goes in the bathroom. He comes out and gets on the phone and tells the front desk they better get somebody up there quick. 'There's no lid on the toilet'."

After getting over his fit of laughter Ted told him about bidets.

It was a Saturday night and Ted found a place downstairs just off the street called The American Bar. Ted was barely inside when Stephen Boyd, famous for his role in *Ben Hur*, called out "Hey Ted!"

He was sitting at a table with two girls and he beckoned Ted over and said "come here and take one. Which one do you want?

Ted said no thanks, that he was going to have a drink – it was past midnight – and head off to bed. Boyd, it turned out, was in town preparing to make a movie.

"I went back to the hotel room," Ted said, "and as I got to the door I heard loud laughter."

He opened the door to find Loftin there with a girl "this big around, and they've got two watermelons opened up and they are sitting there naked eating watermelons." Loftin had also started the bathtub and it was overflowing with water running into the bedroom.

"I said good God almighty, Carey! We're in the George Cinq hotel. You've got to get rid of this girl." Loftin was reluctant but Ted said "look at you. You're both naked and you're eating watermelons. What are we gonna tell the people?"

Loftin shook his head and said "I don't give a shit."

Finally, about 2:00 a.m., they got the girl out of the room "but we never did get the watermelon out of there and I don't know what the studio had to pay for that," Ted said. Soon the two were on another plane flying to Rome and then on to Nairobi, Kenya.

After he had checked into the Nairobe hotel, Ted got a call from Howard Hawks. "Have you had dinner yet?" the director asked. When Ted said he had not, Hawks told Ted to put on a suit and join him in the hotel's restaurant.

"I walked up to his table and was thunderstruck," Ted said. "There sat the woman and the little boy from the plane with her husband, who I later learned was a writer on the film."

Hawks started to introduce Ted and he said "Mr. Hawks, we've met."

The woman turned to her husband and said "This is the *gentleman* who was chewing tobacco on the plane."

Ted recalls that he thought he could see the beginning of a smile on the man's face. "He wanted to laugh but he didn't. He said 'nice to meet you' and we shook hands."

Some ten days later, after the film crew had moved to the little town of Arusha, Howard Hawks approached Ted. "I had a feeling you knew the writer's wife," he said. Ted told him the story and Hawks laughed loudly. "I didn't know you chewed tobacco," he said.

Ted replied that he didn't anymore. "I just quit," he told the director.

HAWKS HAD ASSEMBLED an international cast that included Wayne and Red Buttons from the United States, Elsa Martinelli from Italy, Kurt Muller from Germany, Brandy De la Court and Charles "Chips" Maurey from France, and Luis Francisco Garcia Lopez from Mexico, along with a number of natives of Kenya and Tanganyika.

Ted and many of the others arrived on scene a full month before Wayne who was busily completing work on *The Alamo*.

In their discussion of *Hatari* a number of sources claim that all the animal captures in the picture were actually performed by the actors and that no stuntmen or animal handlers were substituted onscreen.

Ted White, who was nearly gored by a giant rhinoceros while doubling Bruce Cabot in an early scene, and who doubled Wayne throughout the film, scoffs at that statement.

Screenwriter William Goldman who penned *Butch Cassidy and the Sundance Kid* (1969) and others wrote "now you must know this: stars do not do their own stunts... For many reasons, mainly two: 1. They stink at them, and even if they're vaguely competent, they're not in a class with stuntmen. 2. Insurance. Stunts are dangerous. If a stuntman gets hurt, that's obviously a terrible thing, but there are other stuntmen. If a star gets hurt, there goes your schedule, your budget, possibly your picture, conceivably your career."

"When Wayne arrived we'd been there more than a month," Ted said. During that time the cast and crew who were there shot as many of the animal capture scenes as possible. "Our tight shooting schedule meant we had to be constantly working," he said. "I did everything that Wayne was supposed to be doing, riding in the chase vehicles, trying to capture the animals. In scenes where he had dialogue I'd stand in and say it and the crew would time it so they knew the timeframe he had to do it in. Later, they cut shots of Wayne riding in the vehicles into the scenes. It worked, though it was complicated."

"HATARI," THE Swahili word for "danger," was an apt name for the film, as it turned out.

All of the scenes were dangerous and unpredictable, Ted recalls. The cast and crew worked long, hard days. The scenes of capturing animals were not scripted. "The day's plan might say 'catch zebras, catch giraffe, catch cape buffalo' and that's all it would say."

Normally, scripts go into detail explaining each scene, pointing out locations of vehicles and actors, camera locations and backgrounds. "But animals don't read the damn script," Ted said. "We had a spotter plane that found animals and we'd go to them and try to get our shots but it took forever to get things done."

The nerves of cast and crew were on edge. Even Howard Hawks became ill and was sent back to London to recuperate. Two people died. Ted carried a rifle and a pistol for protection. Mau Mau uprisings were terrorizing the surrounding countries.

In fact, only a few years earlier it was reported that more than 70,000 Kikuyu tribesmen suspected of Mau Mau membership had been imprisoned and that more than 13,000 people had been killed by British troops and Mau Mau activists during the previous three years of the Mau Mau Rebellion.

"We were right in the middle of it all," Ted said, "and we were very cautious."

In addition to the concerns about Mau Mau terrorism the filmmakers were dealing with unpredictable and dangerous animals as they worked hard to get shots that accurately depicted the inherent dangers they encountered on an almost daily basis.

"When we were chasing animals I'd be sitting in that front seat of a Chevy three quarter ton pickup doing 60 miles per hour and I'd have a rope and that's all," Ted recalls. "It puts your heart in your throat sometimes."

There were giant ant hills made of mud that they tried to avoid at all costs because hitting them was like running into a brick wall. Warthogs dug deep holes that would wreck a vehicle.

"After the first two weeks I added a seatbelt because several times I was almost thrown from the vehicle," Ted said. "When an animal takes off, there's no planning. He goes where he wants to go. You don't choose the route." The vehicles raced across the plain, the camera car off to one side trying to keep up.

The villagers were in awe of the film crew. They had seen safaris come through but not a movie production company with cameras and all the people. "Many of them probably had not even seen a movie before," Ted said.

At one point director Hawks decided it would make a nice scene if the truck would go along the edge of one of the many ponds in the area and splash water.

In the film, Red Buttons was the one supposedly doing the driving and Ted was doubling Wayne on the Fender. Ted had found a welder in the town of Arusha and had him build a seat and weld it to the front fender where he could sit and try to rope animals with a loop on the end of a long pole. The safety belt on that seat kept him in the vehicle when it hit holes and bumps.

Hawks said "Ted, do you think you guys could give me a little water spray?"

"We'd just gotten out on the open plains and some of those ponds were maybe 30 yards across," Ted said, "but we didn't know how deep they were."

Hawks told Ted to carry one of the long poles as it would be one of the first shots in the scene.

Ted told Carey Loftin, doubling Red Buttons as the driver, that Hawks wanted some spraying water. He neglected to suggest to Loftin that they stay close to the edge.

"Carey was doing about 40 miles per hour when we hit that water and it was over six feet deep.

That stagnant water went completely over me and the windshield and I was strapped into that seat completely under water"

The camera car had to pull the Jeep out and it wouldn't run anymore. Hawks drove up and "I didn't intend for you to drown. Just thought you'd go along the edge." They got another vehicle and reshot the scene.

In one of the first scenes in the film Bruce Cabot's character ("the Indian) is trying to capture an enormous rhinoceros. Ted White, of course, is doubling Cabot who, in the film, is badly injured and has to be flown to London for treatment.

The scene was shot in the Ngorongoro Conservation Area (a UNESCO World Heritage Site) located about 110 miles west of Arusha in the Crater Highlands area of Tanzania. The Ngorongoro Crater, a large volcanic caldera, lies within the area.

"We had two camera cars," Ted says. "These were not typical camera cars but were flatbed trucks with no cabs so we could put cameras anywhere. For open country like we were in having several cameras with different lenses on a moving vehicle was a big asset."

The object was to get a shot of a rhino goring Bruce Cabot (Ted). When they got ready to do the shot Ted was concerned about having Carey Loftin do the driving because he was the only other stuntman on the scene at that point. Paul Helmick, the associate producer of the film as well as the second unit director, asked Ted why Loftin wasn't to do the driving.

Ted said he didn't want to sound melodramatic but if something should happen and both Carey and he were hurt, the production would be shut down. If only one happened to get hurt the crew could keep going. Ted said he would take one of the white hunters. "All he has to do is drive and listen to me," he said.

He told the new driver that when the rhino came and hooked his horn at him "you turn to the right and that way I've got the horn crossing in front of my leg and it looks like a hit." Then Ted would blow the "squid" strapped to his leg and it would look like blood is spraying everywhere. "Just turn to the right," he said. He wouldn't wear the seatbelt for this shot in case he needed to leap away from the animal.

They picked out a huge rhino, knowing that when they got within 30 feet or so it would charge. Nearing the rhino, a call on the radio from the camera car said "he's coming."

Ted told the driver to get ready but when the rhino hooked his horn the driver turned to the left and the horn went well under Ted's welded seat and flipped the Jeep several feet into the air. Both passengers flew out of the Jeep and hit the ground looking for the rhino. He had stopped and was turning back. The driver of the camera car thought quickly and pulled his vehicle between the two stranded men and the rhino. It charged the camera car and as it pulled away the rhino followed it.

Paul Helmick quickly came to the men. "Help me turn this Jeep over," Ted said. "I think I can get it started again."

"Why? We're through for the day. Everybody's upset. That was a close call and we're lucky everyone is alive."

In what would become his signature stance, Ted turned to Helmick and said: "Paul, we came here to get this shot and I'm still working. Let's go again."

"Are you sure you want to do this again?" Helmick asked.

Ted took a deep breath. "I can't be anymore scared than I was the first time. If we lived through this last thing we'll be okay trying again."

The original driver, though, refused to go again. Ted said he didn't blame him. However, another of the white hunters volunteered to drive the second time. "Turn only when I tell you to," Ted told the man. "And turn to the right."

They located the rhino and went after him. This time the horn hooked under the seat again and as the driver turned the right way, Ted tripped the "squid" and blood spurted into the air. The horn supposedly pushed him upwards and the shot was a "take."

After he called "cut" Helmick got Ted on the radio and asked "how bad is it?"

"What do you mean?" Ted replied. "You just don't know good acting when you see it."

Later Helmick called director Hawks and said "we got the shot but we almost lost Ted White."

"That was a thrill," Ted said in an understatement.

THROUGHOUT THE FILM, Ted snagged giraffes with the loop on the end of that long pole, chased zebras, cape buffalo and rhinos. But one day he roped a cape buffalo and earned world-wide notoriety.

The news spread quickly that a Texas cowboy had actually roped a cape buffalo, one of the most dangerous animals in the African Veldt with ferociously large curved horns hiding enormous flapping ears.

A reporter flew from London to Nairobi and found his way to Arusha to report the story. When he got there Ted was on location in the Serengeti Plain and the reporter had to get the story second hand.

"If you want to know just how to rope a buffalo," the story began, "ask Ted White, stunt actor with Paramount Pictures corporation, and he'll give you a very first-hand account of just how it's done."

To hear Ted tell it, it was something that just came naturally.

He said "I'd gone out to a game farm way out in the county to see

51

the animals, and while I was there a cape buffalo was to be given a tranquilizer injection."

First the animal had to be caught, however. An assistant at the game farm attempted to rope the animal but missed on several tries.

A series of photos showing one of Hatari's *opening scenes with Ted doubling Bruce Cabot and appearing to be gored by a massive rhinoceros*

Ted quickly shook out a loop and dropped the noose over the animal's horns. The enraged animal fought the rope, which snapped, and then turned on Ted. Ted jumped the fence and the buffalo followed him, chasing him around the compound. Ted dodged him as best he could, sometimes jumping for an overhead beam and pulling himself clear of the maddened beast's horns as it ran beneath him. At one point Ted grabbed its tail, hoping to slow it down enough that handlers could get a hold on the broken rope. But he was thrown across the dirt-packed ground.

Finally, he grabbed the rope and others were able to pull the animal down and tie its legs.

"I was way out in the country, away from any telephones or other communication," Ted said, "but word that I'd roped the animal got back to Nairobi and then to England." It hit the papers – *Cowboy from Texas Ropes a Cape Buffalo*. The story eventually filtered down to the Arusha area.

Ted's feat was publicized throughout Africa and Europe. He's now in the Guinness Book of World Records as the only person ever to rope a cape buffalo.

DANGER PLAGUED the production of *Hatari* from start to finish.

In one scene that remained in the completed film, Wayne is doctoring a large bird (perhaps it was a Flamingo, Ted said). A supposedly tame leopard is tied to a nearby tree with an eight-foot chain. The animal suddenly ran and hit the bird, killing it. "It scared the daylights out of Wayne," Ted said. "It scared us all."

In another scene Ted had to entice an elephant to charge Wayne who shot it. "I walked down as close as I could get," Ted said, "the elephant charged and I turned and ran and was outrun by a cameraman." Wayne shot the animal and all was well.

Many of the rivers in the area teemed with crocodiles and driving across them was an adventure, Ted says.

A white hunter died in a Jeep wreck. He was driving down a dirt road when a large lorry coming the other direction lurched across the center of the road, hit the Jeep head-on and killed the man.

Just as terrible, a lion killed the woman who was doubling Elsa Martinelli.

In the script "Dallas" (Martinelli) is in a cage which is open. She can see through it and lions are lurking around the cage. The actress said she couldn't do that.

"As stunt coordinator, I interviewed several young women," Ted said. "I hired one who said she had a tame lion and that she could get it to come right up to the cage." Ted went to Hawks who said "if it's tame, put Elsa in the cage for a shot or two."

They brought in the lion and put him on a cable about 40 yards long. The double came to the set to meet Martinelli and then said "now let's go meet my lion."

Near the lion, she called to him and he started toward them. "He's acting strange," the double said. "Why don't you move back a few yards?"

The woman stood and waited for the lion which picked up speed and was running full blast the last 15 feet, leaped and hit the woman in the chest. "He opened her up from her chest to her neck," Ted said.

A white hunter just returning to the set with a rifle shot the lion three times, killing it. The crew tried to get the young woman to Nairobi 140 miles away but it was too late.

"Elsa was so shaken up we never did shoot that scene," Ted said.

AFTER THE LOCATION shooting wrapped Hawks approached Ted. "Have you enjoyed yourself?" he asked.

Ted told him it had been the best time of his life.

"Well, maybe we'll do it again," Hawks said. "What would you like to do now?"

Ted says he now believes Hawks was referring to films but that he was thinking along other lines. "I'd like to save enough money to go to India and get a tiger," he replied.

A few days later the cast and crew were in Nairobi heading off in many different directions. Hawks came to Ted, handed him an envelope and shook his hand to say goodbye.

"When I opened the envelope I found the gift of a tiger hunt in India," Ted said.

Some photos of Ted during the filming of Hatari

Bulldogged a Wildebeast.
Camera car in background.

*Ted during his
Tiger hunt in
India*

*H*ATARI REACHED theatres in 1962. By the end of the year the film had earned more than $14 million, almost more than *The Alamo* totaled and providing generous profits for its investors.

Ted would work with Wayne only briefly one more time – when he doubled Jim Hutton in *Hellfighters*. "I had a chance to work with him on *McClintock*, Ted said, "but I was scheduled to go to Europe on another film and had to turn it down. It just happened that way."

The last time Ted saw Wayne was during the filming of *The Shootist* which would be the star's last movie.

"I was at Warner Brothers when he was filming on a closed set," Ted said. The guard said he couldn't let Ted inside. "I asked the guard to please go in and tell Wayne that Ted is here and would like to see him."

Wayne told the guard to let him in.

When they met, Wayne said "Ted, there's no real action in this movie." Ted told him he wasn't there about the film, but just to see him.

"He said 'sit down' and we talked," Ted said. "Both of us knew it would be the last time we'd see each other. He was really sick then. We just talked about different shows. Special kinds of things."

Wayne said "remember the time you almost drowned on the African desert?" The two had a good laugh.

We had talked only a few minutes when Wayne was called for a scene, Ted says. "When we said 'so long' at the end, Wayne asked about the wife and kids. I said they were fine."

He said "well, 'till we see each other again." They shook hands, Ted says, and that was it.

In a publicity photo Ted assumes a tough guy look

10

_____

Television's Heyday

THE PERIOD BEGINNING in the late 1940s and extending to the late 1950s or early 1960s has been dubbed "The Golden Age of Television" in the United States. The popularity of television skyrocketed, particularly in the US, where 77% of households purchased their first TV set during that time.

In those years free televised programming in the home was relatively new. Large antennas sprouted from homes and apartment buildings and in the evenings families came together, not necessarily to converse, communicate and study, but to sit silently in front of that magic picture tube and watch TV.

At the same time the American film industry was changing. It was soon after the end of World War II and movie fans were looking for new ways to spend their money (other than on movies) and occupy their time. They wanted to start families, find nicer homes in the suburbs, buy cars and refrigerators. Douglas Gomery, in his book *Movie History: A Survey*, reports that weekly movie attendance in movie theatres in the U.S. crested in 1946 and then began to steadily fall. By the early 1960s it was half of what it had been in the glory days.

Many generally blame television for this decline in movie-going but Gomery says the analysis is flawed because "it ignores the fact that in most parts of the U.S. television signals did not become available until long after the decline … was well underway." One possible explanation, he suggests, is that many of the returning veterans had less money to spend after the war and that millions of them were looking for that ideal job. In addition, he says, men and women were getting married and starting families, creating the baby boom of the era.

In the meantime, the early days of television saw many hour-long anthology drama series receive critical acclaim. Filmed series such as *Alfred Hitchcock Presents* and *The Twilight Zone* began to appear among the most popular programming. Prime time TV drama showcased both original and classic productions such as the first telecasts of Walt Disney's programs and the first presentations of *Peter Pan, The Wizard of Oz* and even *Cinderella.*

But among the first and the most wildly popular TV shows were more than 100 Westerns. Most of the early ones were in black and white. A few went to color and some even experimented with one hour or 90-minute formats.

Considering the attitudes of American citizens and the political atmosphere in the United States in the fifties, coupled with the history of American film, the popularity of Westerns on television was not surprising to many observers.

Middle class America was still adjusting to life after World War II. The boys were home from the war and women were at home caring for the children and having a cocktail and dinner ready when the male breadwinner came home from work. They found money for good food, automobiles, a home in the suburb, college for the kids. Sales of TV sets rose tremendously in the 1950s and by the end of the decade there were 52 million sets in American homes. Americans devoted most of their free time to watching television broadcasts. Television revolutionized the way Americans saw themselves and the world around them. TV began to affect almost all aspects of American culture -- what we wore, the music we listened to, what we ate, and the news we received.

But not everyone in the U.S. benefitted from the largesse of a country getting used to a peacetime economy. In fact, Harry Truman's government was even reluctant to call the fighting in Korea a "war." Instead it was referred to as "a police action."

In the poorer reaches of the country, and especially in the south and in inner cities throughout the nation, segregation was rampant. Blacks and other minorities fared poorly and a large proportion did not enjoy the prosperous new world of post-war America. *Brown vs. Board of Education* in 1954 offered a gleam of hope but it would be years before significant progress was made toward at least a germ of positive "equal rights" began to become evident.

Life in the 1950s was quite strict, compared to what was to come. Women were relegated to the status of housewife. Children, including teenagers, were to be seen and not heard.

On the other hand, Hugh Hefner launched *Playboy* magazine in 1953. About the same time, many writers, members of the so-called "beat generation" rebelled against conventional values. America was changing and some of these changes were harbingers of the 1960s which would bring about a definite shift in morals, attitudes, family life, race relations and feelings about the government.

To many people (some of them ignoring the true difficulties and "separateness" of certain races and classes), the 1950s are seen as the "best time," when families and morals were intact and times were simpler and enjoyable.

There was leisure time for ballgames, backyard barbeques, dances and – perhaps most significantly – watching television.

Enter the television Western where the good guys always subdued the evil-doers. Here was the self-confident, rugged cowboy who needed only the clothes on his back, his gun and horse, and who had the right answer to every problem. America was the world's super power, we had the proper moral compass embedded in our very being and the future was aglow with unlimited possibilities. Just like the cowboys we adored who braved the frontier of old, we pondered the frontier of a life that promised peace, prosperity and freedom from fear.

Our entertainment had almost always been based on that premise. And the entertainment provided by America's early cinema had largely been Western.

Professor Richard Slotkin in an on-line college-level course called "Western Movies: Myth, Ideology, and Genre," calls Westerns "the oldest American film genre." He says they have also been "the most important modern vehicles for one of the oldest and most significant of American cultural myths – the myth of the frontier."

Phil Hardy, putting "The Western in Perspective," notes that when increasingly complex issues are being raised such as today's economy, jobs, terrorism and nuclear fears (among many others) the Western presents "a simple, unchanging, clearcut world in which notions of Good and Evil could be balanced against each other in an easily recognizable fashion. Moreover,

61

Good not only invariably triumphed but did so with style and grace."

During the 1940s and 50s millions of children and adults joined in a Saturday ritual at matinees of Western movies in thousands of theatres in all parts of the county. That collective experience said something important about twentieth-century America.

Jack Nachbar, writing in *Focus on the Western*, says "Western movies, are thus far the single most important American story form of the twentieth century." He notes that "even during the 1950s, when the feature production of Westerns was dramatically dropping off, Westerns still comprised one-half of American-made historical films."

Western movies trace their roots back to *The Great Train Robbery*, a short silent film directed by Edwin S. Porter and released in 1903. Before that, however, Buffalo Bill's Wild West Show gave life to the idea of the "Wild West" in 1883 and Owen Wister's novel, *The Virginian*, was published in 1902. *The Last of the Mohicans* by James Fenimore Cooper predates all of that, though. It appeared in 1826.

Throughout the 1910s and 1920s, as the cinema itself was developing, the Western became a staple of the business. In the 20s, stars like Tom Mix, Hoot Gibson and Buick Jones helped build Hollywood and their own careers through the success of films about cowboys, Indians and the great American frontier.

By the late 20s, and in decades to follow, more sophisticated and adult Westerns began to appear. These included *The Virginian* (1929), *Stagecoach* (1939) and R*ed River* (1948). At the same time, however, "B" Westerns were playing in vastly popular double features in theatres in cities and small towns every Saturday afternoon. Parents took their kids, or even allowed them to go to the movies alone, to see Roy Rogers and Gene Autry, of course, but also Tex Ritter, John Wayne (in his early roles), Lash LaRue, Buster Crabbe, Bob Steele, Johnny Mack Brown, Wild Bill Elliott (Red Ryder), Tim Holt and many others.

Many of these films made their ways onto television screens. They were soon joined, and eclipsed, by a vast number of weekly television shows that mirrored their action, moral goals and heroic figures.

Almost simultaneously, the motion picture business was changing. With the growing popularity of television, movie revenues began to decline. In an attempt to bring audiences back to the theatres the industry created new film techniques such as the enormous widescreen extravaganzas and 3-D. These exciting visual experiences prompted the production of big budget "sword and sandal" epics such as *The Robe, Demetrius and the Gladiators, The Ten Commandments, Ben Hur* and *Cleopatra*.

Becky Bradley, writing about "American Cultural History: 1950-1959" for Lone Star College, says "the spectacle approach to film-making, Cold War paranoia, public fascination with outer space, and a renewed interest in science sparked by the atom bomb lent itself well to science fiction films."

Despite all that, Westerns prevailed on television and at any one time there were as many as 120 Western series on the small screen. They included, but weren't limited to (in no particular order) *The Roy Rogers Show, The Gene Autry Show, Sheriff of Cochise, Boots and Saddles, Man Without a Gun, Gunsmoke, The Lone Ranger, The Adventures of Wild Bill Hickok, The Rifleman, Wanted: Dead or Alive, Have Gun, Will Travel, Cimarron City, Lawman, Rawhide, Daniel Boone, Wyatt Earp, Bat Masterson, Tales of Wells Fargo, The Range Rider, The Cisco Kid, Bonanza, The Virginian, Wagon Train, The Restless Gun, Trackdown, Annie Oakley, The Big Valley, Maverick, The High Chaparral, Sugarfoot, Cheyenne, The Adventures of Kit Carson, Dick Powell's Zane Grey Theater, Death Valley Days* and many more.

Ted, left, on a Sheriff of Cochise *tour, poses with series star John Bromfield, right, and New Hampshire Governor (1955-59) Lane Dwinell*

T**HROUGH THE** 1950S and early 60s Ted White was being called for many big movies including the John Wayne films and others such as *Giant, The Big Country, The Naked and the Dead, Exodus, Spartacus* and many others.

However, unlike *Hatari*, which required him to spend seven months in Africa, most of the time spent on these films was of much shorter duration, sometimes only a few days.

In the meantime, Ted was working more and more on television shows and soon became, in the words of fellow stuntman and long-time friend Dean Sm, "The King of TV."

"It seemed like every time you turned on the television set, there was Ted," said Leonard who became a top stunt coordinator and second unit director, even hiring Ted to work on several of his projects.

In fact, Leonard's career got its start thanks in large part to Ted's training.

Early in his movie and television career Ted began receiving calls from various studios wanting him to appear in television shows as the double for the leading man or to help plan and carry out a variety of stunts.

"At one time I was contracted for four different Western TV series and I was jumping back and forth between them on almost a daily basis," Ted said.

He appeared consistently on such series as *Cheyenne* with Clint Walker, *Sheriff of Cochise* with John Bromfield, *Man without a Gun* with Rex Reason, *Maverick* with James Garner, *Wagon Train* with Robert Horton, *Lawman* with John Russell and many others *(see Ted's filmography at the end of the book for a partial list of films and TV shows in which he appeared)*.

Ted, left, in one of many TV shows in which he appeared

Ted appeared as Fess Parker's double in dozens of episodes of *Daniel Boone* and became close friends with the actor. He worked closely with Walter Matthau on *Tallahassee 7000* in a series which took him to Florida for long periods of time.

During that period of time he got a call from Columbia Studios. When told he was available, the caller asked him to grow a beard for several days.

The role was to be a drunk who gets thrown into jail on the popular *Andy Griffith Show*. Ted enjoyed getting to work with Griffith, Don Knotts and a very young Ron Howard.

Ted, left, tries to hide from Don Knotts in an episode of The Andy Griffith Show

He also appeared on *The Tonight Show with Johnny Carson* in an exciting way that differed greatly from the usual guest appearance.

Ted and another stuntman were seated in the audience wearing suits. On stage, Ed McMahon told Carson about a man who nearly ran over him on his way into the studio. Carson asked if he called the police. McMahon said "no, but he's at the show tonight and he's brought some idiot with him."

"Where is he?" Carson asked.

McMahon pointed at Ted and his friend and that initiated a bit of dialogue between Ted and McMahon – something like "don't call me an idiot" which prompted a nasty reply from McMahon.

At that point the two started up the steps from the audience. "We can't do this," the second stuntman said loudly, "we'll get thrown in jail."

"I don't give a damn," Ted shouted and pushed the other, starting a big fight.

The fight was so real that people in the audience began trying to leave and had to be restrained by the ushers. On the stage, Ted grabbed Carson by the throat "and his eyes were this big," Ted said, laughing. "We'd rehearsed it, you know. It was funny. We broke chairs – breakaway stuff – knocked each other around. It lasted not quite a minute but we had a great time."

Through the years, in addition to all the TV Westerns he did, Ted appeared on television with the Three Stooges, Groucho Marx, Red Skelton, Karl Malden and a young Michael Douglas, Tom Selleck and others.

Ted, in helmet in back, in a scene from The Three Stooges Meet Hercules

Working in television is quite different from feature films, Ted said. "It's like the difference between daylight and darkness."

Television producers don't have the luxury of taking as much time as they would on a feature film to get just the right shot, the right light, the perfect stunt.

"You have time limits in television production," Ted said. "By the end of each day's shooting we had to have a certain number of scenes shot and we couldn't afford to fall behind because we worked with only a certain amount of money and usually there wasn't any more in the kitty."

The seemingly simple matter of wardrobe illustrates that point. Although the scene being shot may not call for the actors or actresses to fall into a river, for example. the director may believe if they did it would enhance the scene. Wardrobe may not have a second set of clothes for a retake, though, and that calls for a decision. Because the line producer of the show is not usually on the set, the first assistant must call him or her and explain the situation. Told they needed a second set of clothes and that retakes would be necessary causing a certain amount of overtime, the producer had to make the decision about whether or not spend the additional money.

"Films give you more creative freedom," Ted said. "Most shots on TV take only 30 minutes or so to set up. For a feature, it may take half a day, sometimes an entire day, for one shot." He said directors like Howard Hawks weren't afraid to take the time and recalled that Hawks sat for days on *Red River* waiting for the clouds to get just right.

On a TV series the crew must adjust to a new director almost every week. In the early days of television, each series ran for 32 episodes a year. Using the same director too many times would make the episodes look too much alike. Even with the current 15 episodes a year, individual directors will do very few of them, perhaps no more than two or three.

Ted liked the television involvement. Working in TV actually paid better than being in an occasional theatrical film. "On the various TV series you can go on for years with a steady income and you get to stay at home and film in the L.A. area," Ted said. "On films you're often gone for long periods of time."

He said that some stuntmen who have hooked up with one star don't make as much as they would had they taken a variety of roles. "Big stars like John Wayne will do maybe one film a year," he said. "When Wayne did *Rio Bravo* he didn't do another for over a year." In the interim Ted found other jobs. Especially after *Hatari* he was in demand in Los Angeles to do several television series. "I could direct, coordinate stunts and double the leading man," Ted said. "I was on several contracts and it was nice to be home. Especially because I'd been gone so long on *Hatari*."

Several of the TV shows were especially memorable to Ted. At the top of his list was a long-term contract with Fess Parker.

11

Fired – Twice – From Daniel Boone

ONE DAY IN THE mid-60s Ted and another long-time stuntman Joe Yrigoyen (who appeared in everything from the Roy Rogers and Gene Autry movies to *Ben Hur* and *Prisoner of Zenda)* walked through the Twentieth Century Fox Studios gate to interview for a feature film. Director George Marshall, who knew both of the men, saw them and asked where they were going. "You don't want to do that," he said when told about the feature interview. "I'm going to shoot a series pilot called *Daniel Boone* and I need both of you. Forget the feature. There's lots of action, you'll make some great money."

"What do you think?" Yrigoyen asked Ted.

Ted said "we'll take it."

The pilot was to be shot near Frazier Park in Kern County, California. When the cast and crew assembled to shoot the first action scenes the man who had been assigned to double the series star Fess Parker was also to coordinate the stunts. "Unfortunately," Ted said, "the man didn't have the slightest idea of how to go about things. We tried to help him but it just wouldn't come together. The film we finally shot was horrible."

The next morning director George Sherman came to Ted and asked him to double Fess. Ted turned him down. "Why?" the director asked.

"I don't want to take a job away from someone," Ted said. "I just can't do that."

"Don't worry," Sherman said. "We've already fired him."

Ted agreed at that point but only if they had an okay from Fess Parker who had liked the first double. "He was that way," Ted said. "He never fired anyone off the set during all the years we worked together."

Parker agreed and Ted took over the work of the double and stunt coordinator. On the final day of shooting Parker came to Ted.

"If this thing sells," he said, "would you be willing to come back and double me through the series?"

"I'd like to do that," Ted said. In addition to Fess Parker, the series would star Patricia Blair, Ed Ames and a young Darby Hinton.

Several months later Ted got a call saying the series was on and they wanted him.

Ted, left, with Fess Parker, right, and Ted's son Michael on location near Moab, Utah, for a Daniel Boone *episode*

Ten years before the *Daniel Boone* TV show premiered, Fess Parker starred as another American pioneer on five episodes of *The Wonderful World of Disney* as Davy Crockett. Davy was referred to on those shows as "The King of the Wild Frontier". During the 1962-1963 season Fess also starred as Senator Eugene Smith on the series, *Mr. Smith Goes To Washington*. Parker also starred in several movies including *Springfield Rifle, Old Yeller, The Jayhawkers* and *Hell is For Heroes*, among others. One of Fess Parker's closest friends was fellow actor, Governor and U.S. President Ronald Reagan.

Parker, a tall, Texas-born actor who was discovered by Adolphe Menjou at the University of Texas, became the epitome of the frontier hero when cast by Disney as Davy Crockett. After the series Parker became typecast as a frontiersman so he returned to TV in 1964 as Daniel Boone.

Ted ready to shoot a scene for
Daniel Boone

Before Ted fully settled into the role on *Daniel Boone* he was fired – twice.

The first time was during the filming of one of the early episodes. "I'd brought in several stuntmen for a big battle scene," Ted said. "And I gave them the amount of money they should be earning for that kind of work." The first assistant, a man named Ted Shields, confronted Ted and said he wouldn't pay that kind of money." When Ted argued, he said "you're fired."

Shields brought in a man to replace Ted but when Parker arrived for the next day's shooting he said "where's Ted?" Told he had been fired, Parker said "get him back. I want him."

Ted went back for another action sequence and promised the men the same pay as before. Once again Shields fired him. "I don't give a damn about you. I'm not going to pay that kind of money."

When Fess Parker heard about it he said "we're not a bedroom, parlor-shot kind of series. We're an action show. Daniel Boone didn't walk around with a poodle on a string. We're going to need that kind of action to even make it through the first season."

He called the legal department who put together a 20-page contract for Ted. "We want you back on the show fulltime," the attorney told him. "Do you want to sign this contract?"

"No," Ted said. "I want to read it first."

He did sign the contract and showed up for work the next Monday morning. "What are you doing here?" Shields asked.

Ted said he was working and Shields asked if they were going to have the same problems again. "No," Ted said, "because you haven't got a thing to say about it."

"Since when?" came the reply. Ted explained the new five-year contract and the two managed to work together as the show went forward.

In this Daniel Boone *episode Ted saves a young boy from drowning*

In another scene Ted is bulldogged

72

For one episode the studio brought in a young director from New York who had made a name for himself by directing some well-received commercials.

In one scene being directed by the man from New York, Fess was to transfer from horseback to a runaway wagon to save a young girl. Ted was off the set when an extra came to him and said "did you know Fess is about to do a transfer?"

Ted quickly got to the set and went to the director. "Fess doesn't really do that kind of stunt," he told him. "If he gets hurt we'll be shut down."

"Who are you?" the director asked.

"I'm the stunt coordinator and second unit director and I'm under contract. If you don't think I have the authority to stop this, go ahead and see how fast the crew stops."

After calling the studio, the director came to Ted and said he'd do it his way.

Ted said Fess would not have put up an argument. He was too nice a man. "But the potential consequences if Fess got hurt were enormous. The director was right in one respect – it would have been better to have been able to shoot the scene close enough that the viewers could tell it was Fess. But if he had been hurt, we would all have been out of business."

Over the years, Ted has had to take that kind of stand with other directors if he thought the actor was in a position to get hurt. "If you don't you can't live with yourself, knowing its wrong and letting it happen. It's pretty tough to look in the mirror the next day. It's not just me. Other stuntmen do the same thing."

Ted fights to keep from being shot in this episode

Despite his concern for Parker's safety, Ted couldn't keep from playing tricks on the man. "I did so many things to him it's a wonder he didn't fire me or shoot me," Ted said.

At the time, Fess had a condo on the set where he often stayed during the week's shooting because his home was nearly 100 miles away. Frequently his wife Marci would come and stay with him.

One Monday morning Fess was not needed on the set and Ted was supervising a brief action scene when he got a call from Parker. He said "Marci and I are having a talk and want you to come over." When Ted arrived at the condo the actor said "Marci wants a Mercedes and I want a Cadillac. We can't make up our minds. So here's what we're going to do."

He handed Ted a blank check and said "you take this and go buy us a car. Whatever you buy, that's what we'll have."

A few days later Ted went to a local Chevrolet dealer and bought a pickup loaded with everything he could think of. He put a big ribbon on it and parked it in front of Fess's condo.

"When Fess came out in the morning and saw it he almost had a heart attack," Ted said with a laugh. "But Marci laughed until she cried and then went down and bought a Mercedes."

Parker drove the pickup for five years, back and forth to his home in Santa Barbara. Finally Parker advertised it for sale as "Fess Parker's truck" and sold it for several times what Ted had paid for it.

Ted, left, with Daniel Boone *series star Ed Ames, right, and child star Darby Hinton*

DARBY HINTON WAS the child star who played Daniel Boone's son Israel in 110 episodes of the series between 1964 and 1970. In one scene Boone's cabin was on fire and Israel was on the roof. He was to jump off the roof into his father's (Parker's) arms but he refused to make the jump. Everyone, including his mother, pleaded with him to jump.

Finally, Fess Parker asked "what would it take to make you jump?"

"I'll do it if Ted catches me," the boy replied.

Ted was summoned from across the street. He ran to wardrobe and got dressed then appeared on the set.

"He jumped and I caught him and that was it," he said. "Darby was a good kid. He had great manners and was a good actor. He knew his dialogue, would spit it out and hit the mark. Unfortunately, I haven't seen him since the series ended."

Darby Hinton was only six months old when he made his acting debut and he went on to appear in many commercials, film and TV series. His father died when he was barely a year old and he remained close to Fess Parker (Daniel Boone) who became something of a surrogate father to him.

THERE WAS A TIME when Parker wasn't too certain that Ted was exactly suited to be his double.

"One time he made me stand beside him with our butts to the camera," Ted said. "The photos showed that his butt was much larger than mine."

Parker said "look at the size of your butt compared to mine. I think people can tell the difference between us."

Ted said "Hell, Fess. Has anybody complained to you about your big butt?"

"No, they haven't," Parker replied.

"Then my butt is just fine," Ted said, and that ended the conversation.

ON ANOTHER OCCASION Fess was invited by ABC Television to go to British Columbia to hunt a grizzly bear for a segment of *American Sportsman*. Parker agreed, but only on the condition that Ted White accompany him.

In preparation for the trip, Ted suggested that they take the complete Daniel Boone costume and a 35mm movie camera. That way, Ted could shoot some film of Fess in the woods that they couldn't get in the L.A. area.

After a flight in a seaplane they landed in a remote area and stayed in a small two-story hotel that was populated mainly by a group of lumberjacks, all of whom seemed to have a French accent. The first night in the bar the lumberjacks started in on Fess. "See big Daniel Boone," they said. "Big star, tough guy."

Finally, over the objections of Fess, Ted walked to the men and said "Mr. Parker's a very easy going man. He'd like to just have dinner and leave without having any problems."

"What's the problem?" one asked.

Ted stretched to his full 6' 4" height and said "you're the problem and if you don't stop popping off I'll take each one of outside, one at a time, and beat the shit out of you."

The men quieted down and Fess and Ted got a good night's sleep.

In the morning they boarded the seaplane again and finally landed far to the north on the Kispiox River. ABC had set up camp nearby and provided tents for both Fess and Ted, two professional hunters and the entire ABC film crew. ABC also brought along a professional chef and the group was served an outstanding lunch.

"About 3 or 4 o'clock I was sitting in the tent when I heard Fess ask one of the crew if there was a restroom around," Ted said.

The crew member politely replied that, no, there was no restroom. "You go up this trail about 50 yards," he said, "and there are two trees that have been felled and they're close together. On one of the trees there's a stick with toilet paper." He made sure that Fess understood that he should be rather quiet but that he needed to make a little noise as he approached the area. "Salmon are running in the river," he said, "and bears are in the area. You need to be careful in case there's a mother with some cubs."

Ted grabbed the 35mm camera and ran ahead of Fess. He hid in some dense brush about 15 feet from the "restroom." Fess walked along the trail, whistling, making some noise as he had been instructed while Ted filmed him. He had his pants down and was just getting settled when Ted let out a loud growl, something like a Grizzly might make. Parker jumped up and ran back down the trail, trying desperately to adjust his clothes. Ted got it all on film.

Back at the camp Fess asked Ted to find out how cold the river water was. Ted obliged and found it terribly cold. Back in the tent, though, he told Fess it "wasn't too bad." Fess ran to the river, undressed and jumped in. "You could hear him miles away," Ted said. "He shouted and fought to get out of that river.

After both Ted and Fess, and others, had claimed their bears, they went back to the studio where Ted took the film he had shot to the film department and told the processors that it was private and to keep it a secret. After the film was developed, Ted had several large prints made from the color film's frames. On Monday he hung the pictures on the wall.

When Fess came in the crew was in hysterics. "Where is he?" Parker shouted. "I know he's hiding somewhere!" Ted stayed hidden until nearly noon and when he did show up Fess had all the photos off the wall but the crew had grabbed some.

Fess said "how could you do that?"

"I just couldn't help it."

Parker quickly became a good sport about it and the two remained close friends.

Ted fakes taking a hit from Fess Parker as the two rehearse a scene for a Daniel Boone *episode*

Parker was especially proud of the fact that *Daniel Boone* came in under budget in five of the six years it was on the air. When 20th Century Fox took the show off the air it was still the leader in its time slot.

In an interview on "The Archives of American Television" Parker explained that the company had recently released *Cleopatra* and that it lost so much money Fox wanted to put its television shows into syndication to see if it could recoup some of the losses. The company even sold off its property and the former Fox studios then became Century City.

When it ended its six-year run *Daniel Boone* was ahead in the ratings of such popular shows as *The Donna Reed Show, Perry Mason* and *Cimarron.*

The show was popular for many reasons, not the least of which was its constant use of minority actors, Parker said. The production company made a conscious effort to include as many black actors and actresses as possible. They included Roosevelt Grier, Floyd Patterson, Rafer Johnson, Raymond St. Jacques and even Ethyl Waters.

Ted appeared in episodes with some of them and says the first black actor he worked with, other than on the *Daniel Boone* series, was Nat "King" Cole who, along with Stubby Kaye, sang and played a banjo throughout the film *Cat Ballou* in 1965. He also worked with Sidney Poitier in the 1970 film *They Call Me Mister Tibbs.*

In that film Ted has a pool hall fight in which Poitier "grabs me be the back of my neck and drives me into a pool table and pushes the table across the room." Ted said Poitier was "a nice guy and I liked working with him."

While there are fewer Western movies being produced for the big screen today, the popularity of the genre has not totally diminished. Nor have Westerns completely vanished from television. They constantly show up in reruns and in syndication. In fact, as George-Warren writes, "critically and commercially successful miniseries such as the Larry McMurtry novel *Lonesome Dove (1989)* have found huge audiences. "Though television is by no means as saturated with the cowboy as it once was, it's still unlikely that the Western TV show will ever ride off into the sunset for good."

Other commentators agree that films like Clint Eastwood's *Unforgiven* (1992) proved that the Western was still alive, that it hadn't become a cliché, that the parodies and poor attempts to recreate its glory days had failed to make it a vestige of the past.

"If a man who has given so much of his career to playing a cowboy leaves us asking questions, that's a good sign," says George-Warren. "As long as there is still a new way to look at the great American icon – that individualistic range rider on horseback – whether literally or figuratively, there will continue to be great Westerns."

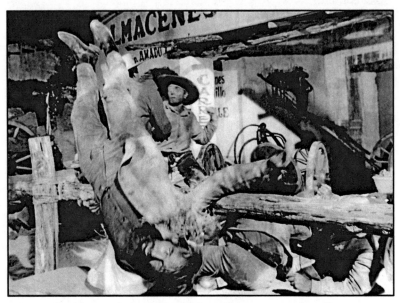

In this scene from another Western Ted appears ready to throw a punch. He's seen in the background in the black hat

12

More TV
The South Pacific

IN THE LATE 1950S it seemed like most television shows featured 19th century cowboy heroes or big city detectives from the 20th century. About that time 20th Century Fox got interested in producing a series featuring a sea captain who roved around the South Pacific. They would call it *Adventures in Paradise*.

During the planning stage for the series Will Milnick , an agent with the Louis Shur Agency dropped by the set where Ted was working. The Shur Agency was one of the biggest in the industry with clients such as Bing Crosby, Bob Hope and other major stars. He saw Ted and asked who he was.

A few days later Milnick called Ted and told him about the proposed series. "Fox Studios is looking for someone like you to do this 30-minute black and white series," Milnick told Ted. "It's about a guy on a sailing ship called the Tiki III in the South Pacific."

Ted said he was grateful but that he "wasn't an actor."

"Well," Milnick said, "with your looks and size and some training I think you'd get the show."

Ted became interested and after working with a drama coach for two weeks he went in for a three-minute screen test. Two weeks later Milnick called and said "come to the office. They want you on the show."

He told Ted that they would go to the studios the next day and sign a contract. "You're going to get $350 a week," he said.

Ted held up his hands. "I can't live on that," he said. "I've got two boys and a wife. I'm making house and car payments, insurance, all the rest."

Milnick tried to soothe him. "The second year, after the show's a hit, you'll make big money, maybe $5,000 a week. You need to take this for a year." When Ted again refused, Milnick said the agency would drop him if he didn't take it.

"I guess you'll have to drop me," Ted said.

Gardner McKay, a good-looking 6' 5" actor, ultimately got the part and, ironically, Ted was called in to double him. They knew one another as Ted had been McKay's double on the 1957 TV series *Boots and Saddles*.

"Gardner didn't have the mental strength to work like we did five days a week, week after week," Ted recalled. "But he did have jillions of girls showing up on the set."

He also had "two left feet," Ted said. And they were big – size 16 shoes.

Fox had constructed a false beach on the back lot with a mockup of the Tiki that was the same size as the real ship. One afternoon, as the crew was setting up for a shot, McKay got a call from the front gate saying there was a woman there to see him. He told them to let her in and she drove onto the fake beach in a large Buick convertible. Gardner went to talk to her and leaned over the door of the car.

Soon an assistant called to him that they were ready to shoot the scene. The girl gunned the car and ran over both his feet, leaving tracks over both his big white tennis shoes.

Ted said McKay fell over backwards moaning and crying that "that damn bitch ran over both my feet!"

They took him to the doctor to see if there were any broken bones, which there weren't.

On another occasion Ted and other stuntmen were rehearsing a fight. The plan, as usual, was to shoot a "master" of the entire sequence and then put the principal actor in at different points for close-up shots.

The shot called for Ted, as McKay's double, to grab a lanyard, swing far out over the ship, come back and hit two other stuntmen with his feet, knocking them overboard and into the water. Gardner watched and said "I want to do that."

Despite Ted's objections, fearing for the man's safety and knowing that he didn't always have the athletic ability to pull off certain kinds of stunts, the director decided it would be a good shot and agreed.

So Ted put tape on the rope where McKay was to grab it and told him he had to run, dive, grab the rope and swing out.

"I got it. I got it," Gardner said, anxious to do the stunt.

Ted then went to the two other stuntmen and said "now listen. He's going to hit you hard. He doesn't know how to do it so you take the hits and I'll make it right with you when the shot's over."

Ted says the director called "action" and McKay let out a warwhoop. "He ran, grabbed the rope, and yelled 'yeehaw!' He swung out and right back, straight into the mast, knocking him out cold."

The two stuntmen Gardner was to hit went into hysterics. McKay's legs were shaking and the director ran to him shouting "My God, I've killed him!"

"You haven't killed him," Ted said. "He's just knocked out."

Ted said the man had a knot on his head like a unicorn. Again, McKay was hauled off to the hospital.

McKay wasn't the only one to be injured on the set. In a scene in which the Tiki has sailed into a small lagoon, several pirates are scheming to take over the ship.

On the island, Gardner is above the pirates on a rock as they pass below him and he is to dive into them, starting a fight. Ted, of course, would double McKay for the shot.

At that time Ted and two partners – Al Wyatt and Red Morgan – had a company called Unit Two (they were all second unit directors and stuntmen). Ted called Morgan in to help with the shot.

"It had been raining for about five days," Ted recalled, "and these were fake rocks, called B52 rocks, and they were mushy from the rain." He told the director that he was concerned about getting a good foothold in the phony rock when he pushed off to bulldog the "pirates." The director asked him to give it a try anyway.

The director called "action" and Morgan trotted into the scene. Ted pushed off and his foot went down into the "rock."

"I was clawing the air and I knew I'm going to be short. But I managed to grab the back of his shirt with my left hand just as my leg hit the ground. There was a real rock hidden beneath the sand and when I hit it, it sounded like a rifle shot. BAM!"

Ted knew his leg was broken but he continued with the shot. "I'm wiped out," he told Morgan, "but I'm gonna hit you once and you roll over."

There was supposed to be a big, long fight but Ted swung, Morgan feigned being hit, and they stopped.

The crew came running and quickly got Ted to a hospital where he learned his leg was broken in two places. "It took them almost two hours before they got me on a stretcher," Ted said. When he got to the hospital he was treated by a man Ted knew, the doctor for the Los Angeles Raiders. He learned he had two fractures. They needed to operate and put in two pins. He would be out of work for some time.

He was in the hospital for two weeks and, because of the swelling, they couldn't put a cast on his leg. When a cast was finally put on he was on crutches and it was nine months before he was able to get around easily. The studio picked up the hospital bills, he said. "In that time I lost a lot of shows." Fortunately, he had insurance with Lloyd's of London and they provided funding based on the previous three years of salary. "It was hard for me to sit still," he said. "But my boys helped care for me, along with some friends."

Later in the series, after Ted was able to return to work, one of the assistants called Ted and said "there's something wrong with Gardner. Will you go talk to him and see what's going on?"

Ted found in him in the middle of a shot in the interior of the Tiki. "He's there with a beautiful blond, kissing her, trying to talk to her." But in the middle of a sentence Gardner would stop talking and break into a kind of hiccup – heh, heh, heh, heh. The director called "cut" and said "you're ruining the dialogue. Let's stop for lunch."

Back on the set Gardner studied the dialogue but continued to bark out the strange "heh, heh, heh." The shot was set up again and he and the woman were on the couch when suddenly he raised up, breathed heavily, ran to the door, off the set and toward Pico Boulevard, a major street that runs from the Pacific Ocean to downtown L.A.

Ted ran after him. "With his big feet he couldn't run as fast as I could," Ted said, "so I caught up and tackled him just before he ran out into the traffic on Pico. He hit his head on the concrete and I thought I'd killed him."

Again, McKay survived but had a breakdown and couldn't work for several weeks.

During the time McKay was off, the crew set up a number of shots with Ted doing action sequences. The plan was to cut to Gardner's face in closeup when he returned. Ted said they worked him hard for weeks – 12 to 15 hours a day.

Finally, McKay returned, "looking good and feeling fine," Ted said. "He apologized to the crew and appeared ready to work."

In one of the first scenes they shot with him, Ted said "I could see his eyes getting bigger and he began breathing heavily." Ted grabbed him as the man began frothing at the mouth. They once more called an ambulance. "He didn't know who he was or where he was," Ted said.

Gardner was unable to continue after that and production shut down. "We were only about halfway through the season and it cost Fox a lot of money," Ted said.

Perhaps ten years later Ted got a call from Gardner who said he was writing stage plays. He asked Ted to come visit him and give him some advice. Ted agreed and drove to McKay's house.

"He had about two acres," Ted said, "with a ten foot chain link fence all around it."

Gardner welcomed Ted and the two were going over one of his scripts in the living room when Ted looked up to see a giant lion walking toward him.

"I froze," Ted said. "I said Gardner, I can't talk right now. There's a lion here and I can't talk."

Gardner shrugged. "I'll get the sumbitch out of here," he said. He walked to the lion and slapped it and it left the room.

"I think I'd better go home," Ted told him. "I left and that was the last time I ever saw him. He was a strange guy. You meet all kinds."

Gardner died in November of 2001.

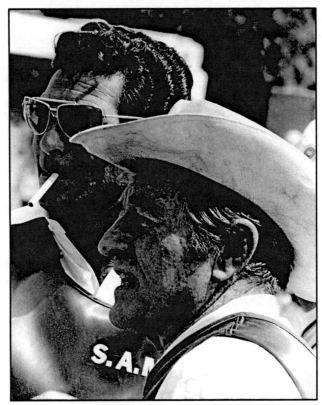

Ted, left, with fellow stuntman Boyd "Red" Morgan

13

More TV II
From Florida to the Frontier

THROUGHOUT THE 1950S Ted worked on a number of television series at any one time. Even when he was working for Fess Parker on *Daniel Boone* he was able to take other roles when the Boone series was between shootings. However, all of that was about to change.

In 1960 he got a call from Columbia Studios saying they wanted to send him to Florida to double Walter Matthau in a new series called *Tallahassee 7000*. In that show Matthau played Special Agent Lex Rogers of the Florida Sheriff's Bureau who traveled the state to help local police departments fight crime in their jurisdiction.

Matthau would later gain fame for such films as *The Fortune Cookie* (1966) and *The Odd Couple* (1968). He was a major star for decades appearing in both dramatic and comic roles, several of them with Jack Lemmon. However he battled heart disease and was eventually diagnosed with two forms of cancer.

He was in good shape, though, when Ted journeyed to Florida to sign on with him in a role that would last for three full years. The contract with Columbia for *Tallahassee 7000* was an unusual one. Normally, Ted had been called in for individual projects or for perhaps several shows in a series. In Florida, though, he was under contract for the entire run of the series. "The stars pretty much got to say who they wanted to work with," Ted said. "When the star says I want this particular individual, the studio has to make sure that person is available. The best way to assure that is to put him under contract."

To Ted's knowledge, no other stuntman has been under such a contract to a major studio. But even on *Tallahassee 7000* Ted was able to take work on a feature film now and then when the series was shut down for periods of time.

The studio hired the main male and female leads from New York or Hollywood. All the other parts were cast locally. To find people to take the bit parts and act as extras a casting director was hired from Hollywood. "In Hollywood, when you're looking for people to appear in films in whatever kind of bit parts," Ted said, "all you do is run an ad and open your door and people start applying."

In Florida, though, the new casting director opened an office and no one showed up. When the show was ready to begin the director asked where the cast was and she said nobody came to sign up. The director said you have to go out and find them. "I don't know how," she said. "When I'm in Hollywood . . ."

"Well, you're not in Hollywood," the director said, and fired her. The Studio brought in a man to replace her but the same thing happened.

On the third week the show's associate producer and director approached Ted and asked if he'd like to be the casting director. "Why me?" he asked. They said he had been around the business long enough to know how to do it. They said they'd give him a car and an additional $750 a week for taking on the job. Ted told them he'd do it but only for an extra $2,500 a week. Trapped, they settled for $2,250 a week.

Ted was in seventh heaven. "All I did was call the Chamber of Commerce and put an ad in the papers saying I needed actors and extras. I had about 200 people lined up almost immediately. It was no problem at all." At that time extras earned $50 a day. When they needed someone for a speaking role Ted would give a part to anyone who read well. "I had a big time with that and I did it for three years."

At one point, Ted needed to go the airport to pick up two stars who were flying in from New York City. His usual car was being serviced at the time and the studio gave him a convertible. The man would be the leading heavy in one of the episodes and the woman had a similar role.

At the airport "this guy steps off the plane and he has a cape over a shoulder, a mustache that curled down low and he looked like a Duke or something," Ted said. "The girl was a flashy New York chick with a short dress and a low cut blouse."

Ted said the woman got in the front seat, the man in the back. When they got on the freeway to head toward town the car was going perhaps 45 miles per hour when the man in the back seat began to shout – "Yaaah! Yaaah!"

When Ted turned around he saw that the man's toupee had blown off. The woman in the front seat went into spasms of laughter. Ted pulled the car to the side of the road and stopped. "I'm walking in the ditch and along the road to see if I can find the damn thing," Ted said. "Finally I find it and a car has already run over it."

Ted brought it back and the man stuck it on his head but got it all wrong.

"The woman is laughing so hard she's crying," Ted said, "and I'm thinking to myself that I'll get fired for sure."

At the set the pair went directly into wardrobe, Ted said, "but the man turned me in to the director and told him we were doing 100 miles per hour." Fortunately, nothing came of the incident.

Ted says working with Matthau "was a kick. What a great guy."

Matthau was a gambler. "He'd bet $10,000 or $20,000 on basketball games," Ted said. "He'd listen to the games while we were working. Every week the bookies would fly in from New York or elsewhere in Florida to collect their money or to pay off. He finally had to borrow against the residuals the show was to pay him to pay off the bookies."

Matthau seemed always to be in debt to his bookies. "We'd been in "Florida only about two months when the dog races started," Ted said.

"Let's go," Matthau said. When they arrived Matthau was recognized and the track owner took the star to his office and marked his card.

Walter won every race and left about $15,000 richer. "We went back the next night," Ted said, "and he lost it all and then some."

Ted said Matthau would bet on anything. One day he saw two birds on a high wire. "See those birds?" he said to Ted. "I'll bet you $500 the bird on the left flies away first."

"I can't bet that much," Ted said. "How about $50?"

He said okay and about that time they called him to the set for a shot. "I'll be there after one of those birds flies away," he told them.

Ted won $50.

"I saw him several times after we finished the series," Ted said, "but never did get to work with him again."

Matthau was a professional, Ted says. "When he came on the set he knew the dialogue, knew the scene and when they said they were ready he was up on his feet, he hit the mark and said his dialogue. I put him in the same category as Wayne and other big stars."

Matthau served in the Army Air Corps during World War II as a radio cryptographer in a heavy bomber unit. He finished the war as a sergeant with six battle stars.

His health was not good, however, and after heart bypass surgery, double pneumonia and the removal of a benign colon tumor he was hospitalized again in 1999 and diagnosed with cancer. He died on July 1, 2000. He was 79.

ANOTHER TELEVISION SHOW involving Ted was a 12-episode (26.5 hours) special that has remained famous since its airing in 1979 – *Centennial.*

Based on the novel by James Michener, the story is of the town of Centennial, Colorado, and follows the lives of people who lived in the area. The show also includes a murder mystery that takes 100 years to solve.

The impressive cast included many notable actors and actresses of the day, including Raymond Burr, Barbara Carrera, Richard Chamberlain, Robert Conrad, Alex Karras, Sally Kellerman, Donald Pleasance, Lynn Redgrave, Dennis Weaver, Andy Griffith, David Janssen, and other big name stars.

The show was nominated for several awards, including a Best Actor Golden Globe for Chamberlain and Best Television Series Golden Globe Drama in 1979.

Some of the filming took place near Pittsburg, PA, on the Ohio River. In one scene, set supposedly in the 18th century, Ted was paddling down the river in a canoe, with other "Indians." He said he looked up and was staring at what was then called Three Rivers Stadium, the home field of the Pittsburg Steelers pro football team. That "Golden Triangle," at the heart of downtown Pittsburg, is at the confluence of the Monongahela, Allegheny and Ohio rivers and the site of Fort Pitt which was built to replace Fort Duquesne after it was destroyed by the British in 1759.

Near Pittsburg the production company had built a Western town on the riverbank. In the town's saloon the crew is to stage a large-scale bar fight that involves one of the series' stars, Robert Conrad. A stuntman was assigned to double him in the fight in which Conrad's character would get hit and knocked through a big plate glass window, landing in the street.

When they were about to shoot the scene a group of newspaper people showed up and wanted to see Conrad, Ted said. He called the stuntman over and said "see all those newspaper people? I've got to do my own stunt."

"It's not up to me," the stuntman said. "Talk to the producer."

Conrad said he didn't need to talk to anyone about it. He did talk to the director, however, and told him to tell the stuntman to get out of his costume (like Conrad's) and get away. He didn't want the press to know he was being doubled.

Stuntmen had been through similar situations with Conrad before. "He was tough to work with," Ted said. In the television series, *The Wild Wild West* (1965-69), Ted recalled, Conrad had been hurt several times because he wanted to do stunts himself.

Ted was too large to double Conrad, who was not a very big man, but he was frequently on the set in various roles. In the episode in which the cast and crew were to stage a large fight in a saloon Conrad's character would be on the second floor near a chandelier. The stuntman doubling Conrad was to dive off the balcony, catch the chandelier and swing out and drop down feet-first on the other side where he would beat up the bad guys.

"Conrad got it in his head that wanted to do that stunt and argued with the director who said he couldn't take that responsibility. While he was on the phone calling the producer, Conrad set up the shot himself. "He was the star and really ran the show," Ted said. He told the first assistant to get the cameras ready.

"OK," the man said, "but you're gonna get me fired."

Conrad promised he wouldn't let him get fired and ran to the balcony. The cameras rolling, he dove off the balcony and caught the chandelier. But his hands couldn't hold on and he fell straight down on his back.

"It knocked him cold as a mackerel," Ted said. "He broke some vertebrae, hurt his neck and shoulder and shut the show down for several weeks while he recuperated.

So, Ted said, after Conrad insisted he would crash through the window in the *Centennial* scene, the stuntmen got together and said "what can we do to teach him a lesson?"

Conrad's double who had been kicked off the set, went to the special effects crew. "How thick is the candy glass in that window?" he asked. Told it was tissue-paper thin, he asked them to replace it with some much thicker glass.

Some of the newspaper people were outside the window to get photographs of him as he was knocked through it, while others stayed inside. Likewise, two cameras were filming – one inside and one outside.

Conrad was to take two or three punches and then the one that was to knock him through the window. Ted said he faked taking the punch and let out a warwhoop as he dove toward the window.

"But only his head and one knee went through and there he was, hanging there half in and half out for all the world to see."

The special effects man said "oh, shit!" and Conrad started crying, Ted said, "real tears."

"You SOBs, get me out of here," he yelled. When he was free he said "what happened?"

The special effects crew said they didn't know, maybe he didn't have enough momentum to get through.

"Momentum, my ass. This is like a piece of wood," Conrad said.

Ted said the reporters loved it and pictures were in the papers the next day.

From that day on, Ted said, Conrad treated the crew like kings. "He knew they had him."

In another episode, Ted was among several who were playing the role of Indians, including Michael Ansera who played an Indian chief.

"We were in the snow up in Wyoming," Ted said. "And we were wearing nothing but breechclouts." He said they had a trailer where they dressed and where the crew sprayed them with a dark brown color. "For the shot we rode bareback with bows and arrows."

The "Indians" were to ride across a creek that was about four feet deep and 20 feet wide. The creek had frozen during the night so the crew chopped it up and got water running. "Some dead trees had fallen in the

92

creek and they had lots of sharp branches sticking out," Ted said.

The scene was to be a running fight with the Indians shooting arrows at the bad guys.

They put the reins in their teeth, pulled arrows from their quivers and shot.

"About halfway across, the stuntman in front of me was bucked off his horse," Ted said. "He barely missed one of those sharp branches but his back hit a rock. He was wiped out."

The crew tore the door off a nearby outhouse, laid him on it and carried him to a car which took him to a hospital.

The director asked for a retake and the stuntmen complied. But again there was a mishap. One of the men was nearly across the creek when his horse went down and he went over the horse's head. The director asked for one more try but the stuntmen refused.

"It was ridiculous to keep shooting under those circumstances," Ted said. "It was too dangerous and the horses were local and not trained to deal with those kinds of conditions."

In another scene, the company brought in a stuntman for a special shot. He was to play an Indian facing away from the camera with a bow and arrow, getting ready to shoot.

Two other stuntmen, riding two horses with a long rope between them would race up behind him and stretch the rope between them, catching him behind the legs and stretching him out.

"It was a hard, tough, stunt," Ted said. "A dangerous one."

When it came time to make the shot, the stuntman who was to play the Indian couldn't be found. Billy Burton, the stunt coordinator on the show, asked Ted to take his place.

"I was standing there after I'd fired an arrow, then I reached back and got another," Ted said, "notched it and pulled back to fire when they hit me with the rope. It flung me like a rag doll up in the air and I landed straight down on my back."

As he painfully got up the cameraman said "I think I missed it." He had thought Ted would fall forward but instead he went straight up in the air. Burton shook his head and asked Ted to do it again.

"I didn't want to," Ted said. "My back and both my legs were hurting. I looked like someone had hit me with an iron bar."

But Ted "soldiered up" and did it again only this time he landed on his face. "We got the shot that time," Ted said. "Then they found the guy who was supposed to do the stunt and sent him home."

Another incident during the production of *Centennial* involved fellow stuntman Tony Epper whose list of film appearances rivals that of Ted. "Tony was very strong," Ted said. "He could take a 16-pound sledge hammer, hold it out at arm's length and bring the metal down to touch his nose and take it back out to arm's length again. "Others of us tried it but couldn't do it." Epper also played the guitar.

One evening, after quite a few drinks in the five-star hotel where the cast and crew were staying, Epper approached the Mexican guitar player who was performing and demanded that he be allowed to play his guitar. The guitarist refused. Epper grabbed the guitar and broke its neck. The performer fell to the floor in tears. When Epper went to the paymaster the next payday he found his envelope was empty. The paymaster told him he had no money coming. "That guitar you broke is a forty thousand dollar instrument," he said, "and the guy can't fix it. You're going to pay it off."

Epper tried to grab the paymaster but was restrained by Ted. They started for the door and found it closed. Epper kicked his foot through the door and "broke doors all the way down the hall and out of the building," Ted said.

Ted was on another production with Epper a year later in Tucson. This film starred Lee Marvin. Ted, Epper, Terry Leonard and others were in a bar when a fight started because a local cowboy thought one of Ted's friends had been "making moves" on his girlfriend.

"A large number" of cowboys had "the six of us" backed up to the bandstand, Ted said. "Tony picked up a captain's chair and hit someone in the head with it. The man fell, and eventually died.

Back in Los Angeles Tony was arrested. Fortunately, Lee Marvin testified on their behalf and explained that Epper and the others, including Ted, were badly outnumbered. Epper was, as a result, found innocent of murder. "He was so strong it was unbelievable," Ted said. "People pitted us against one another for twenty years. They wanted us to fight but it never happened. On many shows they'd put us together to stage a fight and we'd tear the place up." Ted and Epper remained good friends and visited on the phone regularly. Epper died in 2012.

94

14

Meanwhile, Back at the Ranch...

IN THE 1950s and 60s Ted was busy running from one TV western series to another, sometimes to three different shows in one day. Hollywood was also infatuated with Westerns – audiences couldn't seem to get enough of them.

During those two decades he was also busy with films of a more contemporary nature. He worked on such blockbusters as *The Man in a Gray Flannel Suit* with Gregory Peck, *Pillow Talk* with Rock Hudson and Doris Day, *Portrait in Black* with Anthony Quinn and Lana Turner, *Cleopatra* with Elizabeth Taylor, and *The Cincinnati Kid* with Steve McQueen, among dozens of others (*see Ted's filmography at the end of the book*).

Still, Ted's early resume included more Westerns than movies set in modern-day situations. And that was fine with him. He'd grown up a very real cowboy, after all, and he had a Professional Rodeo Cowboys Association (PRCA) membership card. He grew up on a ranch, could ride and rope as well as anyone. Besides that, he was 6'4" in his stocking feet and looked every bit the part of a rugged cowboy.

At that time Ted was one of a relatively new breed of individuals coming onto the movie scene – men who were natural on horseback, who were athletes, who were more or less fearless and who tried to learn every aspect of the business.

A few of them, Ted included, would make themselves invaluable to the industry by immersing themselves in learning the trade and becoming, in addition to stuntmen and actors, stunt coordinators, second unit directors and sometimes even directors and producers.

Ted formed friendly relationships with many of the top stuntmen in the business and even trained some of them. Two of those men who have

95

remained especially close friends over the years are Terry Leonard and Dean Smith. Both were athletes. Leonard, for example, attended college at the University of Arizona and played professional football in Canada for the British Columbia Lions. He was injured early on, however, and decided to go to California to "try that stunt business."

Dean Smith was an Olympic athlete. He won an Olympic gold medal for the 400-meter relay in the 1952 Helsinki games and finished fourth in the 100-dash in the closest race in Olympic history.

When they showed up in Hollywood, the main opportunities for them were in Westerns. Because Ted White had been one of the early arrivals, the relative newcomers often turned to him for training and advice.

Everyone was busy in those days. "Warner Brothers, at that time, had at least seven different series going," Ted said. "I spent several years with them going from show to show to show and doing features in between. It wasn't unusual to be doing something on *Cheyenne* when casting would call down and ask when I was going to be finished there." The *Cheyenne* production crew might say he's just finished a piece but they would probably need him later on. Casting would say "he's on the grounds so have him go over to the *Maverick* set, get to wardrobe, get changed and report."

Ted said that sometimes he might do as many as three shows in one day. "In those days a stuntmen got $55.00 a day but everything you did stunt-wise paid above that. I usually averaged around $350.00 or $400.00 a day which was pretty good back in the 50s."

Almost all the studios were "Western-oriented" back in those days, Ted recalled. "For every ten scripts that showed up eight were Westerns." Westerns were relatively inexpensive to make, he explained.

At one time there was a company called Fat Jones' Farm that stocked animals and everything a studio needed to rent to make a Western. "It was originally called Hudkins Brothers Ranch," Ted said, "but the owner, Ace Hudkins, sold it to a man called Fat Jones. He had maybe 60 or 70 wagons, stage coaches, buckboards, all kinds of saddles.

A "nondescript" horse could be rented for $25.00 a day and a good horse would go for $50 a day. "Now," he said, "it costs the studios anywhere from $750 to $1,500 a day for a good horse." In addition, studios would rent saddles, saddle blankets, bridles, wagons. Everything was rented. And with the horses came a wrangler who belonged to the Teamsters Union."

A rare photo of Clarence "Fat" Jones (left) at his Hollywood horse stables on Sherman Way in North Hollywood. Jones founded the stable originally in Edendale (now Silverlake) in 1912 and rented horses to movie companies for 51 years. (Photo courtesy of Boyd Magers www.westernclippings.com)

When stuntmen like Ted went to work in the morning, they often didn't know what they would be asked to do. He recalled one day when he, Terry Leonard and some other stuntmen were on the *Wells Fargo* series set. "Dean Smith was stunt coordinator on that show," Ted said. "The crew was to film a stunt the next day and the stuntmen flipped a coin to see who got it and Terry Leonard won."

The next day Leonard showed up with a young, good-looking blonde girl on his arm. "Who's the girl?" Ted asked. Dean Smith said he didn't know but that Leonard showed up now and then with a different girl.

Leonard, who wore false teeth, was to fall from the top of a two-story building, hit a portico that extended out over the street and then fall into a "porta pit" that cushioned the landing in the street. When the lighting was ready and the crew called for Leonard, he ran to Ted and handed him his false teeth. "As soon as I hit the ground get me my teeth right away," he said.

As Leonard prepared for the stunt, Ted and Dean Smith saw the girl he had brought to the set wringing her hands and looking very nervous. "Are you OK?" Ted asked her.

"I'm worried to death for Terry," she replied. "He told me only two other men have ever done this stunt and that one died and other was so torn up he never worked again."

Ted recalls that Dean looked at him and slightly rolled his eyes. Ted said "don't worry, dear. He'll be fine." What Ted didn't tell her was that this was a very simple stunt. "Your mother could do it," he said.

Near Ted were several horses and one dropped a "whole bunch of horse apples." He found a shovel and moved it into a nice pile. As Terry turned his back in preparation for the fall, Ted shoved the man's teeth into the pile.

Terry did the jump but landed four or five feet away from the porta pit. Ted reached in the pile and grabbed his false teeth. Terry shoved them in his mouth, gasped, cursed and began running away. "The girl came to me asked how badly he was hurt," Ted said. "I told her he was OK and that he was going down to the production manager to see how much money he would make for that stunt."

Terry came back and said "if it's my dying act, I'll get you for this." He said he could taste horseshit for a week.

Ted, left, and good friend Terry Leonard when Ted received the
Reel Cowboys Silver Spur Award in 2011

Ted didn't know how much money Leonard made for that stunt but recalls that in the early days the going rate was $55 for a fall from a saddle.

He might do eight or nine saddle falls a day, he said. The rate went up to $125 after a few years and later went up again to $250.

"Now, when you walk into the studio the fee is $850 and everything you do is above that," he said. "Today a top stuntman has no problem making up to a million dollars a year."

He admits that only a few stuntmen make that much, but many earn $500,000 to $600,000 a year.

"But you have to have a lot of skills," he said. "That might include all kinds of stunts for Westerns, but also fast car driving, sword fighting, fire work, high work, whatever it calls for. If you're doubling a leading man and he has to parachute out of a plane and you haven't done that, you learn fast."

Neil Summers, in the introduction to his 1996 book *The Unsung Heroes*, notes that professional stuntmen and stuntwomen are not daredevils. "They are highly trained and experienced professionals who make the dangerous and spectacular look easy." Summers points out that "In 1995 alone, two women were killed performing for the cameras and on any given day there are dozens of knocks and bruises by the talented athletes that make their living doubling for actors and doing stunts."

Because there has been no "school for stuntmen" most, like Ted, have learned their trade through "on-the-job training." In fact, Ted has helped train numerous stuntmen, including men like Terry Leonard as well as total newcomers, at his home near Los Angeles.

"I learned a lot of my craft from Ted," Leonard said. "He had a mini school at his house and several of us would go out there and he'd teach us sword fighting and other tricks of the trade."

"I do it because they ask me," Ted said, "and because I want to be of help."

As an example, several years ago he received a call from a friend and fellow stuntman Bob Burrows. Burrows was in the last stages of a serious illness and asked Ted for a final favor. "I want you to train my son to be a stuntman," he said.

Ted, reluctant to turn down a dying man's last request, agreed. He called the son, Brian Burrows, and told him he had agreed to work with him but that he would have to promise that he would stay with it no matter how tough it got. Brian agreed and Ted worked with him and a friend, Jimmy Lewis, in his back yard for seven months.

Ted mounted a camera on a tripod and filmed the two as they practiced. He started with the basics such as a motion picture fistfight, moved to knife fights, sword fighting and even driving cars.

Finally, satisfied that the two were ready, he had them print business cards and took them to various film studios where they were introduced to casting directors and others.

A few months later Brian called to say he had been hired to be a stuntman on a show with Billy Crystal -- *City Slickers II: The Legend of Curly's Gold* – and that among the stunts he was being asked to do was a transfer from one horse to another. Ted gave him a "step" to give him a push when he jumped so he could get high enough in the air. A "step" replaces a stirrup and is L-shaped so a boot won't get caught trying to get out of a standard stirrup.

Later, Brian called Ted to say he was stunt coordinator on a movie called *Robin Hood: Men in Tights* to be directed by Mel Brooks and he wanted Ted to work with him. Ted asked him what he wanted him to do and learned there was to be a big fight that Brian needed help setting up. Ted told him to bring the script and he would help him choreograph the fight but that Brian was the stunt coordinator and he should be the one to carry it out. "The proof is in the pudding," he said. "The fight came off just fine."

Ted said he wanted the young man to be successful but he didn't want to take away any of the responsibility or any of the good feeling he would have when the fight was done properly, and under his own direction.

"We don't get a lot of recognition," Ted said, "so we want to do things right. Naturally we want to be recognized for our work and I wanted Brian to have some of that recognition."

Some struggling stuntmen are reluctant to take advice or help from those who have been successful, Ted said. It may be because they just aren't capable of doing some of the things they are asked to do or their personality might not be quite right and they can't get along with people.

"Maybe one percent of all the guys trying to be a stuntman actually make it," he said. "You get busted up and you can't feel sorry for stuntmen who end up with broken bones, or worse. They make big money. They work with the best people in the business and, they travel all over the world first class. What more could you ask for? It's a good life."

Ted said he knows some stuntmen who made a lot of money and

spent it on fancy cars, big homes and even airplanes. "Most of the younger generation seems to have wised up, though," he said. "They're putting their money away."

Some stuntmen make well over a million dollars a year, he said. If they live a moderate life they can save a great deal of it. "Your airfare is paid, your hotel bills are paid, you get a weekly per diem and the only thing you've got to take care of on location is your laundry bill. I can't tell you how many towns I've left and my laundry is still there."

Westerns have changed considerably over the years, Ted said. The early films were made with little or no research. The Westerns made by Tom Mix and Hoot Gibson, for example, and even Roy Rogers and John Wayne (when he made the B Westerns), were filmed just to make money with little attention given to authenticity.

"Sixguns would fire fifteen times without being reloaded," Ted said. "Horses would run for miles as fast as they could go. But that was what the kids paid a dime to see."

In the 50s, he said, there were very few fast car scenes. "Now it's largely cars or jets and the films are almost all action with little character development."

And the films were inexpensive to make. The production costs of *The Alamo* were among the highest ever to that point. "Now," Ted said, "the newest *The Lone Ranger* cost around $250 million. And it's a picture that's been made at least four times before." As movie fans know by now, this version of the story of the famed masked man did not do well at the box office, despite the on-screen presence of Johnny Depp and heavy advance promotion.

Ted played the Lone Ranger's father in *The Legend of the Lone Ranger* in 1981. His death (in the film) set the Lone Ranger on his quest to do good and right wrongs.

Ted loved doing Westerns. His experiences on various TV series were full of fun and excitement. The early feature film Westerns he worked were some of the highlights of his career, he says, recalling *Rio Bravo, The Horse Soldiers* and *The Alamo*.

Others had just as much of an impact. They included *Lone Star, The Big Country, Giant, Smoky, Will Penny, Cat Ballou, Blazing Saddles, Conagher, Sunset, The Misfits,* (among many others) and two that have special memories for him, both good and bad – *Comes a Horseman* starring James Caan and Jane Fonda; and *Silverado* with its star-studded cast of Kevin Kline, Scott Glenn, Kevin Costner, Danny Glover and other big name stars.

On *Comes a Horseman* (1978) James Caan and Jane Fonda didn't especially get along, Ted said, "but the film turned out well and earned critical acclaim so their problems didn't interfere with the final product."

In the film Ella Connors (Fonda) is a single woman who gets pressured to sell her failing cattle ranch to her corrupt ex suitor, Jacob Ewing (Jason Robards). She asks for help from her neighbor, Frank Athearn (Caan). As Ella and Frank fight back through stampedes, jealousy, betrayal, and sabotage they eventually find love.

Paul Helmick, who had been the associate producer of *Hatari*, was the first assistant director on this film. He got to Montana ahead of the cast and happened to be in the transportation area when Jane Fonda walked in. Stars of films were provided their own vehicles for the duration of filming. "What kind of car do you have for me?" she asked. Helmick had never met the actress before and, without turning around, he said "we have several here. Let's pick one out."

He then turned around and asked: "What do you do on the show"

Fonda was flabbergasted, Ted said. She said "my name is Jane Fonda and I'm the female lead on the show."

She wouldn't talk to Helmick throughout the production after that.

Another incident involving a vehicle further intensified Fonda's dislike of Helmick. In the film Fonda's character drives an old pickup. It was the only version of that pickup that the prop department had. She had brought her two children with her to the set and, on Sundays when they weren't shooting, she took the kids for long drives in that particular pickup.

Helmick was frightened that she would tear it up. "If it blew a motor or had some other kind of problem everything would have to stop," Ted said, "because they didn't have a double for it."

Helmick decided to talk to Fonda about the potential problem. Instead of helping, however, it made her angry and she again refused to speak to him.

That dustup was minor, however, compared to a tragedy that occurred on the set. Near the end of the film, while the ranch house is burning in the background, Jacob Ewing, played by Jason Robards, is shot off his horse. His foot hangs up in the stirrup and the horse drags him through a gate and out onto the prairie.

"When you do a drag," Ted said, "you have a cable running up your leg, through your shirt and into your hand. In your hand is a short piece of wood that, when it is pulled at the end of the drag, will release the hook on your boot that's holding you to the stirrup and you're free."

There were railroad ties on each side of the gate Robards' character was to get dragged through. One was made of balsa wood, though, and the plan was for Jimmy Sheppard, the stuntman (playing Robards) to hit the balsa wood post and break it. He had to make a turn just before the gate, however, to miss a large barn.

"We rehearsed the scene carefully," Ted said. "We even had half a dozen horses out in the pasture where the runaway horse was supposed to go and each time he turned toward that group of horses." That would be the end of the shot because when Jimmy released himself the horse would be running free.

Before the shot Stunt Coordinator Walter Scott said "Ted, just to be on the safe side, get a good horse and go behind the barn out of sight of the camera but where you'll be in a position to help if anything goes wrong."

With the house burning in the background director Alan Pakula called "action!" Jimmy, the stuntman doing the fall and the drag, thought he was through the gate and pulled the pin to release himself too early. Director Pakula was not pleased and called for a reshoot.

"The house was burning wildly," Ted said, "and the horse was antsy. Jimmy weighed only about 150 pounds and when he hit the bend the horse swung him way out and, instead of turning to the left as he had done in rehearsal, the horse turned to the right."

Sheppard went fullforce into the real railroad tie.

"I spurred my horse," Ted said. "Jimmy was still hooked up, of course, as he hadn't pulled the pin. I caught up to the horse and got him loose. He was crushed." Walter Scott called for a helicopter which arrived in minutes but Sheppard died within hours.

The next day, when no action was scheduled, Ted told Walter Scott that, although he wasn't the same size, he didn't think viewers could tell as he was being dragged.

"I'll do the shot," he said. But Scott refused the offer.

The entire company was torn up on the incident and Jane Fonda was badly shaken. But she continued on and did a good job, Ted recalled. "She was very good at dialogue," he said. "I worked with her when she was only 19 or 20 years old on *Cat Ballou* and she was wonderful. She tore a gaping hole in her career when she went to Vietnam but she survived that, too."

The film was completed on schedule and on budget, despite those mishaps, Fonda's run-in with Paul Helmick and other difficulties. In addition to Caan and Fonda not getting along, Caan didn't much care for the director, Alan Pakula, who hadn't directed a modern-day Western. Ted said the man did things that "weren't exactly right" but because he was the director he could get away with them. Caan often balked, Ted said, but the director had his way.

Another fine actor in the film was Richard Farnsworth, a stuntman who after 30 years in the business moved into acting and became an acclaimed and respected character actor.

Ted happened to be in the office reading for a part (one he didn't get) when Farnsworth came to read for a part in *Comes a Horseman* with director Pakula and Fonda.

When he was finished Fonda said: "That was beautiful, Dick. Have you been acting long?"

"No," he said. "I've been an extra and a stuntman."

After Farnsworth read some more Pakula told him he had the role of the fourth lead in the movie.

Pretty soon everyone was talking about Farnsworth's success. "Did you hear about Dick?" Walter Scott asked Ted.

Ted had been among the first to know. "He did a hell of a job in that movie," Ted said.

That was just the beginning. Farnsworth went on appear in many films including *Tom Horn, Independence Day, The Natural, Rhinestone, Misery, The Getaway* and *The Straight Man.*

15

Back in the Saddle Again

IN THE MID-FIFTIES Ted was heavily involved in series Westerns for TV but still found opportunities, and time, to work a feature film.

In 1956, for example, he was called to double Rock Hudson in the hit feature *Giant* which also starred Elizabeth Taylor and James Dean. "I was there to double Rock but never had to," Ted recalled. "I did help him work out a routine for a fight but I was also involved in the movie in many other ways." Ted would have other chances to double Hudson, however.

One way he was involved in *Giant* was helping James Dean perfect a Texas dialect. "Jimmy often came to me, knowing I was from Texas," Ted said, "to ask how I would say a particular line. That went on throughout the course of filming."

When the film had wrapped Dean presented Ted a gold belt buckle. It was inscribed: *To Ted -- thanks for all your help. Jimmy Dean.*

The movie, as film lovers know, was a majestic epic, covering the life of a Texas cattle rancher, his family and associates, along with his continuing battle with James Dean's character who strikes it rich in the oil fields. The movie was directed by George Stevens and was based on the novel by Edna Ferber.

"It was a big movie," Ted said, "with a lot of location work. It was also a big film for Rock Hudson. It was his first major role and he came off very well in it."

Ted said Rock was "a lot more of a man that most people know. He wasn't afraid of anything." Hudson did lots of Westerns in his early acting career, and played many roles as an Indian that required bareback horse riding and other tough stuff (including the bare-chested "Young Bull" in the 1950 film *Winchester 73*). "He never backed away," Ted said.

Almost 30 years later, after acting, doing stunts and serving as second unit director in dozens of films and TV shows including many Westerns, Ted found himself deeply involved in another Western that would prove to have special meaning to him – *Silverado.*

Ted as Hoyt in Silverado

"When we did that movie it was considered one of the big Westerns," Ted said. "It was shot entirely on location in New Mexico. The crew built the town of Silverado from scratch and it was on a hill where you could film a full 360 degrees and not see a telephone pole, a road or any sign of civilization."

"The town had three main streets in it," Ted said. "Most towns that are built as Western sets have only one." The reason, he said, is obvious to anyone who has seen the film. Near the end Scott Glenn's character rides his horse down one street and viewers see another street from between the buildings. "It was pretty authentic," Ted said.

The town was used in a number of other films because, by photographing it from different angles, it could represent a variety of locations. Unfortunately, most of the movie town was burned to the ground during the filming of *Wild Wild West* (1999) which starred Will Smith, Kevin

106

Kline and Kenneth Branagh.

One scene in that film called for a building in the town to be set on fire with flames coming out of the windows. The manager of the set told stunt coordinator Terry Leonard that the wind usually came up in the evening and they shouldn't shoot a fire after 4:00 p.m. Terry told Director Barry Sonnenfeld about the warning.

However, several days later the crew finished a scene earlier than expected and Sonnenfeld decided to shoot the fire scene. "We shouldn't do this," Leonard said. "It's too windy."

Sonnenfelt suggested in no uncertain terms that Leonard was "just a stuntman" and shouldn't try to tell him what to do.

"Terry said okay," Ted said. "They started a fire, the wind came up and burned the place down. I don't know how much it cost to rebuild the town of Silverado."

SILVERADO WAS PRODUCED and directed by Lawrence Kasdan who also wrote the screenplay with his brother Mark. In the film, a group of cowboys meet by chance and, in the town of Silverado, thwart the plans of a corrupt sheriff who is in cahoots with a ruthless rancher. The movie features an ensemble cast, including Kevin Kline, Scott Glenn, Danny Glover, Kevin Costner, John Cleese, and Brian Dennehy.

Early in the production process Ted learned he would play a tough, unshaven ranch foreman named Hoyt. He also learned that all the costumes had to be approved by Kasdan, the director.

"When I went into wardrobe for the part of Hoyt they put me in an outfit but the director wasn't happy with that look. So they put me in long brown coat with a bigger hat." The two Kasdans (the director and his co-writer brother) finally accepted the outfit but they asked Ted how long it would take him to grow a beard.

"You have too good a look for the rough person the character is supposed to be," the director told him. Then he asked: "Would you be willing to wear a patch over one eye? It would give you that look of a man who would do what you're to do in the movie."

"At that point I had no idea how much I was going to enjoy working on that motion picture," Ted said. "I never worked for a better director. From the beginning he was very strict about dialogue, saying it had to be spoken as written.

Three years earlier the movie had been presented to Warner Brothers, but the Kasdans were told the cost was too high. The studio bosses liked the story and the characters but said the proposed cast would cost too much and it would be too expensive to build the town of Silverado. When they finally agreed to terms with the Kasdans, every line of dialogue had been approved by Warner Brothers, and their permission would be required before any changes could be made.

"That was very strange to me," Ted said. "So many times you need to change dialogue to fit the location, the character, or what precedes or follows that scene. But Kasdan made it work by putting people in the right places and setting up specific scenes very carefully."

At one point during the filming Ted suggested a change in the way his character (Hoyt) says a line. In the film Hoyt is about to shoot Ezra, the father of Danny Glover (playing Mal). Ezra is played by longtime screen actor Joe Seneca. "I'm standing on a rock getting ready to shoot the old man," Ted said, "and I've got a line of dialogue that just didn't sound right to me."

Ezra says to Hoyt: "You're lying again."

Hoyt's line that follows is the one in question. "No," he says, "this time I've got my orders."

"I just didn't feel that was a strong enough way to tell him I had to kill him," Ted said. He went to Kasdan with a suggestion but the director and others told him to do it the way it was written. Nearly three months later they called Ted to the studio to redo it because the sound of a nearby river had covered some of the dialogue. "You should have let me say it the way I wanted to," Ted told them. Kasdan laughed and said he still liked it the way he wrote it.

Most big-name stars will adhere to a script and repeat dialogue the way it was written, Ted acknowledged. They have the right to suggest changes but need to make their requests during rehearsals. "Sometimes the way dialogue is written reads well in the script but, verbally, it doesn't really fit an actor's style," he said.

On *Starman* (1984) starring Jeff Bridges Ted made a suggestion that Director John Carpenter accepted on the spot. Ted was able to make his role as the deer hunter rougher and more believable by, instead of saying "I'll be

108

darned" he would say "that dirty sonofabitch."

"I wasn't trying to take anything away from the writer," he said, "but that dialogue just didn't fit me in that particular scene. I'm six feet four and a roughneck in the film."

Likewise, in the opening to *Romancing the Stone* (1984) starring Michael Douglas and Kathleen Turner Ted plays a scoundrel of a cowboy bursting in on a fantasy of a romance novel writer and was able to convince Director Robert Zeneckis that a dialogue change would make his character more believable. His changes stayed in the film.

"Sometimes the writing is good but the place, time and situation demand changes to make it work," he said.

Before filming of *Silverado* began the director brought everyone who had a speaking role together to read through the entire script from beginning to end. "Every actor was there," Ted said. "There were no excuses. If you were alive, you were there."

This gave Kasdan a chance to listen to, and refine, each line of dialogue. "If you were too nonchalant about it, it wouldn't work," Ted said. "We had to do the lines like we believed it, staying in character. If there was to be a change in any of the dialogue that would be the time and Kasdan could get it approved before shooting began."

Finally, they were ready to begin filming.

"When they first put that patch over my eye I knew it wasn't going to work," Ted said. "I couldn't see a thing through it and I had to have good depth perception for some of the dangerous horse-riding scenes I was going to have to do." He got the prop department to make one for him that was a tight mesh that he could see through enough to get by but that the audience thought was completely opaque.

Ted thought director Kasdan was one of the finest he had worked with. "You never heard a cross word from the man's mouth," he said. "He didn't yell or curse at anyone."

There were only a couple of times when Ted saw Kasdan upset.

One dramatic scene called for a cattle stampede. The cattle (about 150 head) were to run down a long narrow street between the barn and the ranch house to the cookshack where it made a turn. "We tried for six days to get those cattle to stampede through there and couldn't do it," Ted said. "Walter Scott, another stuntman, and I were the only ones who had dialogue in that scene."

Finally, after the crew brought in some dynamite, they got the cattle running in the right direction. Scott's role called for him to be in the house and, when the cattle began to stampede, run outside and shout at Ted, whose movie name is Hoyt. The script calls for him to shout: "Hoyt, Hoyt! Stampede, stampede." At that point Ted is to run out of the house, guns at the ready.

Simple enough.

But when the cattle finally began running Scott ran outside and shouted: "Ted, Ted! Stampede, stampede!"

"I thought the director was going to have a heart attack," Ted recalls. He walked over to Walter Scott, who had his head down and said "Walter, what's Ted's name in the script?"

Walter replied "Hoyt."

"Then for Pete's sake, why did you call him Ted?"

Scott looked up sheepishly and said: "Because the big dumb bastard looks like a Ted."

After the location shooting had ended they brought Scott to the studio, ran the sound of the cattle over the original soundtrack and redubbed the shout with the correct name.

Another instance that riled Kasdan involved actress Rosanna Arquette who was originally slated for the second female lead in the film. She was to be Kevin Costner's girl in the movie and her role was to have been a good one.

"But she had a mouth," Ted said, "and she was using the F word too much." The film also features a young boy who appears in many of the scenes. "On about the second day I went to her and said 'we've got this young boy here. Do you think you could tone down the foul language a bit?' Others also asked her to back off on that kind of language."

But Arquette looked at Ted and said "just who the hell are you?"

"I'm just a stuntman," he said, "but I've got a little more sense than to talk that way in front of this young boy."

From that point on Arquette wouldn't ride to the set in the same vehicles with the rest of the cast, requiring a special car of her own.

Somewhere in there, Ted said, her language also got to Kasdan and he cut her out of about 80 per cent of the scenes she was originally scheduled to do. Her part became a relatively minor one.

During the filming the weather turned cold. "It was miserable much of the time," Ted said. "Kasdan's feet felt so frozen that the producers got him some boots with batteries and warming socks in them."

In one scene Danny Glover's character was in a river that was frozen at the time and had to be broken up for the scene.

"Everybody was down about that time," Ted said. People were cold, spirits were low and it was hard to muster up a lot of enthusiasm. At one point the crew is to shoot a scene that includes a big party, a dance at the wagon train where Rosanna Arquette's character is introduced. During the dance Ted's gang is to ride in yelling and shooting and break up the party.

"The director had been sick and we were all worn out," Ted said. So he went to the prop department and asked them to make up a large eye patch like the one he wore. "I'm gonna put it over my horse's eye," he said.

The prop guys weren't too sure it was a good idea. "Are you sure you want to do this, Ted?" someone asked. "You're taking a big chance. You know what it will cost to rebuild that set if you break it up."

Ted said he would take the blame if anything went wrong. He got the eye patch.

"So the party's going on, all the fiddling and the dancing, and the director hollers 'action!' and all 30 of us came riding in," Ted said.

"When they saw that patch over my horse's eye just like the one I was wearing everyone went into hysterics," he said. "It brought the whole scene to a standstill."

After things got settled down Ted took the eye patch off the horse and they did the scene again. "Kasdan thanked me for it later on," he said. "He said it lifted the company up to where it should have been in the first place."

That scene, along with several others in the film, required some special horses.

For example, when Ted and his gang rode in among the wagon train party he needed a horse that would rein easily and move where Ted wanted him to go, avoiding running down the cast members who were scurrying wildly here and there and not be unnerved with all the shooting and shouting.

"I needed a horse that would react quickly when spurred," Ted said. "So during the scene I was watching where people were and could spur him

111

one way or another and he would do whatever was required."

"Speaking of spurs," Ted continued. "When I first got into the business I had some spurs that didn't have the right kind of rowel on them." He said a horse trainer for the movies named Frosty Royce ("a great cowboy") watched him for a couple of weeks then came to Ted and said "you're new in the business, aren't you?" He looked at Ted's spurs and said "that's all you've got?"

When Ted said yes, Royce said "look me up tomorrow."

The next day Royce handed him a set of spurs. "I've worn these for years," he said, "but I just got a new pair. I'll sell these to you."

"Sell them to me?" Ted thought maybe he was being fleeced. Not so.

"Give me a dollar," Royce said. "Now, when you buy spurs you can't get rid of them because they weren't given to you, they were sold to you."

Royce told Ted where to take the spurs to have his initials engraved in them. "He must have picked up the tab for it because there was no charge when I went back for them," Ted said. "I've worn those spurs all through the years in Westerns and even when I was rodeoing."

Before shooting began on *Silverado* Ted met with the horse wranglers and told them he didn't want a "deadhead" but one that's lively. They found a five-year-old who, they said, would "climb a tree if you're wearing spurs and tell him to."

If a horse is what is called a "deadhead" and won't react quickly and accurately the whole scene could fall apart, Ted said.

In addition, the director wanted colorful horses for lead actors. Scott Glenn's horse was white, Kevin Costner rode a pinto, Kevin Kline's was black and Danny Glover's was a nondescript brown. "Everybody but Glover's character had been a cowboy," Ted explained. "Glover was a butcher in his past life so he got a horse that wasn't so flashy."

Glenn's big white horse was chosen because he would jump for the scene that required him to leap out of a barn and clip the bad guy off his horse. "He could also be seen well during the scenes shot between the buildings and in the alley," Ted said.

"Everything in that movie was done the way the Kasdan brothers wrote it," Ted said, "with the exception of the river freezing. We had to dynamite it to get the water flowing."

Another thing that changed during filming was the way Ted was shot off the top of the building during one of the climactic scenes. The heroic cowboys are trying to save the young boy who is being held captive in the ranch house and they think Costner's character has been killed. In the scene, Danny Glover is on top of the building and Ted, guns drawn, is sneaking up behind him. Glover is signaled from below, turns just in time and shoots Ted with his rifle.

Ted flies off the back of the building.

's

Ted (Hoyt) attempts to surprise Danny Glover's character on a building's roof in Silverado *but Glover shoots Hoyt who flies off the roof in one of the film's signature moments*
(Photo courtesy of John R. Hamilton, published in
"Thunder in the Dust: Great Shots from the Western Movies")

The original script called for the audience to see him fall all the way to the ground. A decision was made, however, to not show the full fall. A cable was attached to Ted and four big men pulled him back drastically, as though he had been shot and flung backward over the roof of the building. "When I went over they caught me," Ted said. "There was no rehearsal. We could do it fifty times a day with no problem. It's my face, that eye patch and the fall off the roof that people remember."

Ted found great enjoyment in doing that film. "It had big name stars," he said. "This was the first really big part for Brian Dennehy, an ex-Marine who played the sheriff, and it was also the first big role, for Jeff Goldblum, I think, who played the role of Slick. I later worked with Kevin Kline on *The Wild, Wild West* and liked him. They were all good guys."

Both Kevin Costner and Scott Glenn were "very easy to work with," Ted said. He had worked with Glenn on *Urban Cowboy* with John Travolta where Glenn played the role of the bad guy.

Danny Glover was a different story, Ted said. "He had a chip on his shoulder." Ted said Glover didn't endear himself to the producer, the director or many of the others. "When actors got together to have coffee, for example, he wasn't there. He was just a bit stand-offish. I think he wanted to be unique and he just wasn't. And he had a good part, too."

Despite Ted's initial concern about Glover the two had a friendly reunion at an autograph signing session in the Los Angeles area in early 2013. "My wife Jeri was with me at the signing," Ted said. "She walked around the big room we were in at one point and came back to tell me Danny Glover was there. I went over to say hello during a break and he was smiling and happy to see me."

As Ted approached, Glover stood up and hugged him, saying it was great to see him. "This is Ted White from *Silverado*," he told those around him. "He shot my daddy and I killed him for it."

"It was good to see him," Ted said. "Hollywood is a small town but you don't often run into people you've worked with like that."

Silverado premiered in U.S. theatres on July 12, 1985. It had cost more than $23 million to produce and it eventually grossed more than $32 million at the box office. It was met with generally positive reviews and was nominated for Best Sound and Best Original Score at the Academy Awards.

Some critics were especially excited by Kevin Costner in one of his first big roles. Some even felt he stole the show by playing an irresponsible youngster with a lot of "hootin' and hollerin'." They called the ending a "classic, *High Noon*-style showdown" that capped a "rousing retro Western."

New York Times critic Janet Maslin praised director Kasdan. "He creates the film's most satisfying moments by communicating his own sheer enjoyment in revitalizing scenes and images that are so well-loved" and called the film "a sweeping glorious-looking Western that's at least a full generation removed from the classic films it brings to mind."

On the final day of shooting for Ted and fellow stuntman Walter Scott, director Kasdan brought the entire company together and said: "Ladies and gentlemen, Ted White and Walter Scott have just finished *Silverado.*"

"Everyone applauded," Ted said. "It had never happened before in all my years, and Walter and I were moved and humbled."

Normally, he said, stuntmen come and go, but "we were there for the whole run of the picture. What a thrill."

He said that, to him, one of the great experiences in making a picture is watching it unfold. "I was fortunate to be there from beginning to end," he said. "It's a great pleasure to be a part of something like that. You know that millions of people will see it. I looked forward to every day of it.

"It's not just the money you're making, Ted said, "it's the privilege of being there, working with people who are so professional it goes beyond what you think professionalism is. *Silverado's* director was that way and it reflected on the entire company. This was one of great pleasures in life for me."

Ted with Dorothy Killgallin on the Ed Sullivan Show
in 1968. The sponsor was Lincoln

16

Up Close and Personal

BETWEEN *RIO BRAVO* in 1959 and *Silverado* in 1985 Ted rose to the top ranks of Hollywood stuntmen, was credited with many acting roles, earned his stripes as a second unit director, worked with the world's greatest actors and actresses and was actually just getting started. Some of the best was yet to come.

*Ted is an accomplished woodworker and continues
to spend a great deal of time in his personal workshop*

But, at the same time, his personal life was going through some ups and downs and beginning to read like a tragic movie script.

In 1949 he married Rosemary Akers who had won the title "Miss Oklahoma" two years earlier. Because Ted was a football star at Oklahoma University the marriage made headlines throughout the state. Their two sons

– Ted Alex Bayouth (known to the family now as "Ted Jr." even though Ted White's real name isn't Ted) and Michael Bayouth were born in 1951 and 1955. They grew up in the Hollywood movie community and became acquainted with many stars of the day.

Ted Jr. recalls being youthful friends with the sons of Ed Ames and Carol Burnett and playing often with future movie star Kurt Russell. Michael talks fondly of growing up with a father in the movie business and is now a filmmaker and director. Ted Jr. has made a successful career in the construction business and as a leadership and sales consultant.

Rosemary was a fashion illustrator and willingly followed Ted to California at the beginning of the 50s where he would pursue a career that he had no idea at the time would involve making films.

Things went well for more than 20 years. Then they went sour and the marriage that had begun with so much promise ended suddenly.

Despite the unhappy ending to that marriage both sons speak fondly of their mother and recall with some amusement, and even awe, interesting moments in their young lives. "He was a larger than life fatherly figure," Michael said of his father. "When he'd come home at night, we'd be in the family room waiting. If, after the front door shut, it was 15 minutes before he came in to say hello we knew he'd had a rough day."

Sometimes, Michael said, Ted would come home as a Mohawk Indian, his head almost bald except for a strip down the middle, carrying a tomahawk and wearing a tribal outfit. "He'd tell us to be quiet because he wanted to scare our mother. So he'd creep into the house and frighten her half to death. Those were the kinds of things I grew up with."

Ted Jr. says "living with Dad was intimidating on occasion, of course. First of all he would allow no backtalk to our mother. Despite his tough guy image he used to hold what he called 'manner contests.' He hated to go to a home where the kids misbehaved. He made sure we knew how to be polite."

In the "manner contests" at the dinner table Ted required they say "please pass the…," "yes mamn, no sir," and always "thank you."

At that time, the sons say, the men Ted was around were much like him. Life seemed good for the whole family. These stuntmen were inventing themselves, finding out about Hollywood while Hollywood found out about them.

At home, dinner guests included such men as Jimmy Dean (whose recording of *Big John* was at the top of the charts), Caesar Romero, Red Buttons, Fess Parker and others. For the most part, life with Ted and Rosemary was fun.

"When he had stuntmen to the house for dinner there was usually some drinking," Michael said. "I remember a time when, just to settle a fifty dollar bet, a horse from our stable, that was gentle enough, walked in the front door, came through the house and into the kitchen, then walked out the back door. We were used to witnessing this kind of thing."

The Bayouth boys were also comfortable being around big name stars. Jimmy Dean came for dinner and Ted Jr. was encouraged by his father to get his guitar and play something for the singer. "I did and then Jimmy asked for my guitar and sang *Big John*," Ted Jr. said. "I'll never forget it."

Ted Jr. met John Wayne a couple of times, once at NBC when the star was to appear on *The Tonight Show with Johnny Carson*. Ted Jr. introduced himself and Wayne said "Oh my God! How's your dad?"

Other occasions like being out on a boat with their dad or on hunting and fishing trips are important memories. Ted Jr. often went to the studio with his father, especially when Ted was doing *Daniel Boone* with Fess Parker. "Fess had a large ranch in Santa Barbara and we went to visit him," Ted Jr. said. "He took me for a tour of the ranch in his Jeep."

He also recalled frequently going running with Parker's co-star Ed Ames. When I'd be on location with dad, Ames would come by and say 'let's go running.' So I'd go running with him. What great memories."

One year Ted Jr. and his date were invited to attend the Stuntman's Ball with his parents. "At my dad's table with us were Clint Eastwood and Lee Marvin, who had just finished *Paint Your Wagon*, Howard Duff and Ida Lupino. My mom was there, too, of course."

At one point in the evening Ted Jr. said he got up to go to the restroom. "I'm standing at the urinal," he said, "and on one side of me is Clint Eastwood and on the other is Lee Marvin, both of them almost drunk and telling stories. I was too nervous to be able to go."

Marvin looked across Ted Jr. and said to Eastwood: "Do you think that piece of shit movie we just did was any good?"

Eastwood replied: "I don't know but they paid me well."

That was the kind of life Michael and Ted Jr. enjoyed.

But Ted's career frequently took him away from home, sometimes for long periods of time.

"Once, I was on a movie in Europe and had been gone for several weeks," Ted said. "I got home about 2 a.m., got up the next morning and made a pot of coffee. Rosemary got up and I saw her go into the bar and pour a glass of vodka."

When Ted asked her what she was doing she said she was going to have a drink. "It's morning," he said. She shrugged it off.

Ted learned from his sons that Rosemary was often up drinking at night, and that drinking in the morning was common with her.

"I told her I'd take her to a sanitarium to get her dried out," Ted said, "but she refused." He then said she would go or they wouldn't have a marriage. "You can't keep drinking like this," he told her. "You can't take care of the boys in this condition."

When she continued to refuse, Ted told her was going to file for divorce.

"I had built two houses right across the street from each other," he said. "I gave her both houses, all the residuals I would earn from work up to that time, all our checking and savings, everything we had."

Ted said he told her that all he wanted was the two boys and she agreed.

"We had three cars and I didn't even take one," he said. "The boys and I left the house in a cab."

The three of them moved to an apartment. Eventually, Rosemary married her high school sweetheart, a road engineer in Oregon who, it turned out, was also an alcoholic. Without Ted's knowledge, but observed by the two boys, they had been visiting by phone for weeks.

"She had a lot of money after the divorce," Ted said. "She bought her new husband a ranch and some very expensive ranch equipment that was never used. It sat and rusted in the rain. They finally sold the ranch and got only about two-thirds its worth at the time.

One night, after a wild bout of drinking, the new husband "beat the living shit out of her," Ted said. The boys had gone to Oregon to visit her and called Ted to tell him she was so beat up "you can't even recognize her."

Ted quickly caught a plane to Oregon. He went to the house and found no one at home. "I knew she was in the hospital," he said, "so I just sat in the garage for a few hours until the engineer came home, and when he stepped out of his car I beat him up enough that he also ended up in the hospital."

With the police on the outlook for Ted, he made a fast trip to the hospital to check on Rosemary and told his sons that he had to leave quickly to avoid getting arrested.

Over the next few years Rosemary lived with one man for a few years and then with another. One was a gambler who went through her money quickly. She had sold both the houses and had spent all the rest of the money she received in the divorce settlement.

One day she called Ted's house with a request that he buy a house for her which she would live in for a while and then sell and pay Ted what she owed him. He turned her down and her attorney called saying she was entitled to more of Ted's money, including his retirement. Ted told him about everything he had given her in the divorce and the attorney asked if he had papers proving all that. When Ted told him he did have proof, the attorney asked him to mail copies of the documents.

Ted told him to f… himself. "I'm not sending you anything," he said. He hung up and Ted didn't hear from the attorney again.

Then, ten years after the divorce, Ted married a woman named Jeri and all was right with the world.

17

Jeri's Story

TED MET JERI after he was involved in a brawl in her restaurant. That incident got their relationship got off to a rocky start.

Late in the 1960s, Jeri Tamburro graduated from high school in Nassau County, New York, where she had grown up. At that time her parents, Eleanor and Anthony, moved to California to be near some of Eleanor's family and Jeri went with them.

After spending some time at a nearby community college and later at California State University at Northridge, she landed her first real job, as a secretary with an organization called Stunts Unlimited. Ted was not affiliated with that group.

She eventually became an assistant manager at a disco owned by her uncle Charlie Picerni who was also a movie stuntman. Coincidentally, another uncle, Paul Picerni, was also in the film business. He appeared in 89 episodes of TV's *The Untouchables* in the late 50s and early 60s, and was in dozens of feature films.

Jeri's parents both earned real estate licenses and opened Chalet Realty in Tarzana, California in 1975. Jeri also got a license but worked only part time at it after a client of her parents became a silent partner with her in the Terra Nova Restaurant on Ventura Blvd. in Tarzana.

"It was an Italian restaurant and nightclub I bought from an Italian man. Then I met Ted and suddenly wasn't sure what I had gotten myself into," Jeri recalled with a shake of her head.

Ted vividly remembers the incident that led to his first meeting with Jeri.

One Saturday night in the late 1970s Ted was returning home from a rodeo with a buddy and two young women who were barrel racers. Ted suggested they all go to his house where he would make dinner. His friend knew of a nearby Italian restaurant that Ted also liked and suggested they go there instead.

"We walked into this nice place straight from the rodeo," Ted said. "We were wearing Levi's, boots, spurs and had numbers on our backs. We walked by a round corner booth done in red leather that was occupied by two guys and two girls. On top of the table was a bowl of red mints."

The man who was with Ted was a bulldogger who was at least six foot five and two hundred pounds. He quickly excused himself to go to the bathroom. Ted and the women got seated and one of the barrel racers asked him to dance. "We were on the dance floor and the girl said something hit her in the back of her neck. About that time something hit me on the shoulder."

Ted realized it had been one of the red mints he'd seen on the table when they came in. He turned around and the two men began taunting Ted's group. "Big Hollywood cowboys," they called out, among other things.

Ted took his dance partner back to their table and went to the corner booth with the red mints on the table. "We just came in here to eat," he told the foursome sitting there. "I know we're dressed for a rodeo but we don't want any problems."

"What do you mean, problems?" one of the men asked.

"I mean if you keep this up we're gonna have it out, right here," Ted said.

The man nearest Ted pulled his arm back and made a fist just as the bulldogger, returning from the restroom, hurled his entire six foot five frame into the air and landed in the middle of the table. "Spaghetti and dishes and drinks went all over the place," Ted said. "And in less than 15 seconds both of those dudes were lying on the floor.

"We ran out, got in our trucks and drove to my house," Ted said. "We'd been there only about 30 minutes when the police pulled up." Ted had frequently stopped in the restaurant for dinner and was known by the staff.

Ted tried to reason with the officers, saying the other guys had really started the fight. To make sure, the police took him back to the restaurant where the bartender backed up his story. "I still had to pay the damages," Ted said. "A few days later I got a bill for $2,800 and stopped by and dropped off a check."

124

Jeri was about to close on the sale of the restaurant and went by soon after Ted's visit and the fight. When she saw that the corner booth was gone she asked the bartender what had happened. He told her that Ted White, "a really good customer," had "a little scuffle" but that he had paid for it all to be replaced.

"I was a young, single woman taking on this great adventure and I had thought I was buying a nice, quiet family type of place and not one where we'd have brawls," Jeri said,

She told the bartender that if Ted White came again the restaurant should serve him dinner but not alcohol. "I was 27 or 28 years old and didn't want any riff-raff in here," she said.

Soon, Ted showed up again. "What do you mean, I can't have a drink?" he asked.

The bartender told him "the new owner" wouldn't allow it because of the fight.

"Well, who is this new owner?" Ted asked, ready to challenge the ruling.

The bartender pointed across the room where Jeri was in conversation with another customer. "Well, what could he do?" Jeri recalled. "He had his dinner and left, not too happily, I'm afraid."

But he came back – again and again. "A couple of weeks after I'd first been refused a drink, I stopped by," Ted said. "I looked and she didn't have a ring on. She was a beautiful gal. Later I stopped in again and then I started going for lunch, too."

Jeri said the restaurant was open from 11:00 a.m. until 2:00 a.m. "I'd get there around ten o'clock in the morning and find his truck already parked outside," she said. He's not a night owl but he'd try to hang around. He'd go home and come back, try to stay awake until I got off, but he never made it." Ted never worked up the gumption to ask her out.

"We started betting on Monday Night Football games," Ted said, "and I waxed her. We'd bet maybe $100 on the games."

Once, when he left to do a film in Europe, he called the restaurant and told them he wouldn't be coming in for two or three weeks. At that time, they called Ted "the cowboy." The waitress told Jeri that "the cowboy called and said he wouldn't be in for a while."

Ted got home on a Saturday and stayed home to rest on Sunday. He did call the restaurant to say he was back. On Monday, the day of their regular bet, Ted was in the shower when the phone rang. When he got to it there was a message. It was Jeri's turn to pick the team she wanted to bet on. "You big chicken," she said on the phone. "You're just hiding from me."

After several months of that Jeri had a feeling Ted was interested in her but he still didn't ask her out. "I was kind of interested in him, too," she said. "He was older than me but very handsome and in great shape. We had fun times together and all the regular customers knew there was electricity between us."

Finally, Jeri had run out of patience. On a Friday night she invited him to join the crew at a brunch on the beach that Sunday when the restaurant was closed. "That was to be our first real date," she said.

She didn't know much about Ted, just that he was in the movie business, that he had two sons and was divorced, and that he was quite content with his lifestyle.

"This guy had just bought a new white Chrysler four-door sedan," Ted recalled. "So we all got in it, me in the front seat, and I'm chewing tobacco. I rolled down the window and spit and it streamed down the slide of the car."

Recalling it, Jeri shook her head. "He's spitting tobacco out the window," she said. "I was in the back seat telling my girlfriends he's not my type. What am I doing? He's spitting tobacco and it's running down the side of this new car!"

Nevertheless, they began dating on a more or less regular basis. "He broke up with me several times," Jeri said. "He was fighting hard to not get too involved." She told friends on several occasions that she was done with him. Still, they would go out for two or three months, Jeri said, and then "he'd get scarce, hiding." Now and then Jeri went away for a few days, thinking that when she got back she would start a clean slate and be through with Ted.

"But I tell my friends that when I was gone the hook got down to his belly and he couldn't spit it out," she said.

Evidently, he couldn't.

"One day I was bulldogging and roping at a PRCA rodeo in Santa Barbara," Ted said. "At the same time Jeri was manning some open houses for her parents' company about 140 miles south of the rodeo. When she finished with the open houses, instead of going back to the restaurant she chartered a small plane and flew to Santa Barbara to see me rodeo."

Later that day, after they had returned to Ted's house, he was laying bricks around his barbeque pit when she brought him something to drink.

"I was down on my knees working with those bricks," Ted said, "and I looked up at her and said 'well, do you want to marry me or not?'"

Jeri said "that's a real romantic proposal." But she said yes and they were married on September 7, 1980.

Since then, "it's been a very interesting journey," Jeri said.

Ted and wife Jeri with their new Mercedes in the late 1980s

Ted says he made one of the best decisions of his life when he went back to that restaurant after the brawl. He tells Jeri that she's the best thing that ever happened to him. Fortunately, his sons feel much the same way.

"Jeri has been a wonderful addition to his life," says son Michael. "Being a single guy and on his own, he needed to get settled down and get grounded again. Jeri has the personality to match his. At times he can be rough around the edges and Jeri knows how to tame that aspect of his personality."

Michael said he went to her restaurant "and developed a great deal of respect for her as a smart entrepreneur. I watched how she became very instrumental in my dad's life. She's been a great lady in his life and a wonderful person. I'm really grateful that he found her."

Ted Jr. feels much the same way. "We all love Jeri," he said. "She's great for my dad. She takes great care of him and I think he's the luckiest man alive because of her."

Being married to a Hollywood stuntman who is used to having his own way and being the boss hasn't always been easy but Jeri says "it's been quite an adventure."

She was relatively young and independent when they married. Ted tells her he saved her from being a spinster. "I'd been on my own for quite a while and had run my own business," she said. "It has been hard to balance trying to satisfy his needs to be the boss and still keep my own identity. It was difficult in the beginning to not become totally subservient to him. That would have been easy but I don't think he'd have liked it." She said being married to Ted has helped her become a lot stronger.

Jeri sold her interest in the restaurant before they were married, knowing that she would want to travel some with him. "I've been all over the world with Ted," she said. She did get her broker's license and opened her own firm, Crocker Realty. Ted came up with the name when a local bank – Crocker Bank – went out of business, reasoning that the name was a familiar one that people would remember. Jeri has made the business a success and continues to work at it part time.

Early in their marriage she often went to movie sets with him. "But it was nerve wracking and I would get upset because of what he was doing," she said. "I remember watching him do a stunt and thinking I was going to pass out. I'd get rubber legs and start hyperventilating." After those first few times she tried to stay away so she wouldn't be a distraction to him. If the stunt he was doing was an easy one, she might go, she said.

"I never wanted to be the tail-along wife," she said. "Now and then I wanted to be on the set but I didn't want him to worry about entertaining me. I would often just go off sightseeing. I got to meet a lot of wonderful, nice people."

When she was on a film set with him they often went to dinner with other actors and stuntmen. "They always treated me very nicely," she said. "They were very respectful of Ted and appreciated his attention to detail, especially how he always worked hard to make sure everyone on the set was safe and that stunts were done correctly."

Ted was an avid outdoorsman and Jeri soon learned that she needed to be willing to accept some challenges. "One time we loaded up our Boston Whaler with supplies and went four hours up a river into what seemed to me like the wilderness. We set up camp and spent four or five days there. Remember this is a New York girl who didn't camp, fish or do any of those kinds of things. He made me into a pioneer woman."

Another time when they were fishing far off the California coast they got lost in dense fog and "we didn't know if were headed for California or Hawaii," Jeri said. They finally made landfall a full five miles south of where they wanted to be.

On another fishing trip on the Colorado River she fell overboard and had to be pulled back aboard by Ted. "It scared the daylights out of me," she said.

Ted never did anything halfway. Like the time he decided he wanted to have chickens.

"We have an acre of land in middle of Woodland Hills," Jeri said. "The whole valley has millions of people but our property was big enough for livestock. Ted wanted fresh eggs so he bought something like 40 Ancona chickens." (This is a breed that originated in Italy and is noted for its ability to produce large white eggs.)

But Ted was often away on location and it was up to Jeri to care for the chickens. "Often when he was away I was dressed up with high heels and had to go into the chicken coop and feed them before I went to work. This is a person who doesn't even like dogs in the house," she said. "I would go out and feed them but didn't know who was more scared – me or the chickens."

Once when she walked in, the gate closed behind her and she heard the latch drop. She thought: "I'm locked in the chicken coop with 40 hens and two roosters and I'm in high heels." She pulled a feed barrel to the gate but the latch was so high she couldn't get to it. The property was big enough that even the nearest neighbors couldn't hear her calling. Finally, after some time, a friend of Ted's stopped by, heard her cries for help and released her.

"We had so many eggs I couldn't get rid of them fast enough," she said. "Finally, after six or eight months, Ted got rid of the chickens."

Ted always seemed to have horses and Jeri learned to shovel out the stalls. "I had a mountain of you-know-what," she said.

Finally, Ted brought home two steers, a black angus and a Hereford. His plan was to butcher them and "we'd have the best beef we ever had." But, Jeri said, after a few months he said he couldn't bring himself to butcher them and he sold them.

"I used to have a business manager but don't anymore," Ted said. "Jeri is a better business manager than any I know. She's so smart it's unbelievable. "When we bought Crocker reality she never took a lesson. She studied a book for two days and went down and passed the test on the first try. It pisses me off that she's so much smarter than I am."

Even when they weren't off to some exotic location to work on a film, Ted and Jeri found time to explore many of the world's wonder spots. That's how they found Gunnison, Colorado.

In the early 1990s Ted was working on Sam Elliot's made-for-TV movie *Conagher* which was filmed mainly in northern Colorado near Greeley.

Ted had recently bought a 27-foot Pace Arrow motor home and they drove it to Gunnison to visit longtime Texas friends Joe and Margie Barclay and Neil and Jackie Wood. Both couples owned condos along the Gunnison River just outside the town of Gunnison. Ted had been in the area earlier scouting locations for a film.

After a few visits in the Pace Arrow Ted decided it was too small and bought a 36-foot model. They drove it from Los Angeles to Colorado towing a Jeep Grand Cherokee, but near Grand Junction, about 150 miles from Gunnison, the Jeep blew a tire, tearing up the grill and parts of the bumper and radiator. At that point Jeri decided she had had enough of motor home living.

"Well, now what are we going to do?" she asked.

The solution was to purchase a condo near the Barclays and Woods (after renting one for two summers).

For nearly 15 years Ted and Jeri spent most of their summers in their condo by the river. Finally, in 2012, they sold it and now devote their time to their home in Woodland Hills, California, near Ted's sons and not far from Hollywood.

Life was, indeed, an adventure for Jeri and Ted and their life together. For Ted, more adventures would continue to revolve around the motion picture business.

18

Rodeo'n, Racin' and Rowdiness

IN 1958 TED got his PRCA (Professional Rodeo Cowboys Association) card but he had been in the "cowboy" business for most of his life. He grew up on a west Texas ranch, after all, and learned to ride and rope as a child. After the war and even several years into the movie business, he found time to keep his skills honed on the weekend rodeo circuit.

"The money you make at rodeos is nothing compared to what it costs just to be involved," he said. "You've got to have horses, saddles, trailers, travel money and everything else that's required, including entry fees."

Ted stayed at it until one day when he was 62 years old he got hurt bulldogging.

"That's it big boy," wife Jeri told him. "You're through."

So Ted followed her advice (orders) and sold his horses, but he gave away his favorite, Cowboy.

That horse was three or four when he gave him to a children's home. "They had a big circle with a pole in the middle," he said. "They put a harness on Cowboy and the kids rode him around in a circle. It was an easy life for him and I'm sure he made some kids happy."

SOON AFTER HE QUIT the rodeo circuit Ted went to an auction with a couple of buddies. They had an open bar.

When he woke up the next morning Jeri said "Well, big boy, you had quite a day yesterday."

"What do you mean?"

"I mean you bought four race horses and they're being delivered this afternoon."

Of the four, three were stallions. Ted soon called a vet who came out to "cut them." Afterwards, the three were lying on the ground and Jeri thought they were dead.

"No," Ted told her. "I had 'em cut."

Jeri looked questioningly at him. "Cut what?" she asked.

ONE OF THE HORSES – Cuttin' Time – did very well and won five of the seven races in which he was entered. He finished second in the other two. Because he seemed always to be gone on one film production or another, Ted saw Cuttin' Time race only once. But Jeri went to all of them.

"Jeri's normally very calm," Ted said, "but you should see her at the race track. She goes completely ballistic, screaming and yelling."

Jeri took friends with her to the track and once took her mother and father. Her dad bet the whopping sum of $10.00, won and said "Man, this is good money."

Ted's youngest son Michael, an artist, and his son also went with her at least once. Michael bet $50.00 and "won a bundle." Michael's son, only about 12 years old at the time, said "Wow dad. You can quit drawing for a living. Look at all that money."

Michael had to tell him it didn't happen that way every time.

The one time Ted got to see Cuttin' Time race he took his old friend, stuntman and actor Roy Jenson. Jeri and Jenson's wife were also along. The four were sitting at a table in the glassed-in viewing area when Ted heard a conversation among several men sitting near them. One of the men said Cuttin' Time had been winning but "he's out of his class today."

Ted's friends asked him if he was going to bet on his own horse and Ted said he was. "He only runs as fast as he has to win," he said. "He can run faster but he won't do it, just runs fast enough to beat the other horses."

Ted, Jeri and Jenson and his wife bet on Cuttin' Time and the horse won by half a length and paid $44.00. The group was celebrating when the men at the nearby table beckoned to Ted.

"You wouldn't be the owner of that horse, would you?" one asked. When Ted nodded yes he said "well, damn, we were talking about him. Why didn't you speak up.

"I heard you," Ted said. "You said he didn't have a chance and I didn't want to call you a liar."

About a month later Ted put Cuttin' Time in a claiming race for $62,000 and he was claimed.

HORSES HAVE ALWAYS been an important part of Ted's life, from a tyke growing up on a west Texas ranch, to his rodeo days to his work in TV and movie Westerns.

One day soon after the completion of *Rio Bravo* director Howard Hawks called Ted and asked if he had an empty stall in his barn. Told there was, he said he wanted to send a horse for Ted to keep for him for a while.

"It was a one of the most beautiful horses you've ever seen," Ted said. "He was maybe five years old."

For two years Ted didn't hear from Hawks. He fed and groomed the horse, saddled and rode him for exercise. Finally a man showed up at Ted's door saying he was to pick up the horse and deliver him to a certain address. Skeptical, Ted called Hawks who told him it was legitimate. "By the way," Hawks said. "He has an envelope."

The envelope contained a check for $5,000.

Ted recalls that the horse was used later in either *El Dorado* (1966) or *Rio Lobo* (1970).

Another of Ted's horses was used in the 1980 film *Heaven's Gate* and was involved in an accident that resulted in a lawsuit.

Heaven's Gate was a lavish film loosely based on the Johnson County War and was a major box office bomb. It earned less than $3 million domestically after costing nearly $44 million to produce. It also has a reputation as being a generally terrible film. It had a cast that included Kris Kristofferson, Christopher Walken, Isabelle Huppert, Jeff Bridges, John Hurt and Sam Waterston, among others.

Early in the filming of the movie Ted got a call from Rudy Ugland who leased horses to the studios. Ted had known Ugland as a young man and had worked with him on the 1995 TV movie *Dazzle* which starred Lisa Hartman, Cliff Robertson and James Farentino.

Ugland said director Michael Cimino had added a new character to *Heaven's Gate* in order to tie some scenes together and they needed another horse. "You've got a big gray horse about 16 hands tall," Ugland said. "I'd like to lease him for the movie."

Ted had owned the horse several years and knew him to be gentle and easily ridden and he agreed to lease him to Ugland.

The horse was to appear in a scene with gunfire and explosions and Ugland asked Ted how he would react. "I don't know," Ted told him. "I've never had him in that kind of situation." Ugland experimented by firing guns near the horse. He flinched at first but later seemed to relax.

Prior to the action sequence in which the horse (which they named "Ted") was to appear stuntman Buddy Van Horn, the film's stunt coordinator, walked the actor who was to ride Ted through the scene, showing him where mortars were set to explode and areas to avoid. When the scene was shot, however, the actor rode Ted directly over a mortar. It killed the horse and threw the actor who broke his hip, leg and shoulder. The actor sued the studio, the director and Ted White.

He eventually lost the suit, however, because Van Horn was able to prove the actor had been warned and shown the exact route he was to take in the scene.

TED HAD TWO GOOD friends named Roy. Roy Jenson was the "Roy" who went to the horse race with him, and Roy Sittner was another "Roy" who helped make life interesting in the world of stuntmen.

"Those two Roys were hell on wheels," Ted said. "They were tough. They'd get in a bar fight and clean out the bar. They'd take on five or six guys and never give it a thought."

Ted helped Roy Jenson get a speaking role in the film *Smoky* with Fess Parker and that led to other roles in films for more than a decade.

"Roy Sittner was a wild man," Ted said. "He did some crazy things."

Once, after a three-day drinking binge with Roy Jenson, Sittner tried to come up with a story to tell his wife, a Yugoslavian actress named Marina who Ted said was "absolutely gorgeous." About a block from his home, Ted recalled, Sittner stopped at a gas station, filled a tin cup with gasoline and poured it over his head. At the door of his house he said "Marina, I've got to get inside quick. They kidnapped me and were gonna set me on fire but I escaped." Marina quickly got him inside, into the shower, and forgave him.

"About a year later it happened again," Ted said. "He told her 'they got me again' but this time she knew better and beat the hell out of him with a pan or something."

Later, Sittner married a wealthy woman in San Francisco who owned a large home. Ted said he decided the place needed "something to freshen it up so we went to the beach and bought a small cannon."

Sittner then put in a large flagpole and every morning about six o'clock he fired the cannon and raised the flag. "The neighbors went crazy and demanded he quit the cannon-firing," Ted said. "His wife decided she couldn't put up with him anymore and divorced him."

Roy Jenson had played football for UCLA and then professionally for the Calgary Stampeders and the Montreal Alouettes. Interestingly, Jenson played Roman Polanski's henchman in the famous knife-to-the-nose sequence with Jack Nicholson in *Chinatown* in 1974.

"He was one of the toughest men I've ever known," Ted said. While playing pro football in Canada he earned the nickname "the tester." When new players were signed, his coach would tell him to "test this guy."

Ted said he went to visit him after he heard Jenson was sick "but I didn't know the details which turned out to be that he had cancer and only a short time to live."

Ted asked Jenson how he was feeling. "How the hell do you think I'm feeling?" he said. "I'm dying."

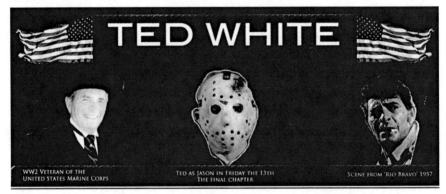

From the Homepage of Ted's website – www.tedwhite.com

19

Jason

A FEW YEARS AFTER Ted and Jeri were married he got a call from Paramount Pictures requesting that he come to the studio for an interview and a reading relating to an upcoming film. Little did he know at the time that his name would soon become associated with one of the world's leading "slasher" films. It almost didn't happen and, even after he completed the film, he tried to keep his name off the credits.

The film was *Friday the 13th: The Final Chapter*, the fourth film in the *Friday the 13th* film series. From the beginning, Ted was conflicted about being a part of the film. Even so, many "slasher" aficionados say his portrayal of the mad killer Jason Voorhees is the best of the entire series.

"Slashers" are among the most prevalent types of horror movies. This is especially true of films presented on video, and they're a particular favorite of modern horror fans. The definition of a slasher film varies depending on who you ask, but in general it contains several specific traits that feed into the genre's formula. Those traits, according to about.com, are the killer; the victims; often a strong, independent female lead; and, of course, violence.

"It took an American film in *Halloween*," about.com insists, "to put all of the pieces together and show that the slasher could be a powerhouse moneymaker in the US." Made on a shoestring budget, *Halloween* became an incredibly profitable independent picture. About.com says its success led to *Friday the 13th* in 1980, which then opened the door for hundreds of imitators during the 1980s.

When Ted went in for the interview at Paramount in late 1983, he knew little or nothing about the *Friday the 13th* series. He was given five pages of a script which was a man's dialogue with a woman. After ten minutes of studying the script, Ted read it with a studio secretary who read the woman's part and then was asked to wait in another room. In that room he came across several other stuntmen who had also read for the part.

Fifteen minutes later Ted was called back into the interview room and told that they felt he was right for the part and that they wanted him to do it. "OK," he said, "but can I have a copy of the entire script so I can work on my lines."

"Well," the casting director said, "this role doesn't actually have any dialogue."

"But I just got through reading it," Ted said.

He was told that what he read was just a small part for another role. "You'll be Jason."

"Who's Jason?" Ted asked.

Instead of answering that question, the casting crew gave him a copy of the script. Ted went into another room and read it. "All I could see was blood and gore and killing young kids," he said. He went back inside and turned it down.

"Listen," he said to the crew. "I appreciate being able to read for the part and I wish you the best of luck in finding somebody, but I'm not right for this part."

The casting people were surprised that somebody would turn them down. "Why?" they asked.

"Because I don't do this kind of thing," Ted said. "I've worked in many features and on television but I've never done anything like this. I don't think I'd like my sons seeing me do this kind of stuff."

"Are you sure?" they wanted to know. Ted said yes, he was sure. They shook hands and he left.

The prop man for the movie, who happened to live only a few blocks from Ted, walked by the interview room later and someone told him that his neighbor, Ted White, had been in reading for the part. He dropped by Ted's house and said he had heard about the reading. "What happened?" he asked.

Ted told him he had been offered the part but turned it down. "They wanted me to do a guy named Jason and that I'd have to wear a mask and kill people."

The prop man's eyes widened. "Ted," he said, "you're crazy." Then he explained. Ted would need to go in for a full body cast, at least from the waist up, and that would take four or five days. Then, he said, Ted would be on hold for about six weeks while they got the cast ready for shooting.

"When you're on hold," Ted said, "you get full pay. I told my friend the prop man to excuse me while I made a phone call."

Ted reached the casting director and said "you know what? I've reconsidered. I don't have anything going right now."

The casting director said "great. We'd love to have you."

Ted Jr. says that, while playing Jason might have bothered his father, the family understood that it was just a movie. But to Ted Jr. it was more than that. It was life-saving.

"I was about 30 years old," he said, "and I had cancer. I had no insurance and the bill for treatment was huge. Dad really didn't want to take on the role but he did it in part to cover the hospital bill for me. I never paid a penny of it myself."

Ted Jr. said he often went to the set to watch the filming. "My dad was miserable," he said. "He didn't much like the director and he was in a bad mood most of the time. But it was interesting to watch. He got through it and did a good job."

Ted as Jason after nearly four hours of makeup

139

Friday the 13th: The Final Chapter was the fourth entry in this successful series. It was supposed to be the final film in the franchise but when the third film in the series grossed almost $33 million against a $2.8 million budget, the studio was convinced to continue with more.

Film critic Bill Gibron says this movie is "perhaps the best of the entire Jason-inspired fright flicks. It's definitely the most focused and the most brutal."

Gibron says it sets up its story well, gets right to the murders and then "makes us guess as to how our horrific anti-hero will finally buy the fear farm." He says Ted's Jason is "all business and waving machete."

The story's plot begins when viewers learn that, though everyone thought Jason had been killed in the previous film in the series, he survived. In fact, while in the morgue he awakens, murders the coroner and a nurse and heads back to Crystal Lake where he had wreaked havoc in the earlier episodes.

The movie was filmed mainly at the Valuzet Movie Ranch (also known as Melody Ranch Motion Picture Studio) in Newhall, California, and at Kelly's gulch, a private residence in Topanga Canyon, California.

Ted went in for the body cast and then was free until the film was to be shot several weeks later. Because he was "on hold" for the *Friday the 13th* film, Ted was drawing full pay. And, because he was free he was able to take part in an episode of *Murder, She Wrote* with Angela Lansbury and to fly to Hawaii with Jeri to be in a *Magnum, P.I.* with Tom Selleck.

Finally, he was called to the set and told to report to make-up at 3 a.m. the next day. "I thought this was great," he said. "It was going to run into a lot of overtime."

The make-up man was Tom Savini who has acquired a remarkable cult following among film fans, primarily due to his ground-breaking special effects in the "splatter movie" explosion of the early 1980s.

"They began gluing pieces on my face," ted recalled. "They closed one eye completely and the other was disfigured. A red lens was put on the 'good' eye. It took four and a half hours!"

Finally, he said, a skull went over all this and was glued to the back of his head. The body cast was necessary, he said, because in the big killing sequence "the machete comes down on Jason's head, goes through the head and half of one eye with blood spurting all over. Tom Savini, the make-up artist, had all this rigged."

A composite showing the makeup process

After the plaster cast of Ted's body had been completed, Savini made a second cast of the head and shoulders. What viewers see is the machete coming down and, as it gets to Jason's (Ted's) head, there is a cut to another shot of the machete penetrating the plaster cast of the head and it appears as though it is penetrating a real head. The inside of the blade is full of blood and it begins gushing out.

When filming began Ted quickly got into the spirit of things.

"When I walked onto the set the whole cast was staring at me," he said. He decided at that point that he would have only minimal interaction with the rest of the cast.

141

"I picked up the chair with my name on it and moved about forty or fifty feet away and sat down by myself," he said. "I didn't want the cast to become too comfortable around me. I thought it would interfere with their performances. They might not be able to act as frightened of Jason as they should."

The fact that he wouldn't associate with the cast got out to the press and they built that up, Ted said. "I didn't want the cast to know me as Ted. I didn't want them visiting with me or having coffee. I wanted the actual fear to set in. It worked."

"To do a scene, I'd come to the set, do the scene and then cover up and leave. I never wanted the public to get close so I turned down all press interviews and wouldn't allow any photos. It made Joseph Zito, the director, pretty unhappy but I persisted."

Before the first scene was to be filmed Ted visited with a prop man and asked him how the other "Jasons" had acted.

"They were all like Zombies," he said.

Ted didn't think that sounded realistic. "If the other Jasons plodded along like Zombies, dragging their feet and slobbering, those kids could have escaped from him pretty easily," he said. "So I speeded up things quite a bit. I decided that if they didn't like what I did they could fire me."

When Zito called "action" to film the first of many killings, Ted said, "I broke into a run, caught the guy and rammed his head into a wall."

The cameraman said aloud "Jesus god almighty!" The director called "cut, print."

"I never said a word but went back and sat in my chair," Ted said. "From that day on that's exactly how I worked."

He did talk to the cast at least once, to make sure they understood his plans. "I'm going to get a good hold on you," he told them, "but I'm not going to hurt you. I've got to hold you tightly enough that I know I've got you and that if you struggle you won't be able to break free of me." He said it worked well and the young actors understood.

The nervousness about Ted's (Jason's) appearance went beyond the set.

The majority of the movie was filmed in Topanga Canyon. Early one morning, about 2 a.m., while Ted waited for a shot to be set up, he decided to visit his "honey wagon," which is a trailer with a bathroom. Because the

142

trailer couldn't get down to where the filming was taking place, it was parked on a road near the top of the canyon.

A car was parked behind the trailer and as Ted walked up from behind the car and past on the driver's side, one of two men in the car said "hey man. What's happening down there?"

Ted, who had forgotten he was in the gory make-up, bent down to the window where the driver could see him and said "we're killin' people."

The driver's eyes got big and he said "holy shit!"

"They trailed smoke from the tires for half a block," Ted said, "and I went into hysterics, laughing."

Ted himself felt fear at least once during the filming. It was the scene in the hospital near the beginning of the movie when everyone thinks Jason is dead. "The thought of lying on that gurney in a real hospital in a real morgue and being pushed into that tiny little cubicle scared the hell out of me," Ted said. "I couldn't wait to get out of there."

During the filming Ted was constantly concerned about the well-being of his co-stars. In another night scene (shot a little after midnight in the dead of winter) a young actress, Judie Aronson, is practically nude in a small raft in the lake when Jason comes up out of the water to kill her. The director wanted a long shot of her in the raft first but had some kind of problem with the camera.

"Mr. Zito, can I please get out of the water and get warmed up?" Aronson asked.

Zito said no, that they would have the problem fixed quickly.

"She was turning blue," Ted said. "We're all standing there waiting. I had a wet suit on because all they were to see of me was my head and my hand."

Ted decided he had seen enough. He walked to Zito and said "you get her out of there right now or I'll quit and walk off the set."

"You can't quit,"Zito said. "I'll turn you into the guild."

Ted said "I'm going to turn you in anyway. That girl is freezing to death. Get her out right now or I walk."

The first assistant director and the executive producer agreed and told Zito to get her out, which he finally did.

On another occasion, actor Peter Barton who played Doug, didn't want to perform the scene where he is killed (when Jason crushes his head against a wall) because he had been hurt doing a stunt on another film and had undergone surgery as a result. Seeing the problem, Ted had the prop crew place a pad behind Barton's head for protection.

In another scene Ted is to chase a girl up some stairs and, when he reaches her, is to grab her by the nape of the neck and throw her over the balcony, a fall of about 12 feet. The stunt coordinator on the show told his grips to dig a hole about 10 feet square and shovel some loose grass over it to cushion the girl's fall.

The stunt girl doubling the actress asked Ted what he thought. "I told her I didn't think it would work," he said.

He went to the stunt coordinator and told him that he thought the landing area had been dug too shallow. "It can kill her," he said. "If she lands wrong she can break her neck." Ted told him the landing area should be at least 12 feet square with a porta pit in it, then a canvass mat over that and loose dirt over the top.

"That would take all night," the stunt coordinator said.

When the director joined them and took the side of the stunt coordinator Ted wouldn't back down. "I've been in this business for quite a few years," he said, "and I know what's going on. I'm not going to let you hurt this girl."

The director finally gave in and the landing area was properly prepared. After the stunt, which came off perfectly, the stunt girl, who was a member of the Stuntwomen's Association, praised Ted for his forcefulness and an article appeared about it in *Variety*.

Another similar scene required some of the same kind of toughness on Ted's part.

"They brought in another stuntwoman for a scene in which I was to throw her through a second-story window," Ted said. "Her body was to hit the top of a car and, as she hit, shells positioned inside would explode and blow out the windows."

The stunt coordinator had brought in an air ram that propels anyone who steps on it into the air. Ted was concerned that the air ram would send the stuntwoman straight up and that she would hit her head on the windowsill. "We probably won't need the momentum of an air ram," Ted said. "I can throw her through the candy glass and with my strength she'll land just right on the car."

144

The stunt coordinator wasn't convinced and decided to try it himself. He backed off about ten feet, ran toward the window, hit the air ram and went through the window. "I could hear him as he went down," Ted said. "He was yelling 'oooh, shit!'"

He missed the car about seven feet, hit the ground hard, tore up his shoulder and scratched up his face. The medic patched him up and he came to Ted and said: "I didn't dream it would put me out that far."

Ted said the stuntwoman and he didn't rehearse the sequence of him throwing her out the window. "She knew what to do," he said. "And the force I used on her would put her on top of that car."

He said he told her two things to do when she went out the window. "Keep your head down and cover your eyes with your forearm. You'll land right on that car and if you turn your shoulders as you fall you'll land on your back."

The director called "action!" and Ted told her to close her eyes. "Here we go," he said, and she hit it just right. Three cameras filmed the action. One showed Ted grabbing the woman and bringing her up to the window and throwing her through it. A second camera, placed outside, filmed her coming through the window from that angle, and a third filmed her as she hit the car.

It was done right and no one was hurt in the process.

Prior to these stunts, Frank Mancuso, Jr., the Producer of the film, approached Ted and said "everyone at the studio is excited about how you're doing this. Don't change anything." He asked if Zito, the director, had said anything to Ted about how he was playing Jason.

Zito hadn't said a word to him.

Later, after Ted had words with Zito over the treatment of the young woman in the raft and on other occasions, he finally was fed up.

He went to Zito and told him that he had done so many things wrong on the show that "when you say the last cut on the film I'm gonna beat the shit out of you."

Zito believed it, Ted said, "because on the last day, after the last scene, he took off and we never saw him again."

Near the end of filming Producer Mancuso came to Ted and asked how he wanted his name on the credits.

"I don't want my name on this piece of crap," Ted said.

"Are you serious?" Mancuso asked. "I wish you'd think about that. This is going to be a hit."

But Ted continued to refuse and, to this day, he is "uncredited" in the role.

"I don't know how, but everyone knew I had done it," Ted said. "So, even though it was known, I preferred that my name not appear."

Ted later turned down opportunities to play Jason in subsequent films in the series. "I was an idiot," he now says. "I could have made a great deal of money. But, for many reasons, I'm now actually glad I didn't do any more of them."

Today, many critics continue to feel that this particular Jason, as portrayed by Ted White, is the most believable of all the Jasons in all the films of the series.

20

Safety First

IT IS 1983 AND TED is on the set of the film *Blue Thunder*. His good friend Terry Leonard is the stunt coordinator for the movie which stars Roy Scheider as a police officer who is in training to be the pilot of a specially modified helicopter.

The scene they are working on involves a wreck at the intersection of a busy highway. Gary McLarty, an expert stuntman and an outstanding motorcycle rider, is set to lay his bike down beneath an 18-wheeler. McLarty has done stunts in more than 100 films which include *Gone in 60 Seconds*, *Lethal Weapon 4*, *Batman and Robin*, *Wyatt Earp*, *Jurassic Park* and *Patriot Games*.

"The crew wet the street down," Ted said, "and we had five cars and an 18-wheeler. At the intersection the cars cut off the big rig and he slams on the brakes and nearly jack-knifes as cars jump the divider and a motorcycle is racing into the scene."

Leonard has told McLarty to "lay that bike down" beneath the 18-wheeler near the large diesel fuel tanks that hang low to the ground. McLarty, known in the business at the time as "the Whiz Kid," comes into the scene doing 35 or 40 miles per hour, lays the bike over and plants it just where Leonard wanted it.

But the shot doesn't satisfy Leonard. "This is not TV," he says. "This is a feature film and you need to speed it up."

Ted takes a deep breath. "Terry, you just said the wrong thing. You're going to get him hurt."

"What do you mean?"

"You'll see," Ted replies.

In the retake McLarty revs the bike up to about 60 miles per hour, lays it down and skids beneath the truck, breaking his leg, and "messing up" an elbow and a hip. He is rushed to the hospital.

Decades of performing movie stunts, working with stunt coordinators, directors and stuntmen has ingrained in Ted a deep awareness of the need for safety and to carefully prepare for even what appear to be relatively simple stunts. He especially knows that dedicated stuntmen like McLarty will often go to extremes to make a stunt look real and to please directors. Sometimes, Ted said, they are willing go too far to get the shot.

Ted has earned a reputation in the industry for looking out for the well-being of the stuntmen and stuntwomen with whom he has worked. "We want to get the shot," he said, "and we know that stunts are sometimes very dangerous. So we want to take every precaution to see that we minimize the risks. But sometimes things happen that you can't control, like the shying horse in *The Horse Soldiers* that resulted in the death of Fred Kennedy and the way Jimmy Sheppard died doing a drag in *Comes a Horseman.*"

Some directors, Ted said, work well with stunt coordinators and with the people doing the stunts, but others, who may not be fully aware of how best to achieve certain kinds of action, are adamant about having their own way.

Ted, left, dispatches a hoodlum - safely! - in the film Going Ape

John Ford, for example, was known as the stuntman's best friend. "He hated to have stuntmen hurt," Ted said, "and he refrained from doing things that were too dangerous." He recalled how upset Ford was with Fred Kennedy's death in one of the last scenes being shot on location for *The Horse Soldiers*. Ted said Ford had complete control of the script and if a stunt appeared to be too dangerous he would take it out completely.

"At Ford's funeral, every stuntman who could possibly be there was in attendance," Ted said.

Other directors aren't always so willing to compromise when it comes to stunts.

"But the whole thing is this," Ted said. "You're there to do the work and if you fail to do it word goes out and it's tough for you to get other jobs." Still, he said, he has always made his concerns known and often argued with directors or stunt coordinators about how a stunt should be set up and performed. There comes a time, though, "when you've done all you can and you have to shut up and do the stunt, regardless of your apprehensions."

Stuntmen and women take many precautions and try to think of everything. "A good stunt person never does anything unless he checks everything out, walks the terrain, goes over the equipment, and makes sure the timing is understood by all involved."

In the 1966 film *Smoky* starring Fess Parker, Ted had a speaking role but was also the stunt double for Parker. In the film, a cowboy finds, captures and patiently trains a beautiful wild stallion until a bond develops between the two. The cowboy's brother, however, needing money to pay off debts, trades the horse, which results in the death of the brother and a long search to reunite the original cowboy and the horse.

A scene from Smoky *with Fess Parker. Ted is standing at the right in the white hat*

Ted said the movie was filmed in Mexico in a national park that was full of prairie dog holes.

"We brought two horses down," Ted said. "One was for Fess Parker and a double for me. George Sherman, the director, was not especially horse savvy and he and I argued from day one about how to do a scene that I thought had some danger to it."

Ted said he often was required to do horse falls or drags and his horse "would drag me down a mountain by one arm. He stepped all over my leg. He shit on me. He did everything you could think of. My left arm got to be longer than my right arm."

For one scene Ted was to make a horseback run down the side of a hill, across a bit of prairie and up a slope before he got to the camera where the director would call "cut" and insert Fess Parker into the shot.

"I walked the route," Ted said, "and it was all prairie dog holes. I went to the director and told him that this was a bad spot because of the holes."

"What other excuses have you got?" Sherman asked.

Ted said he wasn't making excuses but "if a horse goes down in one of those holes with a broken leg, he's dead and we'll have to shoot him right there on the spot."

"You're supposed to know how to handle a horse," Sherman said.

"I can, but at a run I know I won't be able to turn him quickly enough if I see a hole."

Fess Parker overheard the conversation and motioned to Ted to leave Sherman and come to where he was seated. "Don't do it, Ted," he said.

"Fess," Ted replied, "there's an old rule that says if a stunt can be done you do it. I've got to do it."

Parker wanted to talk to Sherman about it himself but Ted asked him not to, saying it would make him look bad. So Ted walked the route three times, noting several places where there were holes that couldn't be seen at a dead run.

"We did it," he said. "By some miracle, we made it."

On another occasion during the filming Ted was to leap from a moving wagon onto a horse and rider as they passed by. The two actors and the horse would fall to the ground. Again Ted went to Sherman to tell him they needed to put sand in the hard road for the horse to land on. Sherman refused and Ted decided he had had enough.

"That's where we draw the line," Ted told him. "I'm not going to hurt that horse because you don't know how to take care of him. If the SPCA were here they wouldn't let you do it."

"They're not here," Sherman said. "Do it."

"I'm not going to do it without the sand," Ted told him, "and you can't make me do it. I'll take all of my stuntmen and we'll get on a plane and head out of here."

About that time Parker walked to the duo and told Sherman "you better listen to him. He'll damn well do it. He's not going to risk hurting any of these animals."

Finally, Sherman gave in and Ted got the sand on the road.

Back in Los Angeles, Executive Producer Aaron Rosenberg learned about the run-ins regarding stunts and fired Sherman from the picture.

"Sherman just didn't have the knowledge," Ted said. "He could very easily have simply called somebody in and asked how to go about setting up a shot, but he tried to bluff his way in and out of things and it didn't work."

THE KIND OF PROBLEM Ted had with director George Sherman was not uncommon at the time. In fact, stuntmen, actors and actresses were being asked to perform more and more dangerous stunts as movie-goers clamored for increasing action and more thrilling scenes of derring-do. At the same time, those performing the stunts were not being paid on a scale that reflected the danger involved.

Ted and some other stuntmen felt it was time to address those kinds of problems.

"Prior to 1961 it was a dog-eat-dog situation," Ted said. "Sometimes a man would go on an interview for a show and give a price and somebody else would cut it. Or the studio would describe what they wanted done and quote a figure that they would pay."

If a stuntman needed work he might often agree to a price and then offer to throw in another stunt or two, just to get the job. "You couldn't really blame him," Ted said. "He was just trying to make a living."

At that time, Ted and two other stuntmen – Boyd "Red" Morgan and Al Wyatt, Sr. – all of whom were stuntmen and second unit directors had a company called Unit Two. The three rented offices and Ted recalls that many stuntmen used to "hang out" there to use the phone and find out what jobs might be opening up. "We'd come in and couldn't even find a seat in our own office. Then we started talking about an association," Ted said, "and we pulled together several men who were always in demand and got together to make plans."

The Screen Actors Guild loaned them the use of a meeting room and the group hired an attorney and began writing bylaws. On February 27, 1961, the Stuntmen's Association of Motion Pictures became official with Dale Van Sickle the first president. Ted was among the original 12 founding members.

The association soon boasted a membership of the top fifty premier stuntmen and stunt coordinators.

The association's website says: "Stuntmen are a rare breed, one of a kind. They plan, prepare and incorporate both the safety and risk factors in their performances . . . It takes tremendous dedication, training and years of experience to become an accepted professional as our well-being and at times our very lives rely on each other."

Today membership is by invitation only and members must belong to the Screen Actors Guild. Ted is now an Honorary Member of the association.

In the early days of motion pictures, along with gymnasts and acrobats, the ranks of stunt performers were filled with rodeo cowboys.

"Because there were so many Westerns being made that was more or less a platform to get into the business," Ted said. "If you knew something about horses you had a good shot at getting some work. "

In those days the director might say "ride that horse up that hill, turn him around and fall down. We'd been doing that all along and not making any money," Ted said.

Early on, the association's members who weren't working at the time would visit sets to see that stunts were being done right, that members were treated well and to keep the name of the association in front of those in charge of making pictures. They would also make sure that any association members who did something wrong or unsafe were reprimanded. Some even lost their membership. Consequently, the association developed a good reputation within the industry. In addition, members fought for fair wages for their work. Another rule dealt with the use of profanity on the set. The association didn't allow it. "In the old days between scenes guys would run off and have a drink or maybe smoke a little pot," Ted said. "We stopped all that. When you're dressed and in makeup you should get there on time and stay there. If it's an hour or so between takes you can go back to the trailer and play cards and be ready when sent for."

The association set standards of excellence and professionalism that continue to exist.

Times have changed, of course, and profanity is more and more prevalent in movies. "It's nearly wide open right now," Ted says. "Language in films has gotten more and more foul. It's a sign of the times and there's not much we can do about it at this point."

In 2011 the Stuntmen's Association celebrated its 50th anniversary. "It was a big shindig," Ted said, "with about 500 people including Harrison Ford and a lot of other big name actors."

ABC televised part of it and the association wanted Ted and Bob Herron, the other remaining original member, to come up on the stage but they turned down the opportunity. "What are they gonna see?" Ted asked. "Two old men standing on the stage." They did read the names of the 12 founding members.

Ted has served on the association's Board of Directors and says today it is a "very solid organization."

Earlier, the men had begun bringing women into the association but only as honorary members. There were several women who were "definitely qualified," Ted said. Among them were Barbara Stanwyk and other leading ladies. In 1967 the women formed their own organization called Stuntwomen's Association of Motion Pictures and in 1984 the United Stuntwomen's Association came into being. Since then other groups of stuntwomen have been established.

Ted, right, with a member of the crew
of the Daniel Boone TV series

21

The double-Edged Ax
And Frightening Children

As in any profession, there are specific methods that are used to make certain the desired outcome is reached. In the stuntman's world, the right method can make a difficult move seem effortless while the wrong one can result in injury or even death.

One production in which Ted was involved and that vividly illustrates that point is a 1982 film called *The Mother Lode* that starred Charlton Heston, Kim Basinger and Nick Mancuso. Heston directed the film which was written by his son, Fraser Clarke Heston (who also wrote *The Mountain Men* which Heston did with Brian Keith).

In this film two young adventurers go in search of a lost friend in the wilds of British Columbia. When their plane crashes they must deal with an old half-mad Scottish miner (Heston) who will stop at nothing, including murder, to keep to himself the gold he longs to find.

Heston plays two roles in the film and one is that of the old Scottish miner who, in the story, is his brother.

The movie was shot entirely in Canada which, Ted says, is becoming a second Hollywood largely because of tax incentives.

Heston's main double for the film was originally to be Joe Canutt whose father, Yakima, had doubled Heston years before. Yakima also doubled John Wayne for years and his horse falls in *Stagecoach* are the stuff of legend. His son Joe was also to be the second unit director but he decided early in the film that he wouldn't be able to double Heston and direct the second unit at the same time. Asked who he wanted, Heston said "get Ted

White." Ted had doubled Heston before (in *The Big Country*) and because he and Canutt were about the same size, Ted was called in to double the star once again.

One of the main scenes is a horrific fight between the old miner and Kim Basinger. Heston's brother tries to kill Basinger's character with a double-edged ax in a very small room.

Throughout the film Heston wears a huge beard that covered his face. Ted doubles Heston in the scene and, when made up, looked just like the star.

"I put on all the hair and makeup and we got to the set where there is to be a big, deadly fight," Ted said. "Then they gave me a rubber ax."

Basinger was sitting at a table when the fight began and when Ted bought the ax down it hit the table and bent.

"Cut!" called Heston. "I can't use that. Any ideas?"

The production manager suggested they use a real ax. Heston said "let's ask Ted."

"I can handle it," Ted said.

"You know it's razor sharp," Heston said.

Ted didn't think that was a problem.

Canutt had brought in a Canadian woman to double Basinger in the scene and she asked for a bit more rehearsal with Ted using a real ax.

"So I start down with that ax and I mean I'm moving and I'm watching her and she turns ashen white," he said.

The woman swallowed hard, shook her head and said "I can't do this." She got up and left the set.

Kim Basinger watched this interplay and stood up and said "I can work with Ted."

"Are you sure?" Heston asked.

"Absolutely," she replied. She was still only in her early twenties at the time.

But Joe Canutt said "not under any circumstances am I going to let Ted wield a real ax with the star."

Heston was perplexed. "So what will we do?" he asked. "I've got three days to film this fight, we can't use a rubber ax, your double just left and Kim says she can work with Ted." He turned to Ted and said "Ted, what do you think?"

Ted said the two of them could make it work. "I just need to talk to her before we go into every phase of the fight, to tell her exactly what will happen."

Joe Canutte was angry. "Not with me on the set," he said, and left.

Ted and Basinger rehearsed for all of one day, over and over and over, and finally felt they were ready to shoot the fight.

"This was very dangerous," Ted said. "But she was a trooper. All of this was done in a small, confined space, in a small cabin, not a big open space. And it's a deadly fight."

On the second day of the fight being filmed Ted had to tell her that she was staying too long in one place. "When that ax starts down you've got to be moving," he told her. "And you know, she listened to every word and did exactly what was needed."

He said the angles Heston picked for the shots were perfect. Heston saw the rushes the next day and said "it's a great fight. You believe she's going to get killed until the last second. You really believe she's going to die."

Ted said that he knows without a shadow of a doubt that a bonding company today would never let her do that scene.

"This turned out to be a truly great fight scene," Ted said. "All the danger was with her but she had the heart to step up. Because she did, it made it more believable than with a double."

"She never saw me as Ted White," he said, "only with all the makeup on."

Later, he heard she was at Universal Studios when he was shooting another film nearby and walked over to see her. She was at a table with another lady when Ted walked up to her and said "Kym?"

Politely, she turned to him and said "yes?"

"How'd you like to do an ax fight?" he asked.

She said "oh my God, no, never. I did one once."

"I know," Ted said. "I'm the guy swinging the ax."

"Ted White!" she almost shouted, jumped up and gave him a big hug. "I've told so many people about that and nobody believes it."

"It was true, wasn't it?"

She nodded. "I went home and was so pleased," she said. "I had about three drinks of scotch."

The Mother Lode was one of three films in which Ted worked with

157

Heston. The other two were *The Big Country (1958)* and *Will Penny* (1968).

The Big Country starred Heston, along with Gregory Peck, Jean Simmons, Carroll Baker, Burl Ives and Charles Bickford. Peck plays a seafaring New Englander who arrives in the Old West to marry Carroll Baker (but ends up with Jean Simmons) and becomes embroiled in a feud between two families over a valuable patch of land. Heston is an employee of Baker's father and quickly comes to dislike Peck's character.

On the set, all the actors and stuntmen were required by director William Wyler to attend an evening showing of the "dailies" (film that had been shot that day) whether they wanted to or not. At dinner one evening Ted visited with Heston about the big fight scene between him and Peck.

"It really wasn't much of a fight," Ted said.

Heston agreed, saying it had a big build-up to it, though.

"Yeah," Ted said, "but when you sit back in a movie theatre and you see two guys six foot three or four and there wasn't that much to it, it doesn't work that well."

"I think maybe you're right," Heston said.

Ted also worked with Gregory Peck on other films, notably *The Man in the Gray Flannel Suit* (1956), *The Guns of Navarone* (1961), *MacArthur* (1977) and others.

In *Will Penny* Heston played an aging cowboy who agrees to take a line camp job on a large cattle spread and finds the cabin, which is isolated in the hills, is already occupied by a woman and her young son. The film was written and directed by Tom Gries and its stars also included Joan Hackett and Donald Pleasence.

DURING THE FILMING a class of 40 or so young students, third or fourth graders, were to visit the set.

Danny McCauley, who was the first assistant director and who "always hung out with the stuntmen," called Ted over and told him about the youngsters. "The scene we're shooting while they're here won't be that exciting," he said. It was to be mainly cowboys sitting around a campfire and talking. "The kids will get bored," he said. "Why don't you come up with something to entertain the kids?"

Ted said he had an idea. He suggested McCauley get a revolver loaded with blanks and put it under his coat. Ted said he would then start an argument with McCauley about the money he was to make on the film.

The plan was for Danny to then become angry and say something like "I'm not going to have any more of this, Ted!" They put the plan into action.

"When McCauley shouted at me I turned away and he pulled the gun and fired two shots at me," Ted said. "I faked a hit and fell to the ground. Those kids scattered like quail. I mean, they went in every direction. It took forever to find them all and even after we got them back together some of them didn't believe it was a fake."

Ted, right, with Charlton Heston in Will Penny

22

Giant Birds
And Smashing Phone Booths

OVER THE YEARS Ted has found himself in some unusual, dangerous and often hilarious situations. He's been nearly killed by a giant falling bird at an Emu ranch, drove a car through a phone booth where a close friend was standing, took 26 takes to make a fight with Will Smith look right and even threw a man in a wheelchair down into the hold of a ship – all for the sake of good film-making.

First, the bird.

The film was *Double Take*, a comedy which was made in 2001 and starred Orlando Jones, Eddie Griffin and Gary Grubbs. In the film a man on the run steals a passport and finds himself stuck with the identity of a street hustler. George Gallo directed and Ted played a highway patrolman. The film included a great deal of action and involved 16 stuntmen.

The movie was filmed on an Emu ranch and when it began Ted had a role as a stuntman but with no dialogue.

"They had hired a comedian from Kentucky," Ted said, "and gave him a part as a highway patrolman. I was in a trooper outfit and played his partner."

In one scene the two were in a saloon with a camera filming them from behind the bar. Ted had gone over the lines with the other and knew the dialogue. "When the scene began the man couldn't talk," Ted said. "I thought he was just nervous and would get over it. After the director had called 'cut' I went outside with the actor and we reviewed the lines again."

Ted told him to take a deep breath and "just say the lines." If it didn't go well they would simply do it again until he got it right.

161

After trying four times with no success the director called the two men aside. "I've got to get the shot and Ted is now going to be the one saying the lines," he told them. The other actor was relieved and Ted did all the dialogue from them on.

In another scene, Joel Kramer, the second unit director, is in charge of a sequence in which Ted and another man are in a car that is destroyed by a giant bird.

"There was this steel bird, maybe 22 feet tall, with a six-foot-long pointed beak," Ted said. "We're in a police car that is being chased."

In a nearby truck is a man with a bazooka. He is to fire it, miss the patrol car and hit the bottom of the tower holding the giant Emu which is then to fall forward and impale the beak in the hood of the patrol car. Timing is critical and Ted said all the stuntmen felt this was a "money shot."

"So another stuntman and I flip a coin to see who drives and the other guy wins," Ted said. "We went to the tower to see what the special effects crew had done."

The two front supporting legs of the tower were on a pivot secured with bolts which would allow the tower and the bird to fall forward the proper distance and hit the car. When it hit, charges would be set off and the explosion would blow out the windows of the car.

On the first try the bird planted its beak in the dirt a good six feet in front of the car. The crew brought in a crane and it took about three hours to reset the bird, put the pins back into the pivot and reset the charges.

Finally, on the second try, the bird's beak hit the hood of the car just right, special effects set off the charges at just the right second – and blew the windows into the car instead of to the outside.

"We had glass in our faces, and our arms and faces were cut to ribbons," Ted said. "They took us to the hospital which was about 70 miles away. I think we made five thousand dollars each. The other man may have gotten $6,500 because he drove."

An even more dangerous stunt was carried out in a 1984 family-oriented science fiction film called *Cloak and Dagger* which was directed by Richard Franklin and starred Henry Thomas and Dabney Coleman. In the film a young boy with a penchant for spy thrillers and video games, finds himself in the middle of real espionage when he's relentlessly pursued by spies after he comes into possession of a video game cartridge containing

162

top-secret government info.

Victor Paul, the film's stunt coordinator and an Olympic fencer, originally hired Chuck Tamburro (Ted's brother-in-law) to carry out some stunts. But the day before filming was to begin Tamburro had to back out due to previous commitments. He told Paul to get Ted White.

In one scene, Ted's longtime stuntman friend Dean Smith is in a phone booth on a street corner with the 11-year-old boy (being doubled by a midget) and Ted's character is out to kill them both by crashing a van into the phone booth.

"I went to Dean and told him I'd be going 55 miles per hour when I hit that phone booth and that both of them had to be out of there."

Across the street from the booth is a jewelry store and Ted's van is to jump the curb and hit the window of the store. Ted is to go through the windshield, through the plate glass window and fall straight down, supposedly cutting his throat on the glass. The crew had reinforced the area below the window with steel and cement so the van would come to a full stop.

Ted attached a cable to himself and to the interior of the van so it would stop him as he went through the windshield and the plate glass window (now candy glass in both cases) at the right point so he would then fall straight down, seemingly cutting his throat.

Every individual on the crew, along with several stuntmen from other shows, came to the set to see the shot. But stunt coordinator Victor Paul was worried. "What is all this going to cost me?" he asked. Ted replied that he wasn't going to do it for peanuts. At that point no price was agreed to and the shot moved forward.

Allan Carr, the producer, came to see the shot and asked about camera placement. He was told there were to be two — one to take the van through the phone booth and another to follow it to the jewelry store window. Carr suggested they put a third camera inside the store to film Ted's head coming through the glass. A camera was placed about three feet inside the building and the cameraman was told "there was no way" he would get hurt. It took half a day to get things rigged up before the crew was ready for the shot.

"Finally, here I come," Ted said. "I get up to 55 and Dean Smith waited and waited and got out just in time. I hit the phone booth, shot across

163

the street and just as I hit the window the cameraman inside shouted 'shit!' and broke and ran. The camera tilted down and I did exactly what they wanted but they didn't get the shot."

The producer was livid, Ted recalled. The cameraman said "listen, if you'd seen what I saw, with that car coming at me, I thought there was no way he was stopping. I thought he was coming through and that I was dead."

Stunt coordinator Paul told Ted they would have to do it again. He said it would take a good three days to reset the shot. "You didn't do it right," he said to Ted. "You looked up when you went through the window."

"That's funny," Ted said. "I had my head down to go through the windshield and it was down when I hit the window."

Nevertheless, Ted was back in three days to reshoot the scene. This time they put a "wild" camera inside the store that they could start remotely. Ted did it just right again but ended up feeling a bit fuzzy this time. "It was a tough jolt," he said.

Paul approved the shot and asked Ted how much he wanted for doing it. "Vic, how about six thousand?" Ted said.

"What?" he shouted. When he was over the initial shock, Paul asked if Ted would settle for $4,500.

"No way," Ted said. "You try it yourself."

"I could do it," Paul said.

Ted looked him in the eyes. "You probably could but you didn't," he said. "I did." He got his price.

Dean Smith, the stuntman who escaped from the phone booth just in time, said Ted was doing every bit of that agreed-on 55 miles per hour. "My eyes were getting bigger and bigger," he said. "That phone booth disintegrated and if we hadn't escaped we'd both be dead."

That wasn't the first time Ted had crashed through a window. In *The Return of Jesse James*, Ted actually rode a horse though a plate glass window. "We took a ping pong ball, cut it in two, painted horses' eyes on the pieces and glued them over the real eyes," he said. "If a horse sees where he's going in that kind of situation, he won't go."

IT TOOK TWO TRIES to get the car scene right in *Cloak and Dagger* but it sometimes takes many more attempts to make a shot look real.

In fact, it once took 26 takes to get one swing of the first at Will Smith to appear as though it really connected.

The film was *Wild Wild West*, a 1999 film directed by Barry Sonnenfeld that starred, in addition to Smith, Kevin Kline and Kenneth Branagh. The film is described as "The two best hired guns in the West must save President Grant from the clutches of a 19th century inventor-villain. "

The scene takes place on the second floor of a brothel. Smith is in a room and answers a knock on the door. Ted and half a dozen other stuntmen are in the hallway. With the camera behind him, Smith opens the door. As he looks out Ted throws a punch, Smith flies sideways, Ted comes at him, he kicks Ted in the groin and the real fight starts.

But each time Ted threw the punch Smith pulled his head back. He looked up at Ted who is several inches taller and asked "how much do you weigh?"

"About 225," Ted replied.

Smith shook his head. "Well, when your fist flies by it seems enormous."

"I can slow it down," Ted offered.

"No, no!" Terry Leonard, the stunt coordinator, said to Ted. "You can't slow it down. It's got to look real." He turned to Smith. "Will, you have to trust him that he's not going to hit you. If you hesitate or turn too quickly it lets the viewer know that you know what's coming."

They tried again and the cameraman said it wasn't a "clean" punch.

"Finally," Ted said, "I think he closed his eyes because the camera couldn't see his face, and it worked. There were a few more punches and then we were out in the hallway. That was the 26th take. It was a long day."

Conversely, on the movie *Ship of Fools* Ted and other stuntmen refused to do a second take. This was a 1965 Stanley Kramer-directed film from Columbia starring Vivien Leigh, Simone Signoret, Jose Ferrer and Lee Marvin. It was based on Katherine Anne Porter's novel.

The movie depics passengers on a ship traveling from Mexico to Europe in the 1930s. The passengers represent a wide variety of society of the time. It was filmed on a sound stage on a large mockup of the ship.

"At one point, the script just said *fight*," Ted said. "There were 13 or 14 stuntmen, the cast and the crew. One of the stuntmen was in a wheelchair."

165

The director called the stuntmen together and said he needed some help in planning and carrying out the fight. "There was a hatch that was about four feet square on the deck," Ted said, "and below the hatch there was a drop of 15 or 20 feet down." The director said he needed something to happen with the hatch "and, at some point, we need to do something with the guy in the wheelchair."

The stuntmen came up with a plan for a big fight, a real "donnybrook."

"The stuntman in the wheelchair was laughing, enjoying himself," Ted said, "because he didn't have to risk getting hurt but was earning the same money as the rest of us."

Ted said the men in the fight were taking falls left and right and going over obstacles. "And on a ship there's no place to put pads for protection. You see the deck of the ship and pads would be visible so you fall on the deck."

At lunchtime the cast and crew took a break. The stuntmen waited until the man in the wheelchair left and Ted gathered them. "Here's what we're gonna do," he told them. "In the last part of the fight we'll take the guys we're beating up and throw them down the hatch. Then we'll grab the guy in the wheelchair and throw him in, too."

The stuntmen followed Ted's suggestion and the director was ecstatic. "That was wonderful!" he said. "I'd never have thought of it. Let's do it again and I'll put a camera in the bottom of the hold."

Ted and the others looked at each other. "We can't do that," Ted finally said. "We'd kill somebody."

23

Fighting Jeff Bridges

As A STUNTMAN, Ted was involved in literally hundreds of fights on screen. He used fists, rifles, pistols, axes, swords, bows and arrows, tomahawks, clubs, vehicles – whatever was called for in a script.

In the 80's it seemed as though Ted was almost constantly in a fight with Jeff Bridges.

The fights were staged, of course, because over the years they had become good friends. Their relationship began in 1981 when Ted worked with Bridges on *Cutter's Way*. It continued through the early years of the decade as Ted joined Bridges on *Tron* in 1982, *Against All Odds* in 1984 and, again in that same year, on *Starman*.

One of the fights in *Against All Odds* won a Taurus Award for Ted.

Starman was an unusual experience for Ted in that, at one point, he actually upstaged the star – not because he tried to but due to his role in an earlier film. He even got the role in *Starman* in an unusual way.

Ted as the deer hunter in Starman *with Jeff Bridges and Karen Allen*

Directed by John Carpenter, the film starred Bridges, Karen Allen and Charles Martin Smith. In the science fiction film, an alien's ship crashes on Earth, and, to avoid detection, the occupant (Bridges) transforms himself into a physical replica of the deceased husband of a young woman. He then must use her help to get to the Arizona crater where the mother ship awaits him. Things get complicated when the two fall in love and the alien is pursued by government agents attempting to capture him.

Ted plays the role of a deer hunter who encounters Bridges and Allen outside a restaurant.

"I got a call from Columbia for an interview," Ted said, "and after I'd done the reading I was about to get into my car when a woman came running after me. She said I had read for the wrong part. I was to have read the part of the hunter but they gave me something else."

Back in the office, Ted took a few minutes to familiarize himself with the script. When he was ready to read, however, the director had left for another meeting. They asked him to wait but, after two hours, Ted was asked to come back another day. Ted had just completed *Against All Odds* with Bridges and was certain that was why he had been called.

Several days later the studio called and invited Ted back for a reading but he was busy on another film and had to ask for a postponement. A few weeks later he got another call and went in. "They needed someone as big as Bridges who looked menacing and I fit the bill," Ted said. "After I'd read and started out the door, the director stopped me."

Carpenter, the director, said "we've had a hard time getting together. You're it."

One the first night of shooting Ted and Bridges arrived at the bus stop outside Manchester, Tennessee where the scene with the deer hunter would be filmed and found 60 cars in the parking lot. As soon as Bridges stepped out of the car "it seemed like a hundred people came running," Ted recalled. "There were newspaper people and movie fans all wanting photographs and autographs."

Bridges wanted to get to the bus stop where the interiors would be filmed and said "why don't you talk to Ted White? He just finished a film."

Disappointed, the newspaper people turned to Ted. "What do you do?" someone asked.

"I'm a stuntman," he replied. "I also play a deer hunter."

168

"What film did you just do?"

"A thing called *Friday the 13th,*" Ted said. "I played Jason."

That got their attention and their stories the next morning included information about Ted and his role as Jason.

The next night when they arrived there were hundreds of cars and people in the parking lot. As Bridges and Ted pulled up Ted said "you're going to ruin your hands signing autographs tonight."

They stepped out of the car and people were shouting "where's Jason? We want Jason1"

"Who the hell is Jason?" Bridges asked.

"That's me," Ted said. He signed autographs until he was "blue in the face.

"That was a fun time," Ted said. He had worked on *Escape from New York* with director John Carpenter and the two had an easy going relationship.

The scene with the deer hunter begins with Ted's character confronting Karen Allen, playing "Jenny," the woman Bridges (Starman) has convinced to drive him to Arizona. The hunter has just killed a deer and has it strapped to the hood of his truck. Inside the bus stop he is beginning to proposition Jenny when he sees through the window that Starman has released the deer, which he has evidently just brought back to life, and it is running away.

Ted runs outside, followed by Jenny, to confront Starman. Bridges doesn't speak English well yet and Ted mocks him. Carpenter had asked Ted how he would do that and Ted told him to turn on the camera. "No speaka da English?" he sneered at Starman.

"That's great," Carpenter said. "Keep all of that."

In the scene, much of the dialogue is made up on the spot. "Sometimes dialogue looks great on paper but doesn't really work on camera. I just added a touch of a bully," Ted said.

After the deer had run off and as Ted and Jenny headed out to confront Starman Carpenter asked Ted if he had any black licorice that he could spit like chewing tobacco. Ted said he didn't have licorice but he sure enough had some tobacco. In the script Ted was to knock Starman down and then spit on him. "And then say 'bingo'," Carpenter said. That wasn't in the script. Ted followed through. Bridges then gets off the ground grabs Ted's

169

shoulder as he is looking at Jenny and knocks him to the ground. Then he spits and says "bingo," mimicking Ted's words. "It was a kind of cute thing that the director put together. It worked well."

In a famous bit of dialogue between Ted, Starman and Jenny, Ted mocks her:

Hunter: [Starman and Jenny are looking at a dead deer strapped to the hood of a car] *Did you cry when you saw Bambi?*

Starman: *Define 'Bambi.'*

Hunter: *Huh?*

Jenny: *He doesn't understand. He's not from around here.*

In another scene Starman jumps in a car, spins the wheels and throws grass in the faces of Ted and another stuntman. They then get into another car and start to chase him. In the meantime, another stuntman is driving a bus which pulls in front of Ted's car, cutting him off, and Ted is to skid the car to a stop near the bus.

Prior to shooting the scene the producer came to Ted and said "listen, under no circumstances are you to touch that bus." The production company had rented a brand new Greyhound Bus for the scene. The bus had only about 12 miles on it and had a unitized body without a frame, meaning if the bus was hit anywhere the company would probably have to buy the bus which sold for hundreds of thousands of dollars.

When the producer had left, director Carpenter came to Ted and asked what the producer had said to him. Ted told him.

"Listen," Carpenter said. "I'm directing this, not him. I want you to stuff this car into the side of that bus."

Ted took a deep breath. "We could both lose our jobs," he said.

"Don't worry about it." The director started to walk away. "It's worth it, considering all the stuff that's led up to this. I need it for the climax."

Ted asked for fifteen minutes so he could get a five-way safety harness on the men in the car because a traditional lap belt as used in those days wouldn't protect them in a crash like he planned to do.

Terry Leonard, the stunt coordinator, had not heard any of the two conversations and came to Ted to complain about the delay. Told he was getting a five-point hookup, Leonard scoffed. "You're just gonna slide up there," he said. "You're a bunch of pussies."

170

Finally, the shot was ready and the cars were in motion. The bus pulled in front of Ted's car and he took dead aim at the big lift on the side that opens to a luggage compartment. "I was doing about 50 miles per hour when I hit," Ted said, "and I mean the radiator blew, it smashed in the front of the car and made this enormous hole in the side of that expensive bus."

His window was down and within seconds he felt two hands come through and grab him by the throat.

"What did I just say to you, you damned ignorant stuntman? I'm gonna tear you apart," the producer yelled as he choked Ted.

The others in the car were in hysterics as the director, John Carpenter, ran up and said "wait, I told him to do it. Ask him."

The producer loosened his grip on Ted's throat. "Did he?"

Ted massaged his throat. "He didn't tell me anything."

As the producer started for Ted again, Carpenter spoke up. "Quit making excuses for me, dammit."

"Okay," Ted said. "He told me to do it."

The producer stepped back, turned to Carpenter and said "I'll talk to you later" and stormed away.

In the meantime, Terry Leonard had been looking at the ruined bus and missed out on the verbal exchanged. He charged to Ted and said "White, what the hell were you thinking about?"

Ted laughed and said "I was thinking about all the money I was going to charge you for doing this stunt."

Carpenter, the director, got Leonard calmed down and told him to give Ted a nice bonus. "After all," he said, "he almost got choked to death."

Spending big money is part of making "action" movies. Another scene in *Against All Odds* features a race between a Porsche and a Ferrari. Both cars were brand new and Gary Davis, doubling Bridges, was driving the Porsche, which Ted believes cost around $130,000. As the two vehicles rounded a corner doing about 85 miles per hour, Davis hit the curb and tore out the underneath of the car.

"Don't give it a thought," said Director Carpenter. "Get the other one."

They had an identical Porsche ready. Davis repeated the race in the second car and made it without mishap.

In another scene Davis is racing along the freeway doing 100 miles per hour with a camera in the car filming the action from the driver's point of view. He had been told that if he could "steal" some shots going that fast there would be a nice bonus in it. The film he got appeared in the movie.

"That was a fun show," Ted said. "When it was over Jeff came to me, shook hands and said 'until the next time.' Well, there hasn't been a next time. Yet."

Bridges was nominated for an Academy Award for Best Actor for his role in Starman, and this was the only film by John Carpenter to receive an Oscar nomination. Bridges was also nominated for a Golden Globe Award for Best Actor – Drama, and won the Saturn Award for Best Actor. Karen Allen also received a nod for Best Actress from the Academy of Science Fiction, Fantasy & Horror Films. The film itself was nominated Best Science Fiction Film. Jack Nitzsche received a Golden Globe nomination for his score.

Starman came hard on the heels of another Jeff Bridges movie, *Against All Odds*, another Columbia film, this one directed by Taylor Hackford and starring Bridges, Rachel Ward and James Woods. It was based partly on a 1947 film, *Out of the Past*, which featured Robert Mitchum, Jane Green and Kirk Douglas.

In the film, a shady nightclub owner and part-time bookie sends a down-and-out ex-pro football player (Bridges) to Mexico to find the owner's girlfriend who has run out on him. But, once he tracks her down, the ex-jock falls for her and then tries to cover it up by saying he can't find her.

At one point Bridges' character, Terry, is sent to break into the office of a corrupt lawyer to retrieve some specific files. He breaks into the office but is discovered by a security guard (Ted) and a lengthy and brutal fight ensues.

This is the fight that won a Taurus World Stunt award for Ted. These awards, according to the award's website, "honor the movie industry's unsung heroes, the world's best stunt professionals. They risk their lives to perform the most daring stunts that bring action and excitement to the movie-going public. The Taurus™ awards go to the industry's best and brightest stunt people for extraordinary performances in feature films. Selected and voted by the members of the Taurus™ World Stunt Academy, who are all in the Stunt industry themselves, the winners are not only recognized for their contribution to the film industry, but also honored by their own peer group, the Academy members."

In the film, Ted walks into the office where Terry (Bridges) is hiding. Terry bulldogs Ted from the back and the two tumble over a desk and the fight begins. But it wasn't Bridges who did the actual bulldogging. It was the film's stunt coordinator Gary Davis. This sequence was shot in one long "seamless" take. In it, the two men (Davis and Ted) fall over the desk but when the two raise up to continue the fight, it is Bridges and not Davis.

The scene was re-shot "eight or nine times," Ted said. "The first few times we tried it Davis didn't get off his feet as he bulldogged me." The director asked him to do it again and be in the air when he hit Ted.

"Remember," the director said to Davis, "you're a pro football quarterback and you are in great shape."

When Ted went home that night he was "bruised all over."

When filming began the next day the fighting continued and was so well done it was recognized with the Taurus award.

But during the fight, Ted knocked Bridges out cold.

"We rehearsed that fight time and again," Ted said. "After we'd laid it out and shot the beginning of it, something happened with the camera and we had a delay."

While they waited, Davis and Bridges got together. Bridges told Davis that if Ted would throw a left at one point instead of a right he would be in a better position for the next punch he was to throw. Davis agreed and said he would tell Ted.

But, in the midst of setting up the shot, he forgot to mention it to Ted.

"In the fight, I threw a right as we'd originally planned," Ted said. "I weigh 225 pounds and I was in good shape. I caught him on the chin and he dropped like a dead duck."

Ted said "oh, my God." He'd never really hit anyone in a picture before and he said you could hear a pin drop on the set. Finally, after some attention from a nurse, Bridges blinked his eyes open and a knot popped out on his chin.

"Damn," Ted thought. "I hope I didn't break his jaw." Ted was "sweating bullets" when Bridges shook his head and spoke.

"What happened?"

Ted told him he turned his head the wrong way.

"You were supposed to throw a left," Bridge said. "Didn't Davis tell you?

Davis was standing nearby and rolled his eyes. "Damn," he said. "I forgot to tell him."

"I could have killed him," Ted said. "If I'd hit him one way it could have driven a bone right up into his brain."

That ended the shooting for the day. In the break room where Bridges was taken to rest, Ted hovered over him. The star's eyes were still glazed over. "I hope we never have a real fight," Ted said.

"Don't worry," Bridges replied. "We won't."

Eventually, Bridges recovered enough that they were able to finish the fight scene which ends when a woman pins Ted's hand to a wall by stabbing him with a letter opener.

"They took a plaster cast of my hand and made a replica of it that looked absolutely real," he said. "Then my hand goes up and the palm is spread and they cut."

At that point viewers saw the fake hand in close-up, the letter opener pinned it to the wall and there is another cut to Ted screaming.

The two other films that Ted did with Bridges included *Cutter's Way* which was filmed in 1981 and also starred John Heard and Lisa Eichhorn. It was directed by Ivan Passer and had Bridges playing a man whose car breaks down in an alleyway where he sees a figure dumping something into a garbage can. When a young girl is found brutally murdered in the alley where he had abandoned his car he becomes a suspect.

In 1982 the film's screenwriter Jeffrey Alan Fiskin won an Edgar Award from the Mystery Writers of America for Best Motion Picture Screenplay.

A year earlier Ted had appeared in another Bridges film, *Tron*, a science fiction adventure in which a hacker is literally abducted into the world of a computer and forced to participate in gladiatorial games where his only chance of escape is with the help of a heroic security program.

Considering today's extensive use of computer graphics, it is ironic that the year *Tron* was released the Motion Picture Academy refused to nominate it for a special effects award because, according to director Steven Lisberger, "the Academy thought we cheated by using computers."

24

Marilyn, Clark and Monty

As MUCH AS TED enjoyed working on films with Jeff Bridges and on others such as *Hatari* and *Silverado*, for example, there were some movies that were simply no fun for him. One of the films that he particularly disliked working on was *The Misfits*.

"There were so many things about the production of that movie that I disliked," Ted said. "At times I wished I'd never signed on. So many things distracted us from doing it right – Marilyn Monroe's problems, the director's problems, just one thing after another."

The film, which was released in February of 1961, starred Marilyn Monroe, Clark Gable and Montgomery Clift with a supporting cast that included Eli Wallach and Thelma Ritter. It was written by Arthur Miller, based on one of his short stories, and directed by John Huston.

The plot revolves around a sexy divorcee (Monroe) who falls for an over-the-hill cowboy (Gable) who is trying desperately to maintain his independent lifestyle in Nevada. This "modern" Western is set in the early 1960s. Gable and his buddies, Guido (Wallach) and Perce (Clift) plan to capture a herd of wild mustangs and sell them to a packing company for dog food.

The day-to-day production of the film was plagued with problems, not the least of which was Monroe herself.

"I knew Marilyn long before she made it big in the movies," Ted said. "I knew her when she was a brunette walking around Hollywood searching for jobs, interviewing for commercials, looking for anything that would help her pay rent. We'd occasionally run into each other on interviews.

Then, after she became a blond, she came to my house several times." After she signed a contract with Fox, Ted recalled, she told him that "now that I'm under contract I can tell the rest of 'em to go to hell."

However, as all movie fans know, Monroe married baseball star Joe DiMaggio and then playwright Arthur Miller, the screenwriter for *The Misfits* and, over a span of time, began sinking further and further into alcohol and prescription drug abuse and depression. She would die of a drug overdose a year and a half after the film's completion. She had been born in 1926 and named Norma Jeane Mortenson (which she later changed to Baker).

Monroe's tardiness to the set and her mental state during the filming was compounded by other problems. Temperatures in the northern Nevada desert often reached upwards toward 110 degrees, reports say director Huston gambled and drank and occasionally fell asleep on the set, and screenwriter Miller constantly revised the script during the shooting.

Some reports also say that Gable insisted on doing his own stunts including "being dragged about 400 feet (120 m) across the dry lake bed at more than 30 miles per hour (48 km/h)."

A website called "Dear Mr. Gable" that bills itself as "the site that celebrates The King of Hollywood, Clark Gable," is more specific about claims that Gable "insisted on doing" his own stunts. An article titled "Clark Gable: Desert Sunset for the Star of 'The Misfits'" by Anne Edwards is reprinted on the site from the April 2000 edition of "Architectural Digest."

"Gable wore heavy Western garb," the article states. "He had lost thirty-five pounds before starting the film, and although he suffered some minor heart problems the previous year, he considered himself to be in excellent condition. Despite there being an expert stuntman and a double on hand, he insisted on doing most of the stunts himself, which included wrestling a wild stallion and becoming ensnarled in a lariat and dragged face-down for several feet. He came out bruised but pleased that he could still do "a man's job".

Ted recalls the circumstances a bit differently and photographs show that he did much of the difficult work of wrestling the horses himself.

"It's not uncommon for the big stars to claim they did their own stunts," Ted said. "Wayne did it on *Hatari* and even Fess Parker, as nice and honest as he was, often was reluctant to admit he had a stunt double."

He said because much of the movie-going public sees these big names as larger-than-life heroes, they want to believe that what they are seeing is real and that the stars are capable of super-human acts. The stars often think of themselves in the same light and don't want to do or say anything that would detract from that kind of hero-worship.

Stuntmen and stuntwomen have come to accept that attitude on the part of some of the stars they double, Ted continued.

"For us, many times, it's all guts and no glory."

Ted doubling Clark Gable in The Misfits

As to Gable being dragged, Ted says it was director Huston's fault and not Gable's wishes.

"They lied to me," Ted said. "I went to the director early on in the production and told him that Gable was in no shape to do the drag. I said I would do it and they could insert some tight head shots of Gable."

Director John Huston told Ted that "I don't need to be told how to direct. But we'll see."

"That's all he said," Ted said. "But when it came time to do the drag they didn't put it on the call sheet so I didn't know it was in the works. When I got in that morning one of the assistants came to me and said they needed me to go to town and get a number of things. He said there was nothing that day but simple stuff and that I wouldn't be needed."

While Ted was gone on the errand they shot the scene of Gable being dragged. When Ted got back the star was hurting and perspiring heavily.

"Where have you been?" Gable asked.

"They sent me to town," Ted said.

"Why would they do that?"

"It was a phony trip," Ted said. "I see that now. They knew if I was here I wouldn't let 'em drag you."

"I asked where you were," Gable said, "and they said they didn't know."

"Well, now you know," Ted said.

The man was beat, he said. "I know they hurt Gable bad. So many things distracted us -- Monroe, the director and other things. But there wasn't a better man in the world than Gable. He was down to earth and great to be around."

Monroe was habitually late in showing up for work but "Gable would sit and wait and never say a cross word to her," Ted said. "You have no idea what it's like working on a multi-million dollar set and you want to start shooting at 6:30 or so in the morning and the time comes and your lead's not there. It would sometimes be 8:30 or 9, or later, before she showed up. Everybody would be up and ready to do their dialogue, ready to hit the mark, and suddenly it's not happening."

Production was originally slated to begin in Nevada in the spring of 1960 but was late in starting due to Monroe's emotional instability, Edwards' article reported. "Monroe, accompanied by an entourage of thirteen, showed up two hours late to work the first day that she and Gable were to do a scene together. When she stepped before the camera, she took violently ill and had to repair to her trailer dressing room. When she finally returned to the set, she apologized to him and said, 'Please don't hate me for being so late. I've

178

loved you all my life.' Gable took her aside. 'Look, honey, you are worth the wait,' he assured her."

William Goldman, who has written a number of books about screenwriting, says that studios may not want to get involved with a star who is difficult to work with, even though the star may be ideal for the script. "More often," he says, "if a poisonous atmosphere invades the sound stage, if crucial people are not speaking to each other except through intermediaries, the quality of the film can be affected. This is no law – some of the happiest sets produced the unhappiest results, and vice versa. It may not hurt your movie, but it probably won't do it a whole lot of good either."

Ted said he believed part of Monroe's problem stemmed from the fact that this was her first time working with someone the stature of Gable. "She was scared to death," he said. "She would come on the set and if you watched her you could see her hands actually shake as though she had a great fear of being in his presence."

As the picture progressed, it got somewhat better, Ted said. "Gable joked with her and tried to help her relax."

Production was stopped at one point while she went to a hospital for two weeks. Huston shut down production in August 1960 to send her away for detox. Close-ups after her release were shot using soft focus.

Montgomery Clift was another tough case, Ted said. "He was recovering from a terrific car wreck and his whole face had been caved in. They did reconstructive surgery on him and his face was still puffy. He wore a bandage that was written into the script."

Director John Huston was "another story," Ted said. "I still don't have much use for him because he lied to me about dragging Gable."

Huston gambled and drank and occasionally fell asleep on the set. The production company even had to cover some of his gambling losses.

Filming was completed on November 4 of 1960 and the movie was released the following February. Despite all the problems, critics generally agree that Gable, Monroe and Clift delivered performances that were superb. Some critics even think Gable's performance was his finest and, after seeing the rough cuts, Gable agreed.

However, the movie did not do well at the box office. Despite being filmed in black and white, final production costs were about $4 million. It barely earned more than that during its US release but has brought in more profits since its DVD release.

The "Overlook Film Encyclopedia: The Western" edited by Phil Hardy and published in 1994, says the heart of the film lies not in the characters' talk with each other "but in the relationships they form."

While Gable is the aging cowboy, Monroe is "the jaded divorcee he meets and Clift the has-been rodeo performer whom Gable persuades to join him in rounding up 'misfits', horses too small for riding."

Together, the review of the film suggests, "they form a society apart, united by their shared dissatisfactions with modern America."

The Misfits was the final film appearance for both Gable and Monroe, and the third-to-last for Clift.

Within two days after filming ended, Gable suffered a heart attack and died ten days later.

Monroe and Clift attended the premiere of the film in New York in February 1961 while Monroe was on pass from a psychiatric hospital. Within a year and a half, she was dead of an apparent drug overdose.

Ted White, meanwhile, was on to other projects that were more fun.

25

─────

Fun Stuff

TED WHITE IS A serious man who loves to have fun. He puts his heart and soul into every endeavor and tries to do the very best he can whether it's performing a stunt, acting or directing. But he's also a man who enjoys life and loves to laugh, often at himself, but seldom at the expense of others.

The Misfits didn't provide much laughter, or fun, for Ted or for the other actors. But Ted found humor and enjoyment on many other projects, even when they didn't always go as he had expected.

One day in the 80s Ted received a call asking if he was working or if he could get to the airport in Los Angeles within the next hour. He replied that he could and was told they would have a plane waiting for him. He would fly to a major city where another plane would take him to his destination.

"I didn't know where I was going," he said, "how long I would be there or what I would be asked to do." He doesn't even remember the name of the film.

"So I flew to a big airport, got on another smaller plane that took me to a very small town where we landed on a dirt runway. There was a car waiting and I asked where the hotel was."

"We're headed to the set," the driver said.

Ted wanted to clean up a bit first but was taken immediately to the set where Jimmy Casino was the stunt coordinator. Casino told Ted they needed him in wardrobe. They handed him a coat, as he was to be in a car and would be seen only from the waist up.

Back on the set he was pointed to a car. "That's the car," Casino said. "You're coming down this dirt road and there's a bend in the road. Nail it broadside and get around the bend and that's a cut."

Ted got in the car, drove it fast, slid around the corner and the director called "cut."

"That's it," he was told. "You're done. We just needed you for that one shot."

The driver took him back to the plane but he had to spend a night in a hotel as the regularly scheduled airline didn't have another plane out that day.

"I was in that one scene for a few seconds," Ted said. "The scene was probably added at the last minute. I don't even know if it ended up in the actual film. They paid me more money for the time I had to lay over than I made doing the actual shot."

IN THE MID-50S Ted had received another call, this one wanting him to be gone for a maximum of three days. Shooting was to be done in several locations throughout California. He was to fly to the set where *Friendly Persuasion* starring Gary Cooper, Dorothy McGuire and Anthony Perkins was in production. The film was based on a novel by Jessamyn West and was directed by William Wyler. It was produced by Allied Artists Pictures with a budget of around $3 million.

Ted went to the studio and was told they were sending him to the set to do a buggy race. "You have one day down there, you'll do the chase and then you'll come back," they told him. They said they would pay him $1,000 a day with no adjustments and no overtime.

The story is of a family of Quakers in Indiana in 1862. Their religious sect is strongly opposed to violence and war. It's not easy for them to meet the rules of their religion in everyday life but when Southern troops pass the area they are in real trouble. Should they fight, despite their peaceful attitude?

"When I got there," Ted said, "I went to the director and he said 'what are you doing here?' I said I was there for the buggy race."

"Buggy race, hell," director Wyler told him. "We've got a battle to put on. Get some stuntmen out here and help me do this battle."

Ted was there for eleven weeks.

"I brought in a bunch of stuntmen to do the big battle, Ted said.

"The director asked how much I wanted for doing the scenes. I said I didn't know because I did know that if all this got back to the studio and they looked up my contract they'd see I was supposed to be getting $1,000 a day and they'd put me on a daily or a weekly basis and I'd make a third of what my original contract said."

In all that time, he spent only the final three days filming what he was originally sent there to do -- the buggy race sequence.

Interestingly enough, and unrelated to Ted's role in the film, the adaptation of the book into a movie and credit for the film's screenplay resulted in considerable controversy. Allied Artists was the first studio to insert a little-known "anti-Communist" clause into the basic Writers' Guild of America (WGA) agreement in 1952. This clause, which resulted largely from the investigation of "Hollywood radicals" by the House on Un-American Activities Committee (HUAC) in 1947 and 1951, barred individuals (especially some screenwriters) with suspected "Communist" leanings from working on Hollywood films.

HUAC charged that Communists had established a significant base in the dominant medium of mass culture. Communists were said to be placing subversive messages into Hollywood films and discriminating against unsympathetic colleagues. A further concern was that Communists were in a position to place negative images of the United States in films that would have wide international distribution.

The "blacklist" was officially broken in 1960 when Otto Preminger, and then Kirk Douglas, credited Dalton Trumbo for scripting *Exodus* and *Spartacus*. (Ted appeared in both of these films.)

WHAT COULD BE MORE FUN than staging a large-scale Civil War battle sequence in *Friendly Persuasion*? How about playing an Indian in an episode of the TV series *Maverick* and being stumped by the one line he had?

In the film, following a large battle scene, Ted is one of many Indians who ride into the fort they've just besieged.

Leslie H. Martinson, the director, called the "Indians" together and said "Okay, now when you're in the fort, you look up at all those dead bodies lying over the walls and you say something mystic in Indian dialogue."

Ted is slated to be the first "Indian" in line and he works on what he might say.

183

"There's an old collection of syllables that doesn't mean anything but sound like an Indian word," he said. "Ya Ta Hey!" This phrase was used often by John Wayne as he waved his hand forward, palm down. "It worked for him," Ted said, "so I decided that's what I would say."

Just before the scene is to be shot the director changed positions and put another stuntman in front of Ted, who had thought he would be the first in line. "Now remember. . .," the director cautioned.

"Okay, okay, we've got it," the "Indians" replied.

Martinson called "action!" and the "Indians" charged into the fort, pulled their horses to a stop and look up at the bodies.

"Ya Ta Hey," said the first stuntman.

Ted thought, damn, that's my line. Stumped, he blurted out: "Ooooh, oooh, shit!"

The cast and crew went into hysterics, he said, and Martinson, the director, shouted "cut! I told them to get me real actors! I told them not to use these damn stuntmen!"

And Ted thought to himself, "what an Indian I am."

ON ANOTHER FILM, Ted had to work with the New York Mafia.

"We were filming *Seventh Avenue*," he said, "about the Mafia taking over the garment district."

In the film there is a scene in an alley in Harlem where the Mafia blows up a car. "We shot there for three days and three nights," Ted said, "and the first night all our equipment was stolen. We had to hire a Mafia guy to come in a protect it." There were no more thefts.

TED HAD SEVERAL opportunities to work with Mel Brooks and each time knew he was in for an enjoyable experience. In 1974 Ted worked on the famous Western spoof *Blazing Saddles* which was directed by Brooks and, in 1993, on *Robin Hood: Men in Tights* which Brooks produced and directed. This was a spoof of the Robin Hood films of the past and, especially, of Kevin Costner's *Robin Hood: Prince of Thieves*.

In between those two, however, he worked on Brooks' *History of the World: Part 1*. Again Brooks served as both the producer and director.

Dom DeLuise had a central role in the film and kept the cast and crew in hysterics.

184

In one scene that took several days to film, Ted and another actor are guards standing on either side of DeLuise. It is a festive occasion during the days of the Roman Empire and the guards are wearing short "skirts" and helmets. DeLuise is in a toga.

"Bring me a bird," DeLuise calls. A servant brings him a turkey and he tears off a leg and throws the rest of the bird back over his head. They need to reshoot the scene and Ted said the prop guy is saying "Judas, I've only got two turkeys." So they would retrieve the turkey, wipe it off and put the leg back on with toothpicks.

"When he threw it, there were toothpicks flying everywhere," Ted said. "Finally, they sent someone to the market to "get as many turkeys as you can and bring them right back.""

"The other guard and I couldn't help ourselves," Ted said. "He'd tear a leg off, take a bite and throw the turkey away. That went on for days. We laughed our butts off, could hardly keep a straight face for a shot."

Ted said he has even forgotten what he and the other guard had to do in the scene. "Just standing there watching him was enough," he said.

"YOU NEVER KNOW what you're going to find when you get a call to come to the studio," Ted said. "And sometimes you'll do a bit and still not know what film it was for."

That's how he ended up in the opening sequence of *Romancing the Stone*.

This 1984 film starred Michael Douglas, Kathleen Turner and Danny DeVito. In the film, a romance writer (Turner) sets off to Colombia to ransom her kidnapped sister but soon finds herself in the middle of a dangerous adventure. The movie earned more than $86 million worldwide and helped launch Turner to stardom. It also reintroduced Douglas to the public as a capable leading man and gave director Robert Semeckis his first big success.

The film won Golden Globes for Best Motion Picture and Best Actress (Turner) and several other awards.

It was quickly followed by *The Jewel of the Nile*, which was equally successful with the same three stars.

Ted's involvement began, as usual, with a phone call. Warner Brothers asked him to come to the studio to read for a part. "What I read didn't make much sense," Ted said. "It was something about jewels or gold or other treasure and lines like 'I'm gonna kill you unless I find it'."

Two days after the reading the studio called saying they wanted him for the part. Ted wanted to negotiate a higher price than the studio was willing to pay. After a few weeks and after other actors had read for the part, he was called again and told they would meet his price.

Those who have seen the movie will remember the opening scene. Turner is imagining a scene in a romance novel she is writing. Turner herself is not in this scene but a young actress who looks remarkably like her plays the role of a woman in a house when Ted appears as a mean-looking scoundrel of a cowboy. Turner narrates the scene as though she was reading the novel and describes the action.

"When I got to the set," Ted said, "Bob Semeckis had decided that the young actress and I should not meet before the shot. Actually, I didn't know anything about the film or who the lead actors were at the time."

When he got on the set, Ted saw the crew shoveling dirt into the entrance to the room to make him look taller as he stepped through the doorway. The actress was in a motor home going over dialogue and Ted was afraid it might turn into another situation like *The Misfits* when Marilyn Monroe was usually late to the set. When they brought her to the set Ted was elsewhere so she couldn't see him.

"The first shot was of me standing on that knoll of dirt in the doorway and when I opened the door I looked enormous. When the dialogue began that young woman was actually frightened."

Ted had a double-barreled shotgun and as he threatened to kill her he cocked the weapon. "I didn't know they had another camera on the shotgun," he said. "It wasn't in the script but it worked and appeared in the final film."

Filming started about 11:00 a.m. and finished late in the afternoon.

"I didn't realize at the time, or for some time afterwards," he said, "that I was doing the opening scene for one of the great movies of its time. It turned out to be a big hit and I got a lot of work after that."

Before the movie was officially released Ted got another call, this one from Terry Leonard who had been the second unit director.

"Blanco," he said to Ted (using the Spanish word for "White"), "you old bastard, you're the opening scene in *Romancing the Stone!*"

"Are you sure?" Ted asked.

"I'm positive," Leonard said. "I just came back from the studio showing for the cast and crew."

Ted was also surprised. "When Jeri and I went to see it she was just as shocked as I was," he said.

In 1959, something similar had happened. Ted received a call from Universal International Pictures asking him to come to the studio to audition for a film.

"I got there and they asked about 15 guys to line up, sit down, and take our shoes and socks off," he said. "They walked down the line and looked at our feet. Some guys had flat arches, some had bad toenails. I had a high arch from wearing boots all my life."

One of those studying the feet pointed at Ted and said "You're it."

The next day Ted reported to the studio and, dressed only in shorts, was put in bed "with a good looking gal in a negligee."

The two put their feet up on the wall and it turned into a scene in the film *Pillow Talk* with Rock Hudson and Doris Day.

"I thought, this is a pretty good life," Ted said.

Ted also doubled Hudson in the 1964 film *Man's Favorite Sport* which featured Paula Prentiss. Hudson played a fly fishing expert in the movie and Ted doubled him in a scene where he carried a canoe over his head. His face is not seen.

He later doubled Hudson in the TV series *McMillan and Wife* which ran from 1971-77. In one scene, Ted rides a bicycle at "what seemed like 60 miles per hour down one of those San Francisco hills. It was plain scary."

In the 1960's *Batman* was a popular TV series starring Adam West and Burt Ward. Ted appeared in several of the episodes.

One of the stories took place on a submarine and was shot at what Ted called the "ranch" at Twentieth Century Fox Television studios.

"Fox had a man-made lake on the grounds and there were three of us playing German sailors standing in a real sub tower," Ted said. "In the scene a plane comes down and strafes us and we act as though we've been hit and fall about eight feet into the water which is only about two feet deep."

The director of the episode is on a large wooden platform near the sub tower. Because there is no real plane in the scene (viewers see only the actors in the sub tower) the director makes the sound of airplane machine gun fire – "ack ack ack ack."

"So we're in the tower and the director hollers action," Ted said. "He shouts 'airplane's coming, airplane's coming – ack ack ack" and he starts backing up and falls off the platform into the water. He comes up shouting 'cut, cut!'"

The cast "went bananas," Ted said. "We couldn't get a shot for two hours. We'd look up and shout 'airplane's coming, airplane's coming' and crack up again."

Ted later appeared in the 1989 film *Batman* which starred Jack Nicholson, Michael Keaton and Kim Basinger.

ANOTHER INCIDENT involving an overbearing director occurred during the filming of an episode of the Western TV series *Cheyenne* which starred Clint Walker and ran from 1955 to 1963.

In the scene Ted is shooting at Walker with a rifle. After several shots the rifle is empty and Walker tells Ted to come out with his hands up. Ted walks into the street, hands up and holding the rifle in his right hand. After a cut, Ted is handed a rubber rifle. When Walker is close enough Ted swings the rifle at him but Walker ducks, Ted misses, and a fight begins.

The director yelled "Cut! Cut!" and hurried to Ted.

"Don't you know how to swing a rifle at his head?" he shouted at Ted. "You're not doing it right." He demanded the rifle and told Ted to play the role of Walker. He swung the rifle and Ted ducked. "Do you see how I did that?" he asked. "Now you take the rifle and I'll be Clint Walker."

Ted did as he was told and swung the rifle but the director didn't duck. "I wrapped that rubber rifle around his head and he fell over backwards," Ted said.

The director lay on the ground shouting "Assassin! Assassin!"

While the crew tried to stifle their laughter the director was taken to the hospital. "He came back with a bandage around his head that made him look like a wounded soldier," Ted said. "He looked at me and said 'you assassin. I'll never forget this'."

Clint Walker had to sit down and get his laughter under control before they could resume filming.

DURING THE FILMING of the 1966 movie *Smoky* with Fess Parker, Ted had a brief and angry encounter with co-star Katy Jurado. Jurado, who was once married to Ernest Borgnine, had a film resume that included many popular films such as *One-Eyed Jacks, The Westerner, Trapeze, Broken Lance, Arrowhead* and *High Noon* among others.

"We were in Mexico City," Ted said, "and I had checked into the hotel." As Second Unit Director he rated a suite. He was just unpacking his clothes when there was knock in the door. It was Katy Jurado.

"You have the only suite left in the hotel and I would like it," she said to Ted.

Ted, who was single at the time, said "fine. Get your clothes and move in."

She became very angry, he said. "No," she said. "I would like for you to move."

"Sorry," Ted said. "I'm not moving."

Jurado stormed away and wouldn't speak to Ted throughout the production process. "I don't know where she ended up staying," he said, "but I kept the suite."

IN 1987 TED was stunt coordinator, second unit director and had a role in RKO Pictures' production of *Hot Pursuit* which starred John Cusack, Robert Loggia and Jerry Stiller. In the film, as summarized on IMDB.com, "Young Danny is following his rich girlfriend's family to the Caribbean. But suddenly he must take a chemistry test and cannot go with them. After they have left, he gets a leave from his professor and takes a plane to find them. But he is not quite sure where they are, and meets smugglers, crazy captains and murderers."

The movie was written and directed by Steven Lisberger, who also wrote and directed the 1982 production of *Tron* in which Ted appeared with Jeff Bridges. *Hot Pursuit* was filmed in Ixtapa-Zihuatanejo, the fourth-largest city in the Mexican state of Guerrero, during the fall in extreme heat.

Nerves were on edge and Ted was forced to use a devious trick to get Loggia to perform one of the last scenes in the movie.

On the beach the crew built a pool about 100 yards long and 60 yards wide, about the size of a football field. In the pool, the crew constructed a mockup of the sailing ship. It was close to the ocean so, even though the action took place in the pool, it appeared that it was in the ocean.

The scene takes place on the sailing ship at sea in a heavy storm.

"Robert Loggia was the lead heavy in the film," Ted said, "and in the final minutes of the film he gets blown overboard and co-star John Cusack dives into the ocean, saves him and pulls him back to the ship."

On the day the scene was to be shot Ted was miles away directing the second unit. As he worked, a car raced to the set, braked to a stop and the driver got out and called to Ted. "They need you on the first unit," he said.

Ted said he was busy with four cameras shooting a scene.

"Shut it down," the driver said. "The director told me to get you."

On orders from director Lisberger Ted shut things down and got in the car. When they arrived on the set it was dark. "What's the problem?" he asked Lisberger. The director pointed at Loggia who was walking around the pool talking to a dozen Mexican crew members who were in the water.

"How long did it take you to build this?" Loggia asked. He was told it took three or four months. "And you were in the water every day?" The reply was yes. "Ever change the water?" No.

Loggia went to the production manager and told him he was not getting in that water. In the meantime a jet was waiting to take him back to Hollywood where he was to report for another film.

"What do I do?" director Lisberger asked Ted.

Ted thought a moment and then said "I've got an idea but you'll have to go along with it."

"Do what you have to do," the director said.

Ted told the director to take Loggia to the bar and get him a drink. While they were gone he assembled the crew. Most of the Mexican crew spoke English and he outlined his plan.

"After Loggia is rescued and gets back on the ship I want you to start clapping and yelling like it's the best acting you've ever seen," he told them. "Don't stop, just keep it up."

When Loggia returned, Ted took him away from the group. "Here's what I'm going to do for you," he told him. "I'm going to get a doctor here and I'm going to put lots of fresh water in your trailer. The minute you get out of that water the doctor will blow out your ears, and freshen up your

190

mouth. You'll take a shower, drink lots of fresh water and get to your jet. Just one shot is all it'll take and you'll be out of here."

"Don't you bullshit me, Ted," Loggia responded.

Ted found a doctor and Loggia agreed.

While Loggia got into costume Lisberger, the director, came to Ted. "What's he going to do?" he asked.

"Just what he's supposed to," Ted said. "But remember what I said. You and everybody else start clapping the minute the scene is over."

When Loggia returned the crew started up four large fans that created large waves in the pool. Loggia, on cue, fall into the water and Cusack dove in after him. When they were back on the ship the director called "cut!" The fans stopped, the wind died and everyone began clapping and shouting.

"Loggia's eyes got bigger and bigger," Ted said. "We reshot that scene time and time again and Loggia was in the water for over four hours. After every shot they're clapping and yelling."

When he finally got out of the water the doctor washed out his mouth and blew out his ears. Loggia took a shower and went to the airport, a happy man.

Ted said years later he ran into Loggia in an airport. "He was walking toward me with his wife," he said. "When we shook hands his eyes didn't register that he knew me."

Loggia's wife asked if he was the Ted White who worked with Loggia on *Hot Pursuit*. She said Loggia had a memory problem and that was why she was with him. That was the last time Ted saw the actor.

After the completion of *Hot Pursuit* one of the producers was getting ready to shoot another film and told the production manager to hire Ted White to direct the second unit. "He saved a show for us in Mexico," he said.

Ted's ever-present smile

26

Blowing Up Pancho Villa
And More fun

TED HAS MANAGED to have fun both on and off the movie set. When not making films Ted found interesting ways to enjoy himself. Like when he was almost arrested for carrying guns into Canada. Or when a young woman in a bar accosted him, thinking he was someone else. Or when he drew a crowd at his newly painted house that glowed in the dark.

Or when he and some buddies blew up a statue of Pancho Villa in Mexico while looking for buried treasure.

But first, there was a chance to buy stolen goods at half what they were worth.

One day early in his career fellow stuntman and good friend Walter Scott called Ted and asked if he had $35,000 in cash. Scott said he was working on a deal with some men who said they had robbed a church of gold statues, candelabra and other material that was worth at least $150,000. They wanted to sell it to Scott for $70,000.

Plans were made for a clandestine meeting with the robbers in Blythe, a town near the California/Arizona border on the way to Phoenix. Scott's father, Walt Sr., was in on the deal but apprehensive and somewhat unsure of whether he wanted to be involved. "This is not right," he said. "All this stuff came from a church."

He needn't have worried. The men drove to Blythe and went to the meeting place on several occasions but nobody ever showed up.

Ted isn't sure how they would have been able to sell the stolen goods anyway.

193

THERE WEREN'T TOO many adventures that Ted shied away from. Especially if they sounded like fun.

"One time soon after I got into the motion picture business but before I was making much money," Ted said, "a friend of mine came to see me with what he said was a great opportunity."

This friend said he had met a man in downtown Los Angeles who was "in pitiful shape" and who said he needed to sell a map of buried treasure in Mexico that was worth millions. He said he was in bad health and too old to go for it himself.

"The map was on a piece of deerhide," Ted said, "and it looked authentic. The more we talked the better it sounded." Ted volunteered the use of some guns he had. Another man had a four-door Chevy sedan.

"Well hell," they said. "Let's go."

Again Ted turned to Walter Scott's father, Walt Sr. (The younger Scott was not involved in this treasure hunt and Ted won't disclose the names of the other three men for fear of implicating them in something they don't want told.) Walt Sr. had been a prospector.

The men told him they needed several sticks of dynamite and told him why. He gave them eight or nine sticks but made them promise not to tell anyone where they got it. But he laughed at their plans saying ninety per cent of those maps weren't worth a nickel.

"We know that," they said, "but this came from a very reliable source."

The men took off for Mexico, travelled for several days and ran out of food and were nearly broke. Finally, one night they arrived at a small village that was roughly noted on the deerhide map. According to the map there was a statue of Pancho Villa on a horse with a sabre in the middle of the town square. The treasure, the map promised, was buried beneath the statue.

The four Americans decided they would have to blow up the statue to get at the treasure. They found some shovels and one night about the stroke of midnight they dug four feet beneath the statue, placed the dynamite in the hole, ran the fuse out and lit it.

"We jumped in the car and drove four blocks away and then heard an enormous explosion," Ted said. "We drove back to the square and there must have been a hundred people standing around."

One of the men said "we can't go back there" so they turned around and quickly drove back north toward the U.S. fearing that if they were caught and convicted they'd spend the rest of their lives in a Mexican jail.

"We kept that story to ourselves for a long time," Ted said. "Then one of the guys told it to another stuntman and we were kidded unmercifully. They'd ask: 'Blow up any statues lately?' The story got around and we were laughing stocks."

One of the men framed the map and has it in his den today. "It was an enormous bronze statue," Ted said. "And there was nothing left of it. Just a big hole. People were circled around it scratching their heads. Was there any gold there? We'll never know. How were we going to find out?"

IN THE EARLY 1990S Ted often carried a gun with him. Those were potentially dangerous times in California because of the anger and unrest spawned by the well-known incident involving Rodney King.

Madison Gray, writing in a 2007 *Time Magazine* article, recalled the circumstances. "While driving down the 210 freeway in Los Angeles with two friends, Rodney King was detected speeding by the California Highway Patrol. Fearing that his probation for a robbery offense would be revoked because of the traffic violation, King led the CHP on a high-speed chase, eventually hitting 115 miles per hour, according to the police. By the time he was caught and ordered to exit his vehicle, several L.A.P.D. squad cars had arrived on the scene. A struggle ensued, and some of the officers quickly decided that King was resisting arrest."

The officers reportedly fired two shots into King with a TASER gun and then beat him with their batons. A videotape of the incident "sent shockwaves around the world and enraged the already frustrated L.A. African American community," Gray wrote. After the acquittal of the officers "all that rage turned into the worst single episode of urban unrest in American history, which erupted on April 29, 1992, and before they were quelled a few days later, had left 53 people dead and $1 billion in damage."

"I was in Los Angeles during that time," Ted said, "and began carrying a gun with me in my car, just in case."

He was carrying three weapons with him when he tried to enter Canada on a vacation.

Ted and wife Jeri were joined by long-time Texas friends Joe and

195

Margie Barclay on the trip, each couple in their own motor home.

At the border, as a matter of course, the customs officials checked to see if Ted had a criminal record. Ted told them he didn't have a record but they said "oh, yeah? What about all those bar fights?"

Jeri crossed her arms. "I didn't know about those," she said.

"That was when I was much younger," Ted said.

The officials asked about liquor or chewing tobacco and then told Ted to pull over to a parking area where they searched the motor home and found two of the three guns he had with him.

"They charged me $750.00 and kept both guns," Ted said. "I should have gotten them back when we left the country but they kept them.

Ted left the customs area and was soon doing 60 or 65 miles per hour.

"Big boy," Jeri said. "You better slow down. If they stop you and find that other gun they'll lock you up for sure."

TED WAS CONSTANTLY being mistaken for someone else and it wasn't just when he was doubling leading men such as Wayne, Gable, Hudson or Garner. Once it happened in a bar.

In Los Angeles there was a bar that was often frequented by Ted's longtime stuntman friend Chuck Roberson. Ted said he and Roberson were almost twins. "We were the same size and had the same facial features," he said. "If you saw him you saw me."

In those days there were two "Chucks." Ted said there was Chuck Hayward, known as "Good Chuck" and Chuck Roberson who was called "bad Chuck." The "bad Chuck" was Ted's virtual twin and had a brother named Lou who was not a stuntman.

One evening Ted was sitting at the bar and Lou was at the far end.

"Suddenly, somebody grabbed me from behind, spun me around and slapped me in the face and my drink went flying," Ted said.

A "good-looking woman" confronted Ted and said "the next time you come around my sister I'm going to come at you again, but that time it will be with a knife or a gun!"

"Lady, I don't even know you or your sister," Ted said.

"Don't lie to me," she said. "I know you. They described you to me completely one hundred percent and that's you."

196

Ted heard laughter from the far end of the bar and Lou Roberson got off his stool and walked to the angry woman.

"Let me explain something to you," he said. "I'm Lou Roberson and this man is not my brother, Chuck."

Ted told her who he was and the woman was very embarrassed and apologetic. "That was my introduction to the Roberson family," Ted said. "Chuck was one of the greatest guys I ever met. He was one of the founding members of the Stuntmen's Association. He was a great cowboy, a super roper, and a good guy. Everybody liked him."

Chuck Roberson died of cancer several years ago. He was only 70 years old.

IN HIS YOUNGER DAYS, when Ted had started to make some money in the film business, he decided to build a house with a pool. He later added a master bedroom that overlooked the pool.

His wife, however, didn't like the color of the house.

Ted told her he had spent all the money he could afford but he got an estimate from a painter who wanted $2,500 to paint the house. "That was a lot of money in those days," Ted said. "We can't afford it."

But one day he stopped in a Santa Fe Train salvage store and spotted two five-gallon cans of yellow paint priced at $10.00 each.

"I bought that paint and worked all week on the front of the house," Ted said. "The paint didn't look that great but I figured it would improve when it dried and would be a mellow yellow."

One Saturday after he had painted the entire front, he took the family out to dinner.

"It was dark when we got back," he said, "and there were forty or fifty people standing in the street in front of our house. We got closer and saw that the entire front of the house was lit up."

The house was glowing.

Ted had painted it with the yellow striping used for painting street lines and when light hit the house it glowed brightly.

Someone asked Ted what he was doing and he told the man he was "making a whore house."

It cost him $5,000 to hire a man to sandblast the house, treat the wood and repaint it.

Another shot from the Andy Griffith Show *when Andy, left, and Don Knotts, right, have captured Ted, center, who is playing a drunk*

27

Lana, Tony and Greg

AMONG THE BIG-NAME stars with whom Ted has worked, in addition to such luminaries as Wayne, Gable, Heston and others, were Lana Turner, Anthony Quinn and Gregory Peck.

In 1960, as he was about to complete work on a Western in Montana, Ted got a call from Universal Studios saying they wanted him back in San Francisco to work on a film called *Portrait in Black* that would star Lana Turner, Anthony Quinn, Richard Basehart, Lloyd Nolan and Sandra Dee.

In the movie Sheila Cabot (Lana Turner) becomes increasingly disturbed as she cares for her ailing, disagreeable husband (Lloyd Nolan). Along the way, she falls in love with Dr. David Rivera (Anthony Quinn), who is tending her husband. This leads to a series of unfortunate events, resulting in the death of the husband and an ensuing murder investigation.

When Ted arrived in San Francisco he was still in the old Levis and boots that he had been wearing in Montana when he was called back to California. He caught a cab to the five-star hotel where the studio had booked a room for him. The reception desk was empty when he arrived but desk clerks came running after he rang the bell.

"I'm Mr. White and I'm with Universal Studios," Ted said. "I want to register."

"There's no need for that, Mr. White," he was told. "We'll take care of it."

"Two bellboys approached and one tried to grab my suitcase but I held on tight so I wouldn't have to tip him," Ted said. "I started toward the bank of elevators but one of the bellboys said I had a private elevator to my room. It took me up to the most gorgeous suite you've ever seen."

In the suite Ted found a bar with a large stock of liquor – "any kind

199

of whiskey you wanted" – and a massive coffee table with an enormous basket of fruit covered in cellophane with a note on it saying "good luck."

"I thought, man does Universal know how to do it right," Ted said. "So when I got to work the next morning I told the crew that they needed to come up to my room. I told them I had so much booze up there we couldn't drink it dry."

That night a dozen crew members came to Ted's room and "we drank until two o'clock in the morning." The next night they came back and drank all evening again.

Soon, the shooting schedule changed to nights. Ted's call was for 8:00 p.m.

"I got there and Anthony Quinn and several men in suits were sitting around a 55-gallon drum with a fire in it."

Quinn called out: "Hey Ted. How're you doing? You going to be doing stuff in this film?"

Ted said he was and one of the men in suits said: "Are you working for Universal?"

"Yessir. I double Tony."

"What's your name?"

"Ted White."

The man stood, stiffened and said: "You sonofabitch. My name is **Ed** White and I'm the Executive Producer of this film. You've got my room and I'm in something that looks like a broom closet."

After the initial shock, Quinn stood up for Ted saying no one had any idea that the mistake had been made.

"The hotel bill was nearly four thousand dollars," Ted said. "It was embarrassing and they even ran a story about it in the *Hollywood Reporter*."

"BEFORE THAT, when I first got to the set I was still in my Western garb and didn't have a place to go to change clothes," Ted said, "I had worked with Quinn before and he knew me so he invited me to his trailer."

Ted went to the trailer to change, took off his boots and left them by the door. Someone came by, saw Anthony Quinn's name on the door, reached in and took Ted's boots, evidently thinking they were Quinn's.

"He bought me a new pair of boots," Ted said. "He was a good guy and great to work with. In fact, most big-name stars like him treat stuntmen

200

very well. They know you're going to make them look good."

ABOUT THREE DAYS into the shoot Ted was asked to go to Lana Turner's trailer and tell her they were ready to shoot her next scene. "I went to her trailer about half a block away and she invited me in," Ted said. "She was sitting at a dressing table while a hair dresser worked on her. She had on a little terrycloth robe that barely covered her. I told her she was wanted on the set and she told me to sit down."

Ted sat down and could see her full length in the mirror. "I tried to look away but she did all she could to tease me," he said. "From that day on, when I got near her on the set there was some more teasing in her eyes."

During the production a special effects crew member unintentionally did something that cost Ted a lot of money.

In one scene Anthony Quinn's character is to run along a ledge far above the ground that is about fourteen inches wide. Far below, the police are to be shining a large spotlight on him.

"I was down below arguing with the Production Manager about how much money they were going to pay me to double Quinn in the shot," Ted said. "I said those lights would be in my eyes and it would be hard to see, making it possible that I'd fall off that narrow ledge."

As they argued, the Production Manager began to laugh and pointed up to the ledge. A special effects crew member, spotlighted in the bright beam from the searchlight, was running along the ledge "like it was a piece of cake. That guy cost me a lot of money," Ted said.

TED LATER WORKED with on other films with Quinn including *The Guns of Navarone* in 1961 which also starred Gregory Peck, David Niven and Irene Papas.

This film, directed by J. Lee Thompson, was based on Alistair MacLean's 1957 novel about the efforts of an Allied commando team to destroy a seemingly impregnable German fortress that threatened Allied naval ships in the Aegean Sea and prevented 2,000 isolated British troops from being rescued.

The film was part of a cycle of big-budget World War II adventures that included *The Bridge on the River Kwai* (1957), *the Longest Day* (1962), and *The Great Escape* (1963).

"Most of the cast in this film were good to work with," Ted said. "I did feel that the director demanded too much of the leading men. There were some very dangerous sequences in the movie and I felt the director put the stars in positions in which they could get hurt."

Ted felt that David Niven was a problem. "He whined all the way through the show," he said.

As described by director Thompson in the DVD commentary track, Niven became severely ill after shooting in the pool of water underneath the cave elevator and nearly died, remaining in a hospital for some weeks as other portions of the cave sequence were completed by the crew. The entire production was in jeopardy, and reshooting key scenes throughout the film with some other actor—and even abandoning the whole project to collect the insurance—was contemplated. Fortunately Niven was able to complete his scenes some weeks later.

"Gregory Peck played the lead in the film and, in actuality, was the leader of the group of stars," Ted said. "I had the benefit of working with some great people. Some of them we'll never see the likes of again. You don't see any Gregory Pecks anymore. These were characters, solid characters. When they came on a show the directors knew they were going to get the best out of them that they could provide. Gregory Peck always gave it his very best."

The cliff-climbing sequences were very difficult, Ted said. Much of it was real but sometimes the director of photography would show a shot of a rope, then a shot of an actor who appeared to be holding on to the rope and climbing. Actually, though, the actor frequently was on a ladder perhaps six feet off the ground. At other times the rope was on a cable and the actor or stuntman was not really climbing but being pulled upwards as he moved his hands as though going hand-over-hand up the rope.

"Anything can be dangerous," Ted said, "and in an action movie you look at situations from all angles and, considering the safety of the actor or stuntman, decide if it's worth the risk for the good of the film."

The Guns of Navarone grossed $28,900,000 at the box office and was the eighth top-grossing film of 1961, earning a net profit of $18,500,000. It won Golden Globe awards for Best Motion Picture and Best Original Score and an Academy Award for Best Special Effects. It was nominated for six other Academy Awards.

Ted also worked with Gregory Peck in the 1977 film *MacArthur* which told the story of General of the Army Douglas MacArthur, Supreme Allied Commander during World War II and United Nations Commander for the Korean War. This Universal Pictures film portrays MacArthur's (Gregory Peck) life from 1942, before the Battle of Bataan, to 1952, the time after he had been removed from his Korean War command by President Truman (played by Ed Flanders) for insubordination, and is recounted in flashback as he visits West Point in 1962.

Ted portrayed one of the soldiers during the invasion of the Philippines prior to MacArthur's triumphant return, immortalized in the photo of him keeping his "I shall return" promise and wading ashore at Leyte in October of 1944.

"We shot some of the big scenes in the San Diego area," Ted said. "We were in landing craft coming to the beach and mortars the special effects crew had planted in the water were exploding all around us. In the first take, the man driving the landing craft stopped the boat and we ran off into about seven feet of water. We got in dry uniforms and did it again, and again."

One evening, after a long day's shooting, Ted and two dozen others were on a bus being driven back to their hotel. "Tony Eppers, a great stuntman, saw a bar and told the driver to pull over saying we all needed a drink." When they left to get back on the bus, Eppers had stolen a large gumball machine. "We had gone about a block when a car wheeled in front of the bus and the driver swerved to miss it," Ted said. "That gumball machine tipped over and the glass broke and we had jawbreakers rolling around everywhere. From then on you couldn't get out of your seat without sliding around and falling down thanks to those hundreds of jawbreakers."

He said the group pitched in and repaid the bar for the machine.

Ted, left, with other actors in the film
What Did You Do in the War, Daddy?

28

Sam, Selleck and Hawaii

TED'S SIZE AND bearing often led to film jobs that had him doubling tall leading men, playing bad guys or rugged outdoorsmen and performing dangerous stunts that required a big, athletic, heroic persona. He also studied film making and learned about directing, the use of lenses and managing people. All of that eventually brought him in contact with two of the screen's larger-than-life personalities – Sam Elliott and Tom Selleck.

Ted began working with Elliott when Sam was an extra at Fox Studios making $12.50 a day. Pretty soon, Ted said, "some agent got ahold of Sam and began getting him some good parts. He is always good in any part he is asked to play. He's a hard worker, knows his dialogue and hits the mark."

In 1969 Elliott showed up in *Butch Cassidy and the Sundance Kid* as one of the card players in the opening sequence. Interestingly, his future wife Katherine Ross co-starred in that film but they didn't meet until they filmed the horror/mystery film *The Legacy* in 1978.

Ted was working with Elliott on an urban action thriller in New York called *Shakedown* in 1988 when Sam told him he had bought the film rights to Louis L'Amour's novel *Conagher*. At the time, Sam and Katherine Ross were working on the script and Sam said he wanted Ted to work with him on the movie.

"That was three years before they finally did it," Ted said. "I said 'that's wonderful' and then basically forgot it. You hear things like that all the time and I figured they meant it at the moment but there was no telling whether it would happen or not."

Sam asked Ted who he thought would be a good director for *Conagher* and Ted recommended a man named Robert Totten who had directed some episodes of *Daniel Boone* and who Elliott had worked with on *The Sacketts* in 1979. This two-part TV adaptation of another L'Amour novel, featured Elliott, Tom Selleck and Jeff Osterhage. It was directed by Totten.

Three years later Ted got a call asking him to come to Turner Pictures to read for a part in *Conagher.* "You never know if something said in passing years earlier will actually happen," Ted said. "In this instance, it did."

Ted was signed to play the foreman of a ranch owned by a character played by Ken Curtis who appeared in more than 300 episodes of the TV series *Gunsmoke* from 1959 to 1975. The series also starred James Arness, Milburn Stone and Amanda Blake. In *Conagher* Elliott plays a cowboy who "rides for the brand."

Tall, thin and wiry, Elliott is the classic picture of the American cowboy. *Conagher* appeared on Turner Network Television in 1991, is rerun frequently and is a popular DVD.

In the movie Mrs. Evie Teale (Katherine Ross) is struggling to stay alive while raising her two children alone on a remote homestead. Conn Conagher is an honest, hardworking cowboy. Their lives are intertwined as they fight the elements, Indians, outlaws, and loneliness. Evie begins tying poetry to tumbleweeds and lonely cowboys throughout the area find her notes and speculate on the writer. "You don't know what music is until you hear the wind in the cedars," she wrote on one of the notes.

The movie was filmed in Colorado and the first morning Ted was on the scene he came down to breakfast in the hotel where Elliott was also staying. In addition to his starring role, Elliott was the Executive Producer of the film. "Hi Ted," he said. "I'm glad you're here. We've been shooting about a week."

"How's it going?" Ted asked.

"We took your advice and hired Robert Totten to direct," Elliott said, "but we've had a few problems."

Back in the studio before filming actually began Totten had fired both members of the makeup crew saying "they didn't do good work." Later he fired the sound man claiming his work was not good enough.

"You can't keep firing people," Elliott told him. "We're going to be shooting in a week."

After another argument Elliott decided that was enough and fired Totten. He moved Reynaldo Villalobos from his position as the director of photography, made him the director and hired another cameraman.

"What a shame," Ted thought. "*Conagher* was going to be tough enough to shoot even without those kinds of distraction."

Having to fire Totten was difficult for Elliott who Ted said seldom got offensive and almost never raised his voice. "But I'll tell you this," Ted said, "you don't want to ever give him any trouble. He's one tough sonofabitch."

Ted, right, with Sam Elliott in Conagher

During the filming of *Conagher* Ted and Elliott met Ted's wife Jeri in a restaurant. Some men who were sitting at the bar began making smart remarks about "candy-assed Hollywood cowboys."

"This is too nice a place to mess up with a fight," Ted said to Elliott.

"It's not gonna be that way," Elliott replied. He walked over to the men at the bar, stood close to them and never raised his voice to a level that Ted could hear. He came back and sat down with Ted and Jeri. The men at the bar paid their bill and left.

"What did you say to them?" Ted asked.

Elliott said quietly: "I told 'em very simply that this Hollywood cowboy would tear their heads off in about two seconds and that they'd look so bad their wives wouldn't know them and if they hadn't paid their check and got out of there in the next few seconds I'd be back and follow through."

Elliott was nominated for a Golden Globe award for his *Conagher* role but lost out to Beau Bridges. Barry Corbin, who played a stagecoach driver in the movie, won the "Buffalo Bill Cody Award" for quality family entertainment and the Western Heritage Award from the National Cowboy Hall of Fame in Oklahoma City for his performance.

During the filming of Conagher *Ted, center, poses with Ken Curtis, left, and the wardrobe director Luster Bayless*

Ted has maintained a friendship with Elliott over the years since then but has worked with him again on only one other feature – *Roadhouse* in 1989 which also starred Patrick Swayze.

TED MET TOM SELLECK in 1979 during the filming of a pilot for a TV series called *Concrete Cowboy*. Unfortunately, near the end of filming the production company fired Selleck and brought in veteran actor Claude Akins to take his role. They managed to salvage most of the scenes in which Ted had doubled Selleck, however. Ted had worked with Akins before during the shooting of *Rio Bravo* with John Wayne back in 1959.

Weeks later, when Ted was in Los Angeles working on another project, he ran into Selleck in the greenroom.

"I'm sorry they canned you from *Concrete Cowboy*," Ted said.

208

"Aw, forget it," Selleck said. "They're sending me to Hawaii to do a show called *Magnum* or something like that."

"That sounds like fun," Ted said.

Selleck shrugged his shoulders. "Well, we'll see," he said.

Magnum, P.I. would make Selleck a multi-millionaire. He became Executive Producer of the show and bought a beautiful home on the beach.

Selleck played the role of Thomas Magnum. Magnum was a former U.S. Navy Officer, a veteran of a special operations unit in the Vietnam War, who had resigned his commission with the USN Office of Naval Intelligence, ONI, and became a private investigator living in Hawaii. The show would go on for eight seasons and 162 episodes until 1988, winning him an *Emmy Award* for Outstanding Lead Actor in a Drama Series in 1984.

Selleck was famous for his mustache, a Hawaiian-style aloha shirt, a Detroit Tigers baseball cap, and the Colt Model 1911A1 .45 ACP Caliber pistol his character carried. Magnum drove a Ferrari 308GTSi in the series. The model became so identified with the role that Ferrari fans now refer to the red-painted model as a "Magnum" Ferrari.

One of the reasons for this series being set in Hawaii is that CBS did not want to close its Hawaii production offices when the original *Hawaii Five-O* ceased production in 1980. Ted was called to double Selleck on *Magnum, P.I.* several times.

"Once I had a big fight to do on a ship," Ted said. "The ship was at anchor and we all went aboard and were setting up the fight when a car came racing down the pier. It was the second assistant director and he told us they were postponing the fight." Selleck had been called back to the mainland to be a presenter on the Academy Awards show and would be gone for two weeks. The company was shutting down production during his absence.

"You've got two weeks to mess around Hawaii," Ted was told. During that time he would be paid expenses and his contracted salary.

"So I got on the phone and called Jeri and said get over here. I've got a five-star hotel and nothing to do for two weeks. We rented a car and drove around the island and had a great vacation."

One night during that time they were in the hotel's restaurant, being served by waiters in tuxedos and listening to an orchestra. Across the way a group of eight men and women were "being loud and obnoxious, disturbing the other diners."

Near Ted and Jeri sat a man and his wife who were in the restaurant regularly. After nearly half an hour of the disturbance, the man walked to the group. "I'm the attorney for ABC television," he said, "and you people are embarrassing beyond words. I can't tell you how ignorant you are. Get up, pay our bill and get out of here now."

The individuals turned out to be a crew of ABC who were on the island filming another project. "We never saw them again," Ted said.

He saw Selleck several times after *Magnum, P.I.* ended its run, once in a Mexican restaurant in L.A. where Ted and his friend, actor John Vernon, were having lunch. Vernon earned fame for several roles but notably as the College Dean in *Animal House.*

After Ted had introduced Vernon, Selleck told them he had just bought an abandoned General Motors plant on Van Nuys Blvd. for his father who planned to turn it into a flea market. His father had died a few days earlier, however, and Selleck was worried about what he could do with the property. Later, Ted was called and asked to replace a man who had been hired as Selleck's double in the TV movie *Last Stand at Saber River.* The film dealt with a man (Selleck) who was trying to put the pieces of his life back together after the Civil War on America's frontier.

Ted turned down the opportunity saying he wouldn't take another man's job. "One of the reasons we formed the Stuntman's Association was to stop that kind of thing," he said. "I wanted to talk to Tom and tell him I hoped he understood but never had that opportunity." Ted saw Selleck occasionally after that but only to visit briefly.

Selleck is probably best known for his role as Magnum but he also plays Police Chief Jesse Stone in a series of TV movies based on Robert B. Parker novels. He also appeared as NYPD Police Commissioner Frank Reagan in *Blue Bloods* on CBS-TV and has appeared in more than fifty film and television roles since his success with *Magnum, P.I.*

On a side note, Selleck's contract commitment to the *Magnum, P.I.* series famously cost him the role of Indiana Jones in the first *Indiana Jones* film, *Raiders of the Lost Ark*, which went to Harrison Ford. Selleck was unable to take the part of Indy because *Magnum* was due to start filming in March 1980. However, because of a writer's strike, the start of production on *Magnum* was delayed until December 1980, which would have allowed Selleck to play Indy.

29

Learning the Craft

TED'S INVOLVEMENT with Selleck on the *Magnum, P.I.* series was not the end of his experiences in making films in Hawaii. However, his roles with Selleck had little to do with the fact that he was asked to stage and film an epic fight on the island of Kauai. That came about due to his skill as a stuntman, of course, but also because he had prepared himself in many other phases of movie-making.

Over the years Ted had risen to the top ranks of a legion of men and women whose largely unsung efforts have made the action in motion pictures exciting and believable. At the same time they have enhanced the careers of many film stars, saved millions of dollars of insurance on them and, no doubt, have saved the lives of actors who couldn't have done what the stuntmen and stuntwomen did for them.

Wendy Pan, in an article entitled "Famous Hollywood Stuntmen: Living Dangerous Professionally," calls these stunt performers "truly artists and innovators." She said Hollywood stuntmen "have captured the hearts and imaginations of millions of moviegoers and television connoisseurs, adults and children alike. Usually remaining faceless and nameless, these heroic acrobats rarely seek the limelight for the deserved recognition of their daring feats."

In other words, they are ***All Guts*** but receive ***No Glory***.

Ted White will tell you there is no one way, or any easy way, to become a stuntman. His own career has been one of "on the job training" although he did have a background as a real cowboy and rodeo rider when he entered the business. Still, there is no stunt school, no academic degree in stunt work; indeed, there is no one clear path to a career in the field.

The "profession" of Hollywood stunt work is an outgrowth of the public's demand for realistic action in the films they pay to see. In the early days of filmmaking little thought was given to how stunts were performed. The Keystone Kops and Buster Keaton learned how to do stunts through trial and error.

Ed Grabianowski points out in an article entitled "How Stuntmen Work" that one of the most famous early stunts was done by Buster Keaton. In one film "the front of a house falls on him, but the window falls around him so he is left standing unharmed. This risky stunt was accomplished simply by measuring very carefully."

Early in the 20th Century, though, in response to the tastes of audiences, movies began to include more and more dangerous scenes and demand grew for experienced individuals willing to double the stars and perform for the cameras.

By mid-century modern stunt technology was evolving rapidly and today the use of computer generated images (CGI) has become more prevalent as directors experiment with stunts they consider too dangerous or expensive to do using live actors.

Ted is among a relative handful of people who have taken their talents beyond horse falls, fist fights, fencing and fast cars to higher levels in the industry. The way he did it is a story of ingenuity, interest and a willingness to expand his knowledge of how movies are made and what makes them work for audiences.

He had to pay his dues as a stuntman first, of course, and it wasn't always easy. After his earliest experiences of leading a billygoat around a set, swimming with killer sharks and banging into barn doors with John Wayne, he decided he would go farther in the industry if he devoted a significant amount of his time to learning the craft of movie-making from the experts he was fortunate enough to work with on an almost daily basis.

There is a lot of "sitting around" on a film set while cameras are moved, actors are made up, sets are adjusted and the crew waits for just the right light when shooting exteriors. Ted took advantage of that opportunity to watch directors, cameramen, second unit directors and others. "When I first got into the business I made up my mind that I wasn't always going to just do stunts," Ted said. "I wanted to get behind the camera and direct but you can't direct without knowledge of the lenses that are available to you."

212

When Ted was on a shoot and wasn't in a scene he stood behind the cameraman, listening to the conversations with the director about which lens to use for a particular shot, how to frame the picture and how to deal with other technical aspects of the filming. Later, when he saw the film that had been shot while he watched, the reasoning behind certain decisions became clear. In addition he spent hours watching demonstrations at a Panavision factory near his home.

"The knowledge of lenses and what you can do with them is critically important as you move through the ranks," he said. "This became more and more evident to me."

Studios rent cameras and lenses because each movie may require a unique set of them. The ones selected can create a specific mood, can film a vast panorama or even show details from across a large room.

"When we went to Africa to shoot *Hatari* we had four cameras and six sets of lenses," Ted said. "The dust was so horrible we had to put a hood over the cameras and even then we could hardly keep the dust out. Every night the camera crew, after putting in a 12 or 15-hour day, would take the cameras apart, carefully clean them and put them back together. We were fortunate to have good, experienced guys and we never had problems with the cameras."

Over the years Ted became proficient enough in many of the finer points of movie-making that he could take over, first as a film's stunt coordinator and then as a Second Unit director.

The "director" is in charge of the movie set but often may not have a background in stunt work, or be too busy on other aspects of the production to handle that part of the process. In this case the stunt coordinator is in charge of planning, rehearsing and filming the stunts. The stunt coordinator also hires the stunt people, plans the stunts, assures that everything is done in the safest manner possible and keeps the stunt crew organized and working well together.

On some films, stunts and other sequences are directed by a "second unit director." In many of these scenes the principal actors may not be involved and the second unit director can shoot those scenes while the director is involved in other aspects of the film, often in locations far removed from where the second unit is filming.

Many second unit directors have a background in stunt work. In fact, some may do double-duty on a film and also act as the stunt coordinator.

"AFTER NEARLY 30 years of standing by cameramen, going to classes and listening to outstanding directors, I knew about as much about cameras and lenses as most directors did," Ted said.

His first directing experience came in the early 1960s on the TV series *Daniel Boone*. Ted had just earned his Director's Guild card. He needed five directors who would "sign" the card for him and two of them were Howard Hawks and John Ford. For this first directing job he was given 26 pages of action scenes. Fortunately, there was no dialogue, just action.

Prior to shooting the scenes he viewed all the film that had previously been shot where scenes would be inserted. He showed up on the set at 5:00 a.m. and got started shooting by daylight. He finished at eight that night. Later, the editing department called to say his film would work well. Several episodes of the series would later include the film he shot that day.

Other opportunities to direct often came up unexpectedly.

In 1980 he was working on the comedy *Used Cars* that starred Kurt Russell and Jack Warden. In the film the owner of a struggling used car lot is killed and it's up to the lot's hot-shot salesman (Russell) to save the property from falling into the hands of the owner's ruthless brother and used-car rival.

Ted's long-time friend Terry Leonard was second unit director and stunt coordinator on the show. It was his first directing job and one day he ran into a problem.

Leonard had 125 cars all driven by young men lined up at an abandoned airfield, ready to shoot an action sequence. In the shot Kurt Russell's double was to transfer from one car to another while travelling at about 60 miles per hour. He was to climb out of one car, get on its hood and jump to the rear of another car racing alongside.

By 7:00 a.m. Leonard was ready to begin filming the scene but his First assistant was nowhere to be seen.

"What am I gonna do?" Leonard asked Ted.

"Give me the script," Ted said. "I can do this."

With Ted directing, the drivers and stuntmen worked all day and got the shots they needed.

214

That night the production manager called Ted to his hotel room and told him he had done such a good job he was to continue in that role.

Later, Ted was involved in a show with the working title of *Reckless* that was shot in Canada (Ted never learned the title under which it was finally released). "It was a very, very tough show because there was so much action," he said. "We had motorcycle racing, hang gliders and fast cars on the street. On top of that the director had never shot action before."

Ted found a dozen of the best "kite flyers" in the world and took them with him to shoot a scene of hang gliders coming off a mountain in bright sunshine and floating down to a river far below. Simple enough, right? Wrong.

Early on the morning of the shoot Ted received a call from the executive producer. "It's raining," he said. "What are we going to do?"

Ted made sure everyone was ready – transportation to the site 50 miles away, the crew, the kite flyers – and said "let's go. We're 50 miles away from the site. By the time we get there the wind and rain will have stopped."

The producer wasn't convinced.

"I'll bet you one hundred dollars that I get the shot," Ted said. The producer, still skeptical, agreed to the bet.

At the site it was still raining. The kite flyers said they couldn't go in that weather. Just wait, Ted told them. After lunch, more rain.

"Let's get set up," Ted said. "I just have a feeling."

The director reluctantly got his three cameras set up. The kite flyers huddled in the rain on the edge of the mountain. Suddenly, the rain stopped and the sun came out.

"It's your show," Ted said to the director who quickly called "action!" The kite flyers sailed off into a blue sky with a bright rainbow in the background of the picture.

That night at dinner, Ted found an envelope being slid over his shoulder. Inside was a one hundred dollar bill with a note that said "lucky."

There was also to be a full-scale motorcycle race in the film. Again, the director had no idea of how to go about filming it properly. The executive producer went to the director and said "listen, you need to turn Ted White loose. Let him direct. He knows what to do and he's already hired all the racers. Just let him do it."

"It was a big sequence," Ted said. "It took several days because it's tough to shoot on a complete race course and to keep all the cameras out of the line of sight. You get a shot you need and then you go through the hassle of moving everything such as the lights, cameras and trucks to get another shot. But it turned out to be a very good part of the film."

Over the years Ted has pushed himself and continued learning about the movie business. "I'm not only one who has ever done that," he said. "Clint Eastwood made Buddy Van Horn, his double for years, a millionaire by having him direct some films. Buddy went through it all with Eastwood, movie after movie, and he paid attention. Terry Leonard came up the same way."

By combining his skills as a stuntman, knowledge of cameras and lenses and experience in directing, Ted has made himself a valuable resource to the production units of which he has been a part over the years.

"Now and then I've been asked to visit a production company that was having difficulty of one kind or another," he said. "Sometimes the company I was sent to was behind schedule or they were having trouble with the action sequences. I'd go there, sit on the sidelines, talk to the assistant director or other senior production crew members and try to figure out what was going wrong."

There were times, he said, when the director would "bull up completely" and not want to hear advice. Now and then, when that happened, the director would get fired. More often than not, however, a director would listen to an explanation of what he or she was doing wrong and be willing to take steps to correct the problem.

"You're walking a very fine line in those situations," Ted said, "and I've had to learn to be tactful. Sometimes a director has become very angry with me and I don't understand that. If someone is not perceptive enough to listen to advice from a man who has been in the business many years longer than him and has worked with some of the finest directors in the world, it can lead to his downfall. He's hurting only himself. If he takes advice, you can make everything seem as though it was his idea in the first place."

Ted said directors like John Ford and Howard Hawks didn't need any advice. However, he said, at one time in their careers they did need advice and the fact that they become so good at their job indicates that they probably listened and heeded good advice.

TED'S INVOLVEMENT with the *Magnum, P.I.* series was not his only film experience in Hawaii.

In 1982 MacGillvray Freeman Films was working on one of the first feature films to be done entirely in large-screen IMAX. The film was *Behold Hawaii*, an adventure story of a Hawaiian family spanning 1,200 years. Essentially, it follows a young Hawaiian's search for his cultural roots. The film was supervised for accuracy by the Bishop Museum's Pat Bacon and Dr. Kenneth Emery.

Most of the cast and crew of Behold Hawaii

IMAX is an abbreviation for **Im**age **Max**imum. IMAX has the capability of recording and displaying images of greater size and resolution than other, more conventional, film systems. It is possibly the most widely used film system for presentation in specially-designed theatres. As of early 2017 there were more than 1,000 IMAX theatres in nearly 70 countries and since 1970 more than 450 million people had attended an IMAX theatre.

Behold Hawaii involved action but the crew did not include any stuntmen. One of the action sequences involved a fight between two men that started on a mountain, went all the way down to a valley, across the valley and partway up the other side. When the film was sent to the mainland for previewing, the Executive Producer found it unacceptable.

The company's management called Ted and asked him to go to Hawaii to plan and reshoot the sequence. Bring two stuntmen, he was told. When he got to Hawaii he met with the first and second unit directors and a skeleton camera crew. He went to the area where the fight would be filmed, started at the top of the mountain and walked the entire length of the fight's proposed path. It started on one mountainside, went down to a valley that was more than 100 yards wide and then partway up a mountain on the opposite side of the valley.

After checking out the span of the fight scene, Ted cornered the Production Manager and asked him to "please listen to what I have to suggest before you say no."

Because they were on an island, Ted knew there were many ship riggers available. He told the production manager he wanted two riggers to run cables from one end of the fight scene to the other. He said he wanted a camera platform that would hold the operator and other required camera crew and, especially, the heavy IMAX camera. In Ted's vision, the camera platform would move across the mountain and the valley at the same speed as the fight and it would be filmed from slightly above the fighters in one continuous shot.

Such a shot would be expensive and Ted had a quote from the riggers that amounted to nearly $90,000. The production manager shook his head. "We can't afford that," he said. After some cajoling from Ted he called the executive producer who gave him the go-ahead.

Shooting with an IMAX camera is difficult under the simplest of circumstances. But filming a fight from a moving platform and going down a mountainside, across a valley and then back up on the other side posed special problems. In the first place, the "average" complete IMAX camera package weighs about 650 pounds and consists of 16 cases. In comparison, the IMAX camera equipment that went into space for the Hubble telescope weighed nearly 4,000 points. However, a modified camera that went to the top of Mt. Everest weighed about 80 pounds.

Secondly, the IMAX wide angle lens sees everything above, below and to either side of the camera. Special care would need to be taken to make sure neither the edge of the platform nor the cables would show in any of the film.

After several rehearsals the crew was ready to film the fight. The

218

entire IMAX staff and crew had come to watch and stood behind the platform, well out of sight of the camera lens.

Ted called "action" and the fight began. The two men fought, gouged and kicked. Blood flew. They fell down, got up, tackled one another, fought madly down the mountainside, across the valley floor and up the adjacent mountain. "Cut!"

The onlookers broke into applause and the cameraman shouted "unbelievable!"

The film was sent to the mainland where the executive producer viewed it, called Ted and said "I can't believe it! What did the helicopter cost?"

"There was no chopper," Ted replied. He explained about the cables and camera platform.

"It's wonderful," the executive producer said. "We couldn't figure out why all the foliage on the ground wasn't being blown around by the prop wash from the helicopter."

When the film was totally approved, Ted received "a nice bonus" for his work.

Nothing like it had ever been attempted before.

Rock Hudson is one of the many stars Ted, right, has worked with in movies and on television

30

Fast and Furious

IN 2002 CHUCK TAMBURRO, Ted's brother-in-law, called to say he had heard Terry Leonard was to be the 2nd unit director and stunt coordinator on *2 Fast 2 Furious*, the second film in the *Fast and Furious* series of movies. Tamburro, a helicopter pilot with many film credits, knew that Ted and Terry Leonard were old friends. "I've done some films with Terry in the past," Tamburro said, "but I don't know if he wants me this time. Will you call him for me?"

When Ted reached Leonard the stuntman said: "Hell yes, I want Chuck. He's the best helicopter pilot in the business. Tell him I was going to call him anyway."

"Great," Ted said.

"Now that I've got you on the phone," Leonard continued, "I want you, too."

"Where are we going?" Ted asked.

"Florida," Leonard said. "We'll be there six or seven weeks. We've got a lot of driving to do."

Tamburro did get the job. In fact he was named the aerial coordinator and helicopter stunt coordinator for the film. His brother, John Tamburro (also Ted's brother-in-law) was named a helicopter stunt pilot.

Ted, by then in his mid-70s, was hired to help Leonard plan and carry out many of the "fast and furious" action scenes in the film that included a number of dangerous driving sequences involving hundreds of cars on Florida city streets and freeways.

2 Fast and 2 Furious is one of a series of action films which centers on illegal street racing and heists. Produced by Universal Studios, the series was established in 2001 and has since been followed by at least seven sequels and two short films that tie into the series. This particular film in the series had a production budget of $76 million and earned more than $236 million in its worldwide release.

The movie was directed by John Singleton and starred Paul Walker, Tyrese Gibson and Cole Hauser.

In the film, former cop Brian O'Conner teams up with his ex-con pal Roman Pearce to transport a shipment of "dirty" money for shady Miami-based import-export dealer Carter Verone, while actually working with undercover agent Monica Fuentes to bring Verone down.

The Skyline GT-R driven by "Brian" was actually Paul Walker's personal car, which he himself customized for the movie. During the filming it had a ruptured oil pan and severe damage on all four rims that resulted from a jump from a bridge. Within a few hours, though, the parts had been replaced and the car was back in action.

Over the course of nearly two months Ted was involved in high speed chases down city streets and on highways and bridges. "We did downtown Miami at high speed with cameras on the ground and in the air," he said. Two film company choppers were flown by Chuck and John Tamburro while the police, the city and television stations had "choppers" above the action.

"We had two choppers filming the action while TV choppers and police were filming them and, even higher, the owner of the helicopter was filming everyone," Ted said.

For the film the studio rented fifty "of the most hopped up cars I've ever seen," he said. "These cars cost well over two hundred thousand dollars and all were individually owned by relatively young people. Where they got the money, nobody knows."

Ted said the film was shot at many locations throughout the state. Locations included Infinite Horizon Studios in Orlando, Boca Raton, Hollywood, Homestead, Key West, Seven Mile Bridge in the Florida Keys, Miami, Virginia Key, West Palm Beach and Weston. Scenes were also filmed at Universal Studios in Orlando and in California.

The studio had to rent the freeways to clear them of regular traffic in order to shoot the high speed action. "I think it cost about $360,000 to shut down a freeway for four hours or so," Ted said.

In one scene eight police cars were chasing one of the special "hopped up" cars down a freeway through a dozen or more "regular" cars. Another 60 vehicles were fanned out across the freeway coming the other way.

"Timing is everything in that kind of action," Ted said. "Drivers and stuntmen must have a great sense of timing and good spatial sense, just like fighter pilots have. You have to focus on cars around you, those ahead and those coming up behind you and you have to determine if you've got room to do what the script calls for. It takes hours and hours of practice."

He said drivers must be especially aware of "bogies," individual vehicles that have slipped through police barricades at freeway entrances and who might end up in the middle of a pack of cars going 100 miles per hour. "If someone spotted a bogie," Ted said, "the action was immediately shut down until the rogue vehicle was removed from the mix."

He said the drivers went down some streets at 120 mph with the side streets blocked off. Even the police cars in the film couldn't keep up," he said. "They'd hit a button and the nitro was so powerful the cars would literally leap ahead. I had driven cars with rockets in them but it wasn't like these cars."

He said some of the cars had boom boxes so big it hurt your ears to listen. The paint job alone could cost up to $20,000.

"After they saw that movie people all over the world got hurt trying some of the stunts," he said.

Most of the main cars were housed in a large warehouse that Ted said was 300 to 400 feet long with many garage doors that were several feet above the ground with ramps leading from the lip of the garage to the concrete below. At one point in the film all the doors open at once and all the cars and trucks race out at high speed.

However, one of the doors did not have a ramp.

Early in the production process stunt coordinator Terry Leonard asked young stuntman Brian Burrows to go to the warehouse and bring out the lead car. "Brian came out the only door that didn't have a ramp," Ted said. He was going very slowly and he ended up with the nose of the car touching the ground and the back wheels perched precariously on the edge of the opening.

"The whole crew was in hysterics," Ted said. "Brian was still sitting

223

in the car when Terry Leonard ran to him and saw that he was unhurt. But he was terrified that the car had been ruined. Brian got out and was white as a sheet."

Ted said they simply repainted the front bumper and all was well. The crew continued to kid Burrows about it throughout the filming, though. "Don't let Brian go after any of the cars," they laughed.

The late film critic Roger Ebert, writing in the *Chicago Sun Times*, called the film "a video game crossed with a buddy movie, a bad cop-good cop movie, a Miami druglord movie, a chase movie and a comedy." He said it was made "with skill and style and, boy, is it fast and furious."

Ted was also involved in the production of *The Fast and the Furious: Tokyo Drift* in 2006. In this film Terry Leonard was again the second unit director and stunt coordinator. The movie was directed by Justin Lin and starred Lucas Black, Zachery Ty Bryan and Bow Wow. It was filmed primarily in California with some scenes in Tokyo.

In the film Alabama teenager Sean Boswell becomes a major competitor in the world of drift racing after moving in with his father in Tokyo to avoid a jail sentence in America.

"Drifting" meant a vehicle could drive straight ahead at high speed, slide to one direction or another, and suddenly be going in that direction, again at a very high speed. The first time Ted encountered it, he panicked.

"They had brought men in from Australia with their own cars," Ted said. "In the first scene I shot, I was coming to an intersection doing about 35 miles per hour. Another car is coming toward me at high speed and is to suddenly drift into a turn, avoid me and speed away."

Ted said when he saw that car coming at him at about 70 miles per hour he couldn't believe he would make the turn and was certain they would collide head-on. "At the last second I turned the steering wheel and sent my car over the cub," he said. "We had a crowd of Asians on the street as this was supposed to be in Tokyo, and they all scattered."

The director was furious at Ted and even Terry Leonard was upset. "What the hell were you thinking?" he shouted.

"I could see him flying at me and I was sure I was a dead man," Ted said.

They shot it again and got it right but the film of the people scattering from the first take stayed in the final film.

224

"Those cars and the drivers were amazing," Ted said. "They would set the cars in a drift and when they were pointed in the right direction would just punch it and straighten it right out." He said some the cars had up to 650 horse power.

After lots of practice the stuntmen on the film could also do the drift but early on it was frightening even to many of the men who had done all types of dangerous stunts in previous films.

"Normally when you break into the business, unless you're some crazy kid who drives cars at a hundred miles an hour just for fun, you don't have experience," Ted said. "Early in my career several of us figured out how to learn to drive and do car chases."

Outside of Los Angeles the group found an abandoned airfield that was all blacktop. Ted and his friends rented cars and used them to practice sliding, skiing and simply dodging one another in high-speed chases.

"Finally, the rental car companies figured out what we were doing and wouldn't rent to us anymore," Ted said. "We got to where we were pretty good at it, and we did it for three or four years."

The Fast and the Furious: Tokyo Drift got mixed reviews but still earned nearly $158 million. Its production budget was $85 million.

*Ted did this dangerous horse-fall for a movie version
of* Scheherazade, *filmed in the Mojave Desert*

31

The Good, the Bad and the.....

AS IN EVERY ENDEAVOR in life, the people one works with can make a job enjoyable or miserable. The memories resulting from those associations, no matter whether they are brief or of a more long-term nature, result in impressions of individuals that are long-lasting and difficult to shake.

For more than half a century Ted has worked with many of the world's greatest actors and actresses, producers, directors, cameramen, stuntmen and women, wranglers, drivers, special effects people, sound crew and others associated in just about any way with making a motion picture.

He holds most of them in high regard and has great respect for those who learn their craft, do their job, practice safety, take advice and are considerate of cast and crew. However, there are those in the industry, past and present, who haven't earned his respect. He is often reluctant to speak in negative terms about some of those with whom he has worked but has often been so upset and frustrated by the actions of an actor or a director that he is frank about his feelings.

Ted enjoys remembering the good times and he loves to laugh. His memory of people, films and details about productions is prodigious. He'd rather talk about the fun and amusing times than about the awkward or uncomfortable times. And he'd much rather talk about the people he likes and respects than about those whom he finds lacking in one way or another.

Here's a sampling of his thoughts about people with whom he has worked and about some of the interesting events in his life.

DEAN MARTIN

"He was very easy going and likeable." Not long after Ted worked with Martin in *Rio Bravo* he doubled Cesar Romero in a film's rapier fight. "I didn't know it at the time," Ted said, "but the man I was fighting had been a fencer in the Olympics. I thought he was just another stuntman." At one point the Olympian slashed at Ted and he missed his parry. The rapier cut Ted's throat, just missing his windpipe.

Sewed up, Ted and Jeri took a vacation trip to Las Vegas and tried to get into Dean Martin's show. It was sold out. "Does it make any difference that I Just made a movie with him?" Ted asked the man at the door. Asked what movie, he replied *Rio Bravo.*

After a quick call to Martin the ushers took Ted and Jeri to "Table Number 1" which was close to the stage.

When Martin came on he walked to the edge of the stage and pointed to the two of them sitting alone at the best table in the house. "Here's a good buddy of mine, Ted White" he said. "Ted, what happened to your neck?"

Jeri spoke up and said he was cut in a sword fight.

Ted had at least three more opportunities to work in a film with Martin but had to turn them all down because he was tied up with other projects.

JOHN WAYNE

There's not much that can be said about Duke Wayne that hasn't already been said, written, filmed or immortalized in some fashion. Ted said he was "definitely the kind of tough person he portrayed on the screen."

Wayne was a proud man and "rightfully so," Ted said. "He started as a prop man and worked his way up to being one of the biggest stars in the business. It all began, of course, with John Ford's film *Stagecoach.*"

He said most people have no idea how much talent the man had. Wayne's immersion in the production of *The Alamo* is an example.

"That was a monster undertaking, having to direct the film and then to act in it. He had to hire the actors and crew, find the locations, build the set, handle the finances, set up the scenes and then walk away from the camera and get in front of it to act. People don't understand. It takes so much talent to do all of that and to do both convincingly."

Wayne was exhausted with the completion of *The Alamo.* He then did *North to Alaska* before heading off to Africa to work on *Hatari.*

MOVIE DIRECTORS

Ted has worked with a number of very good directors, along with some he felt were "not very competent." He is especially proud of the fact that he had opportunities to work with some of the "truly great" ones.

He called **Howard Hawks** "one of the finest directors I ever worked with." He said a good director like Hawks knows his story, his script and his actors and is able to pull all of that together in a way that results in films that "truly work" and that are memorable.

"With Hawks there was never a loud word," he said. "He had the respect of everyone – Wayne included, and the rest of the cast and the crew. He had a string of some of the finest films ever made. *Red River*, for example, was an exceptional Western and is respected to this day. People who worked with him came away saying 'what a gentleman'."

Among the films Hawks directed were such favorites as *Gentlemen Prefer Blondes, Red River, The Big Sleep, The Outlaw*, the so-called Western trilogy that included *Rio Bravo, El Dorado* and *Rio Lobo*, and many others.

Ted especially enjoyed working with **John Ford** on *The Horse Soldiers*. "He was a complex and interesting man who got the very best out of his cast and crew," Ted said. "What a character. He was one of the most unforgettable individuals I've ever met. He was so completely different from anyone else in terms of mannerisms, his speech and especially in his stature. I've never known anyone like him before or since."

Ford's resume includes a long list of exceptional films. A few of them are *Cheyenne Autumn, The Man Who Shot Liberty Valance, Wings of Eagles, The Searchers, Mr. Roberts, The Quiet Man* and, of course, many others including the frontier cavalry movies with John Wayne.

Gerald Mast, writing in *A Short History of the Movies* (not too short at 575 pages including an index) said Ford tended to "use the myth of the settling of the West as his central metaphor for the spirit of Man and the spirit of America, bringing civilization and fruitfulness to the savage wilderness."

Compared with Ford, Mast says "Howard Hawks's films are more brutal and less sentimental, more active and less moralistic."

Although he did not have a chance to work with him, Ted had great admiration for British filmmaker and director **David Lean**. "We had a spell of bad weather during the filming of *The Guns of Navarone* in 1961," Ted recalled, "and I walked over to another set with Anthony Quinn, who wanted to visit with a friend. David Lean was directing a film there and I got to watch him work for a good solid hour. I don't remember what movie it was but I felt it was a real privilege getting to be on the set with him."

Lean, Ted said, was very mild but had a reputation as being a genius in setting up shots and getting the most out of every actor. "He would take the time to get his actors in the right mood, the right position, to get the scene he wanted," Ted said.

Lean is known for such outstanding films as *Lawrence of Arabia*, *Doctor Zhivago* and *The Bridge on the River Kwai*, among many others.

There were other directors Ted enjoyed working with but there were also some who he felt simply didn't measure up.

Some didn't know how to set up a dangerous stunt and wouldn't listen to advice such as **George Sherman**, the director of *Smoky*. Some were oblivious to the stress and dangerous situations they have put a star in such as **Joseph Zito**, the director of *Friday the 13th: The Final Chapter*. Some were not honest with their stuntmen like **John Huston**, director of *The Misfits*, who exposed Clark Gable to danger by having him dragged behind a runaway horse rather than using his double.

Fortunately, from Ted's point of view, there are more positive stories about directors than negative ones.

"Camaraderie on a set is one of the essentials in a successful production," Ted said. "Whether or not the director, cast and crew get along depends almost entirely on one man – the director." He said Howard Hawks and John Ford were among the best at creating that kind of positive atmosphere.

CLARK GABLE

"There wasn't a better man in the world than Gable," Ted said. "He was down to earth and great to be around."

During the production of *The Misfits*, when Marilyn Monroe caused frequent difficulties, Gable was "very patient with her. He never spoke a bad word to her about being late. He was a gentleman from the word go."

Reports say that Gable had just signed a contract for the film that would make him one of the highest-paid performers up to that time. The contract was for $750,000 and ten percent of the gross. However, because of

Monroe's history of lateness and frequent histrionics, Gable's contract also guaranteed him $48,000 a week for "overtime."

STEVE McQUEEN

McQueen was "a good guy" according to Ted who knew the actor for many years, working with him on *The Cincinnati Kid* in 1965 and even racing motorcycles with him. The two became good friends over the years before McQueen died "far too young" of cancer.

Ted often raced motocycles with his friend Steve McQueen

"He was wild," Ted said. "He was also fearless and did most of his own stunts, even in *The Great Escape.*" McQueen did the motorcycle riding in that film except for the jump over the fence as he tried to avoid capture by the Nazis. Ted said a stuntman named Bud Ekins doubled McQueen on the jump.

McQueen, like most stars, was always concerned about how he would be billed on a film. Ted said *The Towering Inferno* (1974) almost didn't get made because of bickering over which of the film's many stars would get top billing. "They solved the problem by putting names side-by-side in the opening credits," he said. The question of top billing was a recurring problem. "They tried and tried to get Wayne and Gable together in a film but it never happened partially because of a disagreement over top billing," Ted said.

"Once a big star's name comes off the top of the list, his or her life changes," he said. "As soon as the word is out producers who earlier could not have afforded such a big name are after them. Once your price drops it can continue to drop, along with prestige."

He cited Lee Marvin as an example. Marvin did *Cat Ballou* and his price shot up. Soon after that, however, he did *The Man Who Shot Liberty Valance* and was listed as the third lead. Ted said his price came down and stayed down after that.

RONALD REAGAN

Reagan was another actor who was "well-liked" in Hollywood, Ted said. "He was an actor who could have gone far in the business but he became President of the Screen Actors Guild and once politics got into his system he couldn't get it out."

Ted said he used to have his haircut every other Wednesday at Paramount Studios and Reagan, then SAG President, was always there in the chair next to him. "I'd get after him every week," Ted said. "I'd ask him when he was going to do something for the stuntmen. I would constantly badger him about that."

Reagan would pretend anger. "Ted," he'd say. "Can't I get a haircut in peace? Do I have to put up with this every week?"

Reagan's ranch bordered the Fox Studios ranch and often, when Ted was working on *Daniel Boone*, the production took place right on Reagan's property line. "He and his wife would ride horseback to the set and join us for lunch. "We'd kid them," Ted said. "We'd say they were too cheap to go out to a restaurant but would come to our set for a free lunch."

"He never got so serious about his position that he became overbearing," Ted said. When then President Reagan was shot in an assassination attempt his wife Nancy said he "probably just forgot to duck."

LEE MARVIN

Ted worked with Marvin on *Cat Ballou in 1965* and again on *Point Blank* in 1967. "He was a wild man," he said, "but also very friendly, honest and down to earth. He was fun to sit and visit with. He was friendly to all and never really considered himself a big movie star." Marvin had a ranch in New Mexico and during the filming of *Silverado* Ted and some of the cast went to see him. "His house had a big porch across the front of it," Ted said. "He sat on that porch with a rifle and shot prairie dogs. He'd sit there all day with a bottle of vodka, drinking and shooting. He was pretty sick when he saw him and a few months later he committed suicide."

232

SEAN CONNERLY

Ted doesn't have much good to say about Connery. He did one picture with the man – *Wrong is Right* in 1982. "It was a difficult picture," Ted said. "I found Connery troublesome. He never had anything good to say about America or the American people."

FRANK SINATRA

Sinatra was, according to Ted, "another bad case." The filming of *Von Ryan's Express* in Europe in 1965 involved a great deal of action that included explosions, machine guns, mortars, and even running down railroad tracks.

"Sinatra would sit in his dressing room and refuse to come out," Ted said, "and we had to use his stand-in to rehearse. I told the director, Mark Robson, that we needed Frank so he'd know where the explosions would occur. The special effects people were also upset because after a rehearsal they had to reload everything."

When Sinatra finally came to the set he asked to see all the explosions. "So we had to do the explosions three times to get one take," Ted said. "We did them once to rehearse with Sinatra's stand-in, another time for him to see them and finally during the shot."

Ted said this kind of behavior was unusual. "Sometimes you get a big star and they take advantage," he said. "But you never saw it happen with people like Gable and Wayne. Sinatra was a big star, sure, but I don't think he carried the stature of those two."

YUL BRYNNER

"Yul was a good guy," Ted said. "He was friendly and easy to work with. He had his pride but he was receptive to advice." Ted worked with him on the 1962 film *Escape from Zahrain* which also starred Sal Mineo and Anthony Caruso.

This film featured a difficult and potentially dangerous piece of action that involved 50 people. Ted is proud of the way it turned out.

The scene involved an army truck crashing through a plate glass window into a crowded restaurant. "The truck is coming down a hill into an Arab village," Ted said. "Besides the driver, there are seven others in it including several standing in the back of the truck as it attempts to escape from terrorists. At the bottom of the hill the road makes a sharp turn to the left. The restaurant is at the intersection and there are 43 people, men and women, inside."

Ted hired stunt men and women to be in the restaurant because the truck was to crash through the window. He also hired stunt doubles for the stars and had other stuntmen in the truck.

The film's director Ronald Neame wanted to know how Ted was planning to avoid "killing people" during the action.

"I'm not going to tell you all my stunt secrets," Ted said, laughing. "All you have to do is stand behind the camera and say 'action.' When it's all over everyone will come running to you with their hands out for money."

But Neame was still concerned, especially about the speed of the truck.

Ted solved that by having the driver hold his speed to about 20 miles per hour while the cameraman shot at "speed," making it look as though it was moving at least twice as fast. "By going that slowly I could have people in the restaurant stay in position much longer than they normally would before they scattered." They also put a camera inside the restaurant but running at normal speed.

"It took a week to put the shot together," Ted said. "I told the women to wear black shoes without high heels and that there should be no dresses below the ankles. I wanted them to be able to move quickly without risk of tripping and getting hurt."

As the diners ran from the truck two stuntmen were positioned to take hits "and go flying" as springs set beneath their feet sent them into the air. "Tables and chairs were flying, people were running and it all worked," Ted said. "We got it on the first shot."

At the time, Brynner had cancer of the throat. He did some commercials begging both youngsters and adults not to smoke. Ted admired the man greatly.

Ted doesn't have much good to say about Sal Mineo, however. He also worked with him on *Exodus*, filmed in 1960 in Egypt, Bagdad and Jerusalem.

PATRICK SWAYZE

"Swayze was a good guy," Ted said. He worked with him on the

1989 film *Roadhouse* which also starred Kelly Lynch, Sam Elliott and Ben Gazzara. "Even though he was going through some family problems at the time and was a bit preoccupied, he was easy going and fun to work with."

Coincidentally, Jeri's brother Charlie Tamburro and uncle Steve Picerni were involved in stunts along with Ted. Charlie acted as stunt coordinator on the show and Jeri's uncle Steve Tamburro also was a stuntman on the production.

Swayze played a bouncer in Gazarra's bar and the movie involved a number of fights. "This was difficult for Charlie, who was the stunt coordinator," Ted said, "because setting up a fight with five or six people calls for a variety of camera angles, resetting lights and choreographing all the action."

Ted was in many of the fights but a scene in a car dealership was the most dangerous in the film. In the scene Ted is walking across the dealership's showroom in front of floor-to-ceiling windows about 20 feet high when a monster car with eight-foot wheels crashes through the windows hits the top of one car in the showroom, bounces off and hits another across the room.

"I managed to duck and then beat it toward the wall out of harm's way," Ted said. "My heart was racing."

While Swayze was easy to work with, Ted said Ben Gazzara was another story. "He believed in the old style movie system where he was a big star and wanted to be treated like royalty," Ted said. "He was upset that he wasn't treated as well as he expected. It was a relatively low-budget film, though."

STEVEN SPIELBERG

Around 2002 Ted was asked to come to Spielberg's studios to tape an on-camera interview. He had no idea what the famous director wanted but took his son Michael, a movie buff, and went to the studio.

"I walked into an elaborate setup," he said, "with two cameras on me and Spielberg behind the main camera. I was told I'd not be given any dialogue because they wanted to hear me straight off the cuff."

He said Spielberg was a gentleman "from the word go." He said they would simply have a conversation and that Ted should be candid in his answers. Spielberg began by asking questions about various producers and directors with whom Ted had worked. He then asked what Ted thought of today's movies.

Ted told him they had "come a long way" and that, at the time it was made, *The Alamo* was the most expensive production ever. That brought on a series of questions about other films Ted had done that were not in the same category as *The Alamo*.

Among the films Ted mentioned was his role as Jason in *Friday the 13th: The Final Chapter.* "What did you think about that?" Spielberg asked.

Ted told him he didn't really care for it, that he initially turned it down but changed his mind when told he would be "on hold" for six weeks. That brought on some laughter from the crew doing the filming.

"How did it turn out?" Spielberg asked.

"I don't know," Ted said. "I've never seen it."

More laughter.

"Well," Spielberg said, "it so happens that we've seen that film but didn't see your name in the credits."

Ted told him that he had asked that his name not be used. "I told them to just say Jason was playing Jason."

Again, more laughter.

When the interview was concluded Spielberg shook Ted's hand and said "I've never met anyone in the history of motion pictures with your background who told a major production studio that he didn't want his name on their picture. That's the best laugh I've had in a long time."

As Ted and Michael left they still had no idea about why Ted was called for the interview. Ted learned later that Spielberg was considering doing a documentary about pictures made for less than $1 million. He wanted to find out which ones made a profit and why.

"I never did hear if he followed through or if anything came from his idea," Ted said. "But he paid me for coming down and I enjoyed visiting with the man."

CLINT EASTWOOD

Ted often has lamented the fact that so many of the great stars of the past are now gone. "Most of the larger-than-life movie stars of past years like Wayne, Gable, Cooper and others haven't been replaced with men of similar stature and bearing," he said. "Oh, there are a few but not many."

236

He did, however, say Clint Eastwood would fit into that mold.

Ted first worked with Eastwood when they filmed the pilot for *Rawhide*, a popular Western TV series that ran from 1959 to 1965. The show was about a continuous cattle drive and featured Eric Fleming as trail boss Gil Favor who was assisted by Eastwood as Rowdy Yates.

Later, Ted worked with Eastwood on his 1980 film *Bronco Billy* which also starred Sondra Locke and Geoffrey Lewis. The movie was about an idealistic, modern-day cowboy who struggles to keep his Wild West show afloat in the face of hard luck and waning interest.

"I had just won a big belt buckle in a rodeo and wore it in a big saloon fight we staged for the movie," Ted said. Someone on the crew went to Eastwood and told him about the buckle and suggested he make an issue of it.

In the middle of the fight Eastwood stopped it and yelled "Ted White!"

Worried, Ted said "yeah?"

"That damn buckle is reflecting light into the camera," Eastwood said. "Take it off."

Ted said "yessir" and began to take it off when he heard the crew begin to laugh and figured out the joke. "They got me again," he said to himself.

"Clint is a good guy," Ted said. "He's a savvy, savvy, savvy director and actor. He's been there from the beginning and he knows what he's doing, what he wants and how to get the best results."

ARNOLD SCHWARZENEGGER

Schwarzenegger became a major star (and the Governor of California) but, before that, Ted worked with him in minor roles, including one on *The Streets of San Francisco*, a TV series that ran from 1972 to 1977 and starred Karl Malden and Michael Douglas.

On the TV show Schwarzenegger was to have a fight with Malden. Ted's first impression of the man was that he was "a big pussy." But he also thought: "Damn, look at the size of him."

Ted worked with him for several days and began to appreciate his skills. "In one scene he had to cry and he did it so well that I took back all I had said about him at first," he said.

He had a later opportunity to work with Schwarzenegger on *True Lies* but had to turn it down because he had a "problem" with the man who was Schwarzenegger's usual double. "He was making well over a million dollars a year," Ted said, "and he got involved with a 15-year-old drum major. His wife found out about it and called Arnold and he was gone."

Jeri, Ted's wife, chimed in. "Little did she know that Arnold was up to the same tricks. He was a big womanizer."

Ted had told people he didn't think Schwarzenegger would make it in the motion picture business. "Of course, that was the second time I'd been wrong about somebody," Ted said.

BURT REYNOLDS

Years ago after a motorcycle race from Barstow to Las Vegas, Ted went by a fellow stuntman's home to pick up his bike where it had been left by a friend. During the visit, at his friend's invitation, he was to meet someone who was interested in the motion picture business. When he arrived he was introduced to a man named Burt Reynolds. After some conversation, the stuntman friend asked Ted if he thought Reynolds had a chance to make it in the business.

"I told them I didn't think so," Ted said. "I said he's too short and he's bald." (This was before Reynolds began wearing a toupee.)

Ted's wife Jeri had met Reynolds before. Years later, at a wedding reception, Ted and Jeri saw the actor across the room. He started toward them and they thought he was coming to say hello to Jeri.

However, Reynolds brushed past Jeri and approached Ted. "You were wrong," he told Ted. "I'm a f…ing big star."

"I was surprised that he remembered our first visit," Ted said. "But he surely did, and evidently held it against me that I had doubted his ability to make it in movies."

JOHN RUSSELL

"Most big stars treat the other actors and crew as equals," Ted said. "Now and then you'll work with someone who thinks he's a big name and becomes indignant and hard to get along with."

In the mid-fifties Ted worked on a TV series called *Soldiers of Fortune* with the series' star John Russell. Later, Howard Hawks, who liked Russell's size and deep voice, hired him to be one of the lead heavies on *Rio Bravo*, in which Ted also appeared.

"I had a chance to get to know him and liked him," Ted said. Russell told Ted he was planning to begin work on the TV series *Lawman*. That series ran from 1958 to 1962. It was the story of Marshal Dan Troop of Laramie, Wyoming and his deputy Johnny McKay (played by Peter Brown), an orphan Troop took under his wing. Ted also appeared on that series.

Like Ted, Russell was a Marine in World War II and earned a battlefield commission on Guadalcanal. He played a number of second leads and occasional heavies in major productions before branching into television where he appeared in, or starred in, several popular series, including *Lawman*.

Russell's appearances were sporadic after the 1960s but he did play the role of a memorable villain in Clint Eastwood's 1985 film *Pale Rider*. Russell was the hired gunslinger who shows up near the end of the film with a gang. He's been hired to kill Eastwood's character.

"Unfortunately, he didn't feel like he was being treated like a star," Ted said. "He got angry and complained." Eastwood finally had to have a talk with Russell and things settled down.

"It's sad when that sort of thing happens," Ted said. "Russell was perfect for that role. He was a good actor. I liked him. John Wayne liked him. It was just too bad."

BRODERICK CRAWFORD

"You form impressions about certain actors based on the characters they play," Ted said. "Most are very nice and easy to work with. Sometimes you run into an actor who is difficult and it's often because of drinking. Broderick Crawford, it seemed to me, was constantly drunk."

Crawford is best remembered for two roles: his Oscar-winning performance as Willie Stark in *All the King's Men* (1949) and as the star of the TV series *Highway Patrol* (1955-1959). Ted appeared on *Highway Patrol* which featured powerful patrol cars and fast motorcycles on America's highways.

"Some actors are better than others at dialogue," Ted said. "Crawford couldn't remember lines. He could say the dialogue but he needed help remembering. And he was a real fast talker."

He said some actors can drink and pull off a scene without difficulty. Lee Marvin was one of those and Ted said his drinking was more comical than anything. But Crawford was a different story. "When he was drinking he'd kind of slur his words and that caused several retakes. Every day, that vodka."

ERROL FLYNN

"Different actors had different quirks," Ted said. "Broderick Crawford's was drinking. With Errol Flynn it was a hatred for Warner Brothers. He had constant battles with Jack Warner. When they finally put him on a contract they told him what he could and couldn't do. He told them to go to hell."

Flynn would do what he wanted, Ted said, and he could get away with it because every studio in town wanted him and he knew Warner wouldn't cancel his contract. "He was the hottest thing in Hollywood, bar none."

Ted recalled that Flynn had a 60-foot sailboat and that he often took several stuntmen and "eight or nine girls out on the boat and they'd get drunk and raise hell."

One day Flynn and his group were sailing up and down the coast near where Warner Bros. was shooting a film. The director asked "who in the hell is that SOB who keeps getting in the background of the film?"

Some of the film crew sailed out and discovered it was Flynn. Told it was Warner Bros. doing the filming, Flynn said he would move out of the way but it would cost them $100,000. The film crew eventually moved a mile down the beach.

"He was famous for that sort of thing," Ted said. "But he was a good worker, knew his dialogue and showed up for work."

Flynn's rambunctious spirit was evident as a very young man. Biographies say he managed to get himself thrown out of every school he attended. During his time as an actor, IMDB.com reports, "his off-screen passions, drinking, fighting, boating and sex, made his film escapades seem pale." He had troubles with lawsuits and with the IRS. Late in life a few good roles came his way but he died of a heart attack in 1959 at the young age of 50.

"Women who worked with him loved him," Ted said. "He was a man's man and I think everyone liked him."

WILFORD BRIMLEY

Brimley was a farmer early in his life, then became a rodeo rider. He gained weight, however, and was a blacksmith before becoming a screen actor.

"I knew him years ago," Ted said. "He would shoe my horses and we'd sit around chewing tobacco and visiting. One day I ran into him at a rodeo and he told me he was going to be in a movie with Robert Redford." The movie was 1979's *Electric Horseman* which also starred Jane Fonda.

"At the time he drove a truck for Redford," Ted said. "He got the part because he had the truck."

The role put Brimley into the spotlight, however, and his agent saw to it that he had many other opportunities, including a good role with Tom Selleck in the TV film *Crossfire Trail* (2001).

FESS PARKER

Ted formed a long-lasting friendship with Fess Parker over the years, working with him regularly on the TV series *Daniel Boone* from 1964 to 1970 and on the 1966 movie *Smoky*.

"Fess was one of the kindest, most warm-hearted and gracious men I've ever known," Ted said. "He was six foot six inches tall, had two left feet and didn't make any bones about it."

Early in the production of *Daniel Boone* Fess's mother was about to be evicted from the mobile home where she lived with her dog. "No dogs are allowed," the owner of the mobile home park said. To solve the problem Fess bought the park and suddenly dogs were allowed.

Parker retired from motion pictures and went into business. He had considerable real estate holdings and a vineyard. "He was an excellent businessman," Ted said.

Not too many years ago some of Ted's friends from the Kansas City area were visiting him at his home in Woodland Hills, California, and asked if it might be possible to meet Fess.

Ted told Steve and Geralyn Kelly that Parker seemed never to be at home but they could visit the hotel he had built in Santa Barbara. Fess had formed a California General Partnership in 1981 called Fess Parker-Red Lion. Among its holdings is the Fess Parker Doubletree Resort, a dramatic mission-style hotel on 24 beachfront acres that includes four restaurants.

"We pulled up in the circle drive at the back entrance and were met by a doorman," Ted said. "He looked down his nose at us. We were dressed pretty casually."

Ted told the doorman he was a friend of Mr. Parker. The doorman replied that "everyone in Santa Barbara claims to be a friend of his."

"I'm not from Santa Barbara and I AM a friend of his," Ted said. "My name is Ted White and I worked with him for many years. I just brought some friends by to see the hotel." The doorman relented and let them in.

"We walked in and, lo and behold, there sat Fess with one of his partners," Ted said. "I introduced him to the Kellys and we sat down for lunch."

Twenty minutes later, when Parker had finished his meeting, he came to Ted's table with a card. "When these folks are finished," he said, "take them out to my winery. Here's a pass."

When they were ready to leave Ted asked for the check and was told that "Mr. Parker" had already paid.

"My friends were thrilled," Ted said. "Fess was such a gracious man." Parker died in 2010.

32

The "One-Legged Jerk-Off"
And Other Tricks of the Trade

STUNTMEN AND WOMEN take great pride in their work and, although they have a competitive spirit and often try to outdo one another, that's not the primary goal of their work. Their goal isn't to accomplish the highest jump, biggest explosion or craziest stunt; their purpose is to create a realistic visual effect on film by performing a carefully choreographed and planned sequence.

It's understood that stuntwork can be dangerous. Injuries are common and deaths happen far too often. While a stuntman won't go out of his way to do something dangerous, creating a realistic stunt often requires high-risk action. Training and technology help make stunts a lot safer than they were in decades past, but if all stunt sequences were perfectly safe, stunt people wouldn't be needed at all.

In the past stunts were often especially dangerous for animals. As more and more animals were hurt on films, the SPCA (Society for the Prevention of Cruelty to Animals) helped put a stop to certain kinds of stunts. Horse falls, like those seen in the movie *Stagecoach* (1939) in which Yakima Canutt performed some of the most famous horse falls in movie history, were called "Running Ws" and involved a cable on a horse's leg that caused the fall. Those kinds of falls and many others have been outlawed.

Canutt invented the Running W but it has now been replaced by more humane methods. It is believed that it was used for the final time in the 1983 Iraqi film *al-Mas' Ala At-Kubra* when the British actor Marc Sinden and stuntman Ken Buckle used it several times in a cavalry charge sequence.

In spite of their efforts to be safe and to keep the stars of films from

243

getting hurt, actors are sometimes not eager to be doubled.

"I've had actors get mad at me because I was doubling them," Ted said. "Sometimes the stunt is something they probably could have done but the production company won't let them because of the bonding and insurance. If a company loses its bonding they have to shut the show down."

"I don't go up to the star or the director and say I want to double him in this scene," Ted said. "They call me in and tell me what they want to do. Oh, on occasion I've had to tell a director that the star shouldn't try a particular stunt but usually they know what needs to be done."

Actors can be touchy, Ted admitted. "Now and then you just have to pull in your wings and sit on the sidelines and not say anything."

Ted said he could name names but wouldn't. "Some of these are pretty big-name people," he said, "and some are still alive so I'll honor them and not say who they were."

SOME OF THE MOST interesting and enjoyable parts of being a stuntman is figuring out how to make a "stunt" happen, have it look real and be believable to audiences. And be safe.

Throughout his career Ted has been concerned with "safety first" and has always stood up for actors and stunt men and women who were being asked by directors to take unreasonable chances.

On an episode of *Daniel Boone* his ingenuity was put to a severe test.

In the story two Indians charge Boone (Fess Parker) on horseback. Boone shoots one off his horse but, in the script, the other comes at him with a lance. Boone stands his ground, parries the lance and the Indian plants a foot in Boone's chest. The script says "Boone grabs the foot, the Indian is momentarily suspended in the air and then falls to the ground."

"How the hell am I going to do that?" Ted wondered. "It's a physical impossibility."

The production manager approached Ted. "Can't do it, can you?"

"Yes, I can," Ted said, accepting the challenge.

The production manager was skeptical. "When that Indian plants his foot in Fess' check he'll go flying backwards and the Indian with him."

"Not the way I'm gonna do it," Ted said.

"I can't wait to see this," the production manager said.

The sequence was to be shot at the Fox ranch and Ted brought in two loads of sand to the part of the stage that was set up as a wooded area, saving a great deal of money because they wouldn't have to go on location to shoot the scene.

"Who in the world are you going to get to do that stunt," Ted was asked.

"I've got a favorite guy," he said. "Terry Leonard."

With Leonard on the horse, Ted cut two holes in the bottom of his right moccasin and attached an eighth-inch cable to a U-bolt in the moccasin. The other end of the cable was attached to a Ford axle about 40 feet back. The plan was that, when Leonard put his foot out he would hit the end of the cable, it would stop him in mid-air and then he would fall to the ground.

Leonard was ready. "What's this called?" he asked Ted.

"I don't know. I've never done it before. How about 'the one-legged jerk-off?'"

"That sounds a big risqué," Leonard said, eyebrows raised.

Ted wasn't deterred. "Just do it like I told you," he said. "Otherwise you'll get hurt."

They got Boone (Parker) in position and tested the length of the cable, making sure that just as Leonard's foot appeared as though it was hitting Boone's chest, it had reached its full length.

"When Leonard's foot touches your chest," Ted told Parker, "it'll feel like a feather and he'll stop in mid-air."

Parker wasn't sure about the stunt. "Ted," he said, "I think maybe you've gone beyond yourself here."

The production manager said he was dubious and wasn't certain he wanted to shoot it.

"It'll work," Ted assured them. The entire crew and members of crews from other shows stopped work to watch the action.

The director called "action!" and Leonard, sweating bullets, rode forward just out of a gallop. As he reached Parker he stuck out his right foot, Parker grabbed it, he hit the end of the cable and it appeared on film as though Parker had stopped him. "I swear he hung there a full second and then went crashing to the ground," Ted said.

The entire crew began applauding.

After the film was processed the executive producer asked "how the devil did you get that shot?

The director said "you'll never believe it so I won't tell you."

Later Terry Leonard was working on a movie called *The Mountain Men* with Charlton Heston, Brian Keith and Victoria Racimo. The film was written by Heston's son Fraser Clarke Heston.

Leonard told scriptwriter Heston about the stunt and said it was called the one-legged jerk-off.

"What kind of nonsense is this?" Heston asked.

Leonard convinced him it was "a great piece of action" and that he'd do it as an Indian against one of the trappers who was coming in for rendezvous. Dubious as he was, Heston wrote the scene into the script.

Leonard followed Ted's example of how to set up the shot but, instead of coming to the end of the cable in a gallop, he hit it in a full-out run. When he got to the end of the cable it snapped and he fell beneath the horse's back legs and was kicked in the head. He lay on the ground unconscious. Finally, tended by the staff medic, he came to.

"You're right," Heston said. "That was the damndest stunt I've EVER seen."

The term "one-legged jerk-off" became a legend around the motion picture industry and when kidded about it, Leonard would reply "it was all that damned Ted White's doing."

ANOTHER STUNT THAT was "all that damned Ted White's doing" involved "skiing" a car down a small town's main street. "Skiing" is when a car is driven while balanced only on two wheels, either the pair on the driver side or on the passenger side. The stunt is generally done by driving one pair of wheels up on a ramp to lift one side of the car.

In the film *Black Oak Conspiracy* (1977) starring Jesse Vint, Karen Carlson and Albert Salmi and directed by Bob Kelljan (and in which Ted's son Ted Jr. has a role), a stuntman returns home to a mining town where his mother is being hoodwinked out of property by a mining company. To show off his skills he drives down off a hill and skis a car down the town's main street.

"None of the stuntmen on the picture, including me, had ever done that," Ted said, "so I called up an old friend, Joie Chitwood."

"You want me to do what?" Chitwood said when he heard Ted's request. "I'm retired."

Chitwood was a long-time stuntman who had worked on films such as *Smokey and the Bandit Part 3, Thunder and Lightning, A Small Town in Texas, Live and Let Die,* and many others throughout his career. His grandson, interestingly enough, Joie III, became President of the Indianapolis Motor Speedway.

Ted told him all he wanted him to do was to fly first class to Sacramento where he would stay for a week in a nice hotel. In addition, he would be paid well. After some discussion, and negotiation of what he would earn, Chitwood agreed.

The car the character in the movie drove was a 1976 Chevrolet Camaro and they needed a "double" for it to use in the stunt. Fortunately, someone had seen a similar car parked in front of the hotel where the cast and crew were staying. It belonged to a young clerk who agreed to lease it to the production company for a week.

The rear wheels had to be altered so they would turn like the front ones and the company promised to restore the vehicle when they returned it to the clerk.

"We did that stunt thirty or forty times," Ted said, "and when it came down it slammed the ground with the whole weight of the car."

The car was returned to the young clerk and on the second day he drove it the dashboard fell off. The company fixed the car, put in a new rear end and did other repairs.

In another scene in the same film Albert Salmi, playing a corrupt sheriff, is in a fight with the returning stuntman Jingo Johnson (played by Jesse Vint) and the sheriff, who is winning the fight, is about get his pistol and kill Jingo. The fight is near a lake at the bottom of a pit mine.

"We needed a distraction so the hero could get the best of the sheriff," Ted said. "That was to be provided by a police car that goes off the top of the mine, flies down toward the lake and explodes as it hits."

The car was loaded with dynamite, the steering wheel locked in place with bungee cords so it wouldn't turn, the accelerator taped down, and the car in gear. When Ted called "action!" the special effects man was to reach in, turn the key to start the engine and then get out of the way as it would immediately begin to roll toward the cliff.

When he turned the key, though, the man's arm was caught in the bungee cord and he couldn't get himself free. As the car hurtled toward the cliff the man grabbed the wheel and was able to turn it enough that the car took longer to get to the cliff face and he was able to free himself just as it went over.

"It exploded about halfway down and then there was dead silence," Ted said. "Then everyone was running toward the special effects man who lay on the ground, dazed." The man, who was in shock, was quickly on his way to a nearby hospital and later returned to the production unhurt.

"Now what?" the production manager asked.

One of the crew had a white four-door car that looked something like the police car that was demolished in the failed first shot. Ted said they could spray paint a blue stripe around the car, put a second bar light on top and try it again, this time using a long stick to start the car instead of actually reaching inside.

They paid an exorbitant price for the car (after objections from the production manager who was in charge of the budget) and were ready.

The production manager still wasn't sure he wanted to risk injury or death again.

"Then I said something foolish," Ted said. "I said I would take responsibility. I had no idea what it might cost me if we had serious problems again."

After some discussion with the director and others, the production manager agreed that Ted could try it again.

"It had been over an hour since the first try," Ted said. "Everyone was nervous but I told them to send the car."

He said the trick with the long stick worked, the car started slowly, picked up speed and headed for the cliff. "Keep goin' baby, keep goin'," Ted said to himself.

It went over the cliff, flew through the air, hit about ten feet from the lake and exploded. One camera was on the car, another on the two fighters and as the sheriff pulled his gun, the car exploded in a burst of fire and smoke. The noise startled the sheriff who fell over backwards and the "good guy" jumped on him to win the fight "and I was home free!" Ted said. "That was the closing highlight of the film."

IN OTHER FILMS Ted would figure out ingenious ways to pull off stunts that no one thought was possible. In one film he fitted a stuntman with a parachute that, when released, pulled him off the back of a racing speedboat as though he had been shot and propelled backwards.

In *Wrong is Right* starring Sean Connery, Ted rigged a cable to co-star John Saxon which would stop him as he ran forward just as an explosion filled a narrow hallway with smoke and flying debris. The crew would pull him away as though the explosion had blown him backwards. The stunt was accomplished over the objection of the director, Richard Brooks, who told Ted that he was not to put a "jerk vest" on the actor.

After the stunt came off successfully Brooks was pleased and said "don't tell me my actors can't do that without a jerk vest."

When he saw one of the grips removing the wire from Saxon he looked for Ted who had quickly disappeared. "It would have been impossible without the cable," Saxon told the director.

The next day Ted and Jeri were in a restaurant when Saxon came in and complimented Ted on the stunt. "Let me buy you a drink," he offered. They visited a few minutes and Saxon told the waiter to "bring me the check."

After he left Ted asked for the dinner check. "I gave it to that other man," he was told. Saxon had planned to buy the drinks but ended up paying for the entire dinner. "I thought he had a funny look on his face when he saw the check," Ted said. "He's a hell of a guy, really nice."

WHEN STUNTS GO WELL, end safely and look real to an audience it is usually because of careful planning and many rehearsals. Ted said he often carried a "stunt bag" that had all the tools he might need – knee pads, gloves, the right kind of shoes and even miniature cars, trucks and planes.

"When we were working with large numbers of vehicles on city streets and highways, such as we did in the *Fast and Furious* movies, we tried to plan each move down to the tiniest detail," he said. "We laid out the miniature cars just as they would be in the film and planned each move. Every driver needed to know where he was at all times in relation to the others. He needed to know what the guy next to him was going to do so he could react to it."

The drivers would set up the scene and do a dry run at perhaps 15 miles per hour before doing it for real at full speed, sometimes up to 100 miles per hour.

When the scene required the use of multiple cameras the planning had to involve putting the vehicles in positions where another camera would not be in the shot.

"Working with animals is just as hazardous," Ted said, "because a horse, for example, might react one way in rehearsal and another during the filming." He said they all have different temperaments and men and women ride horses in different ways. Riders spur and rein differently and this can be confusing to a horse.

In a scene for a western film Ted reaches down from his horse to pick up something from the ground

Sometimes, despite careful planning and long rehearsals, things go wrong. Because of that, when he was serving as Stunt Coordinator or Second Unit Director, Ted was strict with his cast and crew. Before any shooting began Ted told them there would be no drinking or use of narcotics on the set. "I'd tell them that no matter if they were one of my good friends, if I found narcotics on them I would call the Sheriff, fire them and turn them into the guild."

He had only one problem in that regard. A close friend of his, married with two children, came to Ted literally begging for a job. Ted knew the man had been using drugs but he swore to Ted he was clean. Out of kindness, Ted hired him. On the third day of the shoot, however, he found his friend smoking pot in the dressing room.

Ted fired him but because of their long friendship he fired the man but didn't call law enforcement or turn him into the guild. "I felt like an asshole," he said, "but I had to do it."

It has to be done, he said, because people could get killed if their timing is off. "You have to have a clear head. There are many examples of people getting killed or ruined for life because of a simple mistake when they were on drugs or alcohol."

There are times, however, no matter how clear headed the stuntman is or how carefully things have been planned, things go wrong.

An infamous example of this occurred during the filming of *How the West Was Won* (1962). Stuntman Bob Morgan was severely injured and nearly died while performing a stunt. During the filming of a gunfight that takes place on a moving railroad flatcar loaded with logs, one of the chains holding the logs snapped and Morgan was crushed by the falling timber. It took him five years to recover from his injuries. His wife, actress Yvonne DeCarlo, put her career on hold in order to nurse him back to health.

In 1978, during the filming of the movie *Convoy* starring Kris Kristofferson, Ali MacGraw and Ernest Borgnine, stuntman Bob Herron was involved in an accident that nearly took his life.

In the film truckers form a mile long "convoy" in support of a trucker's vendetta with an abusive sheriff. In one scene Herron is driving a car that gets cut off by the trucks. As he flies through the air he is supposed to bury the car in the roof of a house.

"We were setting up the shot and called Bob who was half a mile up the road to ask if he was ready," Ted said. "He said the car didn't seem to be running right."

Some of the cast and crew were skeptical and said they felt like Bob was backing out, "losing his heart." Some of the crew went to the car to check it out and felt that it simply needed to be run faster to clean out the carburetor. Herron agreed to give it a try but realized when he was about to leave the road that he was doing 60 instead of the planned 25 miles per hour.

"He hit the roof of the house at the wrong angle," Ted said, "and went clear through it and beyond the house about 70 yards. The car hit flat on the ground and he broke his back. That's the shot that's in the film. He didn't mess up, the car wasn't running well and he was trying to make it right."

251

Because accidents often result in suits, Ted formed a production company around 1980 to recreate accidents for attorneys. His firm, West Coast Productions, has worked with some of the largest law firms in California.

Among the many accidents he has recreated on film was one in San Francisco when a trolley broadsided a car on one of that city's steep hills.

IN JANUARY OF 1998 "Playbill.com" reported that Michael Crawford, who had originated the title role of *Phantom of the Opera* and was the Tony-winning star of the musical, had filed suit against MGM Grand, Inc., claiming he was unfairly fired from the Law Vegas high-tech extravaganza *EFX!* Crawford claimed he was repeatedly injured while doing stunts for the production.

Playbill reported that in August of 1996, Crawford had visited a doctor and learned that he had "a severe, debilitating and permanent injury," the lawsuit contended. Four days later the hotel terminated the actor's weekly $150,000 contract that was supposed to run through March 1997.

Crawford had begun his performances in London in 1986, continued on Broadway in 1988 and then Los Angeles in 1989. In April of 1991, after more than 1,300 performances into *The Phantom of the Opera*, Crawford left the company.

The law firm handling Crawford's claim, filed suit for $350 million and the court case lasted two and half years. They called Ted who filmed recreations of the accidents that caused Crawford's injuries.

In the MGM production Crawford slid down the banister of a 40-foot staircase. Ted said the man was on a "descender" which could control the speed of his descent but the cable failed and he literally flew down the staircase. Because the stage was a large semi-circle that had no curtain the crew fogged it in to change scenery. When Crawford hit the floor it was slippery from the fog and his feet went out from under him.

"This happened several times and he did other stunts in the show where he got hurt," Ted said. "He tore both hips completely apart and tore the liver lose from his body. He went from making millions of dollars a year to earning practically nothing."

Prior to recreating the accidents, Ted had the law firm subpoena the men who had made the equipment used in the stunt. The firm also brought in engineers who found the equipment was made poorly.

Ted's film proved that with the right equipment Crawford would not have been hurt. "I gave them several copies," he said. "Three showed how it was done the wrong way and three showed how it should have been done using proper stuntmen's equipment. Had they come to the Stuntmen's Association and asked to use our equipment none of this would have happened."

Crawford, then in his 50s and at the height of his career, won the case.

TED SAYS THERE are hundreds of tricks that one learns over the course of years in the motion picture business. "The main thing is that whatever you do has to look real to the audience," he said. "People can spot fakes right away."

Things have changed drastically over the years, he said. Now, much of the action is done with a green screen with the actors or stunt people on wires.

The young people coming up today are very fortunate to have the absolutely best equipment which stuntmen and women didn't always have in the past. "When I started we did high falls into cardboard boxes," he said. "Now they have airbags as big as rooms and we can do eighty or ninety-foot falls with no problem."

In the conclusion to *Sharky's Machine* (1981) stuntman Gar Robinson doubled Henry Silva as he is blasted by a cop played by Burt Reynolds through a plate glass window and falls to his death from at Atlanta, Georgia, skyscraper. Ted said he fell backwards, firing a gun all the way down. After the stunt Reynolds met Robinson on the ground and told him what a great job he had done.

"Want me to do it again?" Robinson asked. Reynolds said it was just fine the first time.

In 1985 Reynolds cast Robinson as the sadistic albino villain "Moke" in the film *Stick*. In the movie "Moke" seemingly falls to his death from a very high balcony, evidently straight into the pavement below.

In actuality, Ted said, Dar was rigged to a complex wire hooked to a drum that "decelerated" his fall.

"The human body falls at about 120 miles per hour," Ted said. "With the decelerator we can control the speed and stop him at any time." The stunt was tried first with a dummy but the cable broke about halfway down. Ted said that, before he actually did the stunt, Robinson made out his last will and testament. He did the stunt, though, and it worked.

Robinson first appeared on screen as Steve McQueen's double when he jumped into the sea off a cliff in *Papillon* (1973). In the following year he once again leapt into the sea, this time on a motorbike as he doubled David Soul in *Magnum Force*.

He died in 1986 in a motorcycle accident.

"Gar was a great stuntman who specialized in high falls," Ted said. "Not all stuntmen can do everything." Many of them specialize in specific stunts like sword or foil work, horse falls, fistfights or car stunts, for example.

Ted was more of an all-around stuntman who could do almost everything, thanks to his half a century in the business and his willingness to experiment.

"As you learn to be a stuntman you figure out what you're good at and what you can't do," he said. "In my early career Westerns were the big thing and because I'd been a cowboy it was a natural for me to do horse falls or other stunts those kinds of films required. Later, we graduated into cars and motorcycles. I raced motorcycles in the desert and on the flat track for nearly twenty years. Cars were second nature to me."

He even became a competent fencer.

On a chance that he might get on a swashbuckling show with Burt Lancaster – *The Crimson Pirate* – Ted took lessons from a man teaching Olympic fencing in Hollywood.

"I worked with him for about three months and got very proficient," Ted said. Years later, he even taught fencing to stuntmen including Terry Leonard and others.

33

Sunset
Wyatt Earp, Tom Mix and Ted White

THERE'S SOMETHING ELSE about being a stuntman (or woman) that is often frustrating to those who practice the craft.

Despite their concern with safety first, with careful planning and consideration for all the potential pitfalls associated with any stunt, and despite what the script says, stuntmen don't always know what they're getting into when they report to the set.

Consider the movie *Sunset* (1988) starring James Garner, Bruce Willis and Malcolm McDowell and directed by Blake Edwards. In the film Wyatt Earp (Garner) has come to Hollywood to act as a technical advisor on a Tom Mix (Willis) movie. The two become partners as they set out to track down a murderer. In reality, Earp did once consult on a movie starring Tom Mix.

At one point during the film's production Ted was asked to report to the set before 5:00 a.m. He was told that he would double Garner in a scene that required a sunrise. That's all he knew about the shot. Half asleep, Ted reported to the set, donned the costume and was taken to a barren field where a small, open-cockpit biplane was warming up.

"It was still very dark," Ted recalled. "A trainee took me to the plane and said I was to be in the front seat. I got in, expecting to get some instruction. I waited while the pilot talked to a couple of men on the ground but I couldn't hear them over the roar of the engine."

He said there was no communication with him. The pilot had a radio to the director but Ted sat alone and uninformed looking at a dirt runway that loomed in the slightly brightening light and ran downhill toward a house.

Finally the sky had brightened enough and the plane moved forward. It gained speed on the dirt road as it headed straight downhill toward the house and, as it finally got within 50 yards of the building it lifted into the air.

"We flew to about four thousand feet," Ted said, "and the sun was coming up. It was a beautiful sunrise. Off to my left I saw a helicopter with a camera pointed at us. The plane did a few lazy turns and the chopper broke off and left. I thought that was simple enough and was wondering how we would land going uphill."

But instead of heading back toward the ground the plane climbed to around 10,000 feet.

Suddenly, there was an explosion and smoke filled the cockpit. The plane banked and began heading earthward in a spiral.

"What a hell of a way to go out," Ted thought. "I was in the front seat so I would take the impact when we crashed. There was no way out. No parachute."

As the plane neared the ground, though, the smoke cleared and the pilot pulled the plane out of the spiral and leveled out.

"We were maybe forty or fifty feet off the ground, getting lower, and straight ahead I see a barn," Ted said. "I was hoping the pilot saw it too when, just in time, he pulled up and we cleared the barn by a few feet. I looked down and saw a camera crew on the ground filming it all."

The plane landed and Ted quickly jumped out, angrily threw off the helmet and coat he had worn, and decided he was going to kill the pilot.

"I grabbed the pilot as he was getting out the cockpit and was about to slug him when James Garner and the first assistant got ahold of me."

Everyone was yelling at Ted to settle down but he was still angry. "You dirty SOB," he told the pilot. "You never explained a thing to me. You had my heart in my throat. We're up there and you blew that smoke bomb. I thought the motor had blown up. Nobody told me anything."

When he had calmed down and the crew had stopped laughing, Garner donned the costume and climbed into the cockpit where Ted had been. The plane taxied up to the camera as though they had just landed and Garner calmly climbed out. That was the end of the scene.

"I don't know what I'd have done to prepare for it but it sure would have been helpful if I'd been told what was going to happen," Ted said.

In another scene supposedly set on Tom Mix's ranch and which was filmed near Gilroy, California, Ted (doubling Garner) is asked to run a horse downhill with Mix (the stuntman doubling Willis) riding behind him on the horse.

Joe Dunne, the stunt coordinator, gave Ted the setup. "Mix runs and jumps on the back and you're really movin' on," he said. "Then you've got to come down a hill."

Ted was worried about the shot and expressed his concern to Dunne. "You can't come down a hill in a run," he said. "That's too dangerous, especially riding double. If the horse's legs go too far under him they'll fold and you'll go end over end."

Asked how fast he thought he could go, Ted said he'd have to study the terrain before he knew for certain.

Finally, when the shot was set up, Ted and the other double rode the horse in a dead run for about two blocks before they got to the hill. In the meantime one of the drivers had pulled a large semi to a location that put it in the shot.

"Fortunately, we had to stop while they moved the truck," Ted said. "We got off the horse, let him stand and loosened the cinch."

When the semi had been moved the two mounted the horse again. "Here we go," Ted told Willis' double. "We took off and I did break him into a run but not full out. We had only one stumble and made it to the bottom of the hill where we both breathed great sighs of relief."

MEANWHILE, SPEAKING of injuries . . .

In this particular scene Garner chases a suspect into a building and upstairs. He looks out a window, sees the man running toward a car, and jumps to the ground, about 20 feet below. Ted is to double Garner in the jump.

"Jim was wearing boots and the ones they gave me were too small," Ted said. "They knew I wore a 12D but they gave me an 11A. I was up there twenty feet and looking down at hard cement and I was supposed to jump."

Ted went to the first assistant and explained the problem. "I weigh more than 200 pounds and something's gonna give when I hit that cement," he said.

The first assistant was unmoved. "I can't tell Blake Edwards that you're not going to wear the boots," he said. "He's a stickler for detail. This

257

picture is costing a lot of money."

Ted's wife Jeri happened to be on the set that day and, while the cameras were being set, Ted went to her. "I'm probably going to get hurt doing this," he told her.

"What can you do?" she asked.

"Nothing. I'm here to work," he said. "I just wanted you to be aware."

He jumped.

"I hit awfully hard," he said. "My toes split clear back into my right foot. The toes didn't have a chance to spread in those tight boots."

His boot quickly filled with blood but even with the pain Ted jumped up and ran forward about ten steps as called for in the script. Then he fell to the ground and shouted for help.

"Get this boot off before you have to cut it off," he said. Before he was taken to the hospital, Ted told the first assistant they needed to get someone else to double Garner as he knew he wouldn't be able to work for some time.

"No need," he was told. "That was the last shot."

Ted was able to attend the film's premiere and he felt it was well-received.

"I didn't see it again for ten or twelve years," he said, "then I saw pieces of it on television. I don't know to this day if they used the film of that jump in the final version."

He's still got a long scar on his right foot but he said "I made good money on that show."

Bruce Willis received the top billing on *Sunset* but much more screen time was given to James Garner.

Garner had played Wyatt Earp in an earlier film, *Hour of the Gun* which was directed by John Sturges in 1967.

TED AND GARNER were long-time friends because Ted had doubled him and done stunts in the TV series *Maverick* (1957-1962).

In one episode Ted is playing a bad guy who comes at Garner with a knife. Because there were to be no fists thrown Garner does the scene himself without a double. As Ted lunges at him Garner ducks under the knife, grabs Ted by the arms and throws him through a window.

"They put a little army cot behind the wall for me to land on," Ted said, "but after I hit the wall and should have busted up the window, I looked up and everything was still in place."

The crew was laughing because the wall had been put on hinges and fell back in place with no damage. They planned to use it again in another scene.

"What do we do now?" Garner asked.

The director said to leave it in and that's the way it appeared in the episode.

Garner and Ted had a great deal in common. Garner, an Oklahoma native, attended OU and in 1995 received an honorary doctorate from the university. He never had acting ambitious but, after the Korean War (where he earned two Purple Hearts), decided to give acting a try. Three years later he was on *Maverick* and reports say he hasn't been out of work since then.

Another publicity photo of Ted

34

Autographing a Breast
(And Other Things)

ONE DAY IN 2002 Ted was attending a convention featuring film celebrities and movie memorabilia vendors. Stars like Ted manned tables where they displayed hundreds of photos of themselves alone or posing with other actors and actresses from movies in which they had appeared. Convention-goers could purchase photos which Ted would autograph or, often, he would pose for a photo with a fan.

At this particular convention Ted's wife Jeri was sitting with him when they were approached by a young woman.

The woman stood in front of the table and suddenly exposed most of a breast. That was startling enough but on her breast was a tattoo of Ted's face as Jason from *Friday the 13th: The Final Chapter.* "I'd like for you to autograph this for me," she said.

"Well, what could I do?" Ted wondered. "She had paid to get in and would pay me to autograph her breast." Ted obliged as Jeri watched, a bit embarrassed for him but also amused at her husband's attempt to write on a woman's breast with a felt-tipped pen.

That experience was one of many "interesting" activities that have occurred at one convention or another over the past several years.

These gatherings have become quite popular and attract literally thousands of fans. Entertainment is a business, after all, and businesses want to maintain their "customer base" for as long as possible. A way to do that is to continually promote celebrity autographs, pictures and memorabilia from Hollywood. Autograph conventions offer fans an opportunity to meet their favorite stars from television and movies. They also offer the stars a chance to get involved in the growing business of celebrity memorabilia.

Producers of these conventions attempt to gather as many different Hollywood celebrities in one room as possible, all eager to sign autographs, pose for pictures, sell merchandise and mingle with their fans. Included are former child stars, Western heroes, sitcom favorites, pop heartthrobs, talk show hosts and even Academy Award nominees and winners.

"The way it works," Ted says, "is that a producer or his agent calls and asks if I would appear at a convention in one major city or another on such and such a date. I always ask for a certain guarantee before I'll agree to go – usually several thousand dollars."

In addition to the amount of the guarantee, Ted is provided transportation to the site and put up in a hotel for the duration of the "show." He is usually at his table on Friday evenings from 4:00 p.m. until 10:30 or so. Then, on Saturday, he will "work" from 10 in the morning until 10:30 at night. "Security officials will often have to close the doors and not let some of the people in late at night.

"They'll often have a costume contest or a tattoo contest," Ted said. "And vendors will sell all kinds of stuff including swords, knives, clothes from movies, action figures and other things related to films."

Fans show up by the hundreds and pay up to $50.00 simply to enter the convention hall. Then they pay extra for memorabilia, pictures and autographs.

Over the past several years Ted has appeared at these conventions in Los Angeles, Dallas, New York, Miami, Nashville, Kentucky, Boston, Baltimore and many other locations in the United States. One of the largest conventions he took part in was in Dusseldorf, Germany, where American films are extremely popular. He was recently invited to be a participant in a convention in Australia but turned it down, dreading the 17-hour flight.

Ted frequently leaves these productions with several thousand dollars in profit.

"People recognize me in three different ways," he said. "As a stuntman, an actor, and as Jason."

In fact, three decades after he reluctantly took on the role of Jason in the 1984 film he still has legions of fans eager to meet him, get his photo and autograph and have their picture snapped with him. They also want photos of him with such stars as John Wayne, Clark Gable, Victor Mature, Fess Parker,

Tom Selleck, Sam Elliott and other big-name stars. He often hears fans saying things like "Oh, my dad loved him," or "my mom will adore this." Often, they are actually buying the photos for themselves. "What I sell often depends on where the convention is being held," Ted said. "In the west fans want more cowboys but in the east they often want more of me as Jason." He said men usually want photos of stars like John Wayne . "Women flip over Sam Elliott and they will buy more pictures of me with Clark Gable."

"Many of the celebrities show up in jeans and sweatshirts," he said. "I always wear a suit or a sports coat and tie. I want to be a positive representative for my industry."

He is often asked to tape a brief television commercial to help promote the convention and one time, when he showed up at the TV studio dressed nicely, the crew didn't believe he had actually played Jason. "I finally convinced them," Ted said, "but it was pretty comical for a while."

Ted never knows what to expect when he gets himself seated at his table with dozens of photos spread out before him.

At one convention a woman and two children came to his table, looked through the photos of Ted as Jason and found one she evidently liked. She turned around and held up the photo so a man standing ten or fifteen feet away could see it. She did the same with several photos and each time he would nod or shake his head. Finally, she had selected a photo which met the man's final approval and asked Ted to sign it.

"Whose name should I address this to?" he asked.

She gave him a name and he signed it "good luck. Ted White."

"It's for my husband," she said.

Ted looked at the man across the aisle. "Well, who is that?"

"My husband," she replied.

"I'll take it over to him and shake his hand," Ted said.

As he started around the table the woman held up her hand. "I don't think so," she said, and wouldn't let him get close to her husband. "He's terrified of you. He watches and re-watches that movie but he is too frightened to get near you."

Ted called out to the man. "Hey," he said. "I didn't really kill anyone. I'm a nice guy. It's all make-believe."

The man backed away. "I'm sorry," he said. "I can't have you come any closer."

As Ted watched, the woman took the photo and they quickly left. He felt sorry for the man and would have liked to talk to him and perhaps quell his fears.

Ted reports that he has fans from all walks of life. "I've had attorneys, police officers and all kinds of professional people come to my table," he said, "along with regular folks who just happen to like movies."

He said one particular New York detective comes to almost every signing convention he attends, including shows in Baltimore, Kentucky, New York, Dallas and others. "He's a real fan and he'll spend several hundred dollars on pictures. He's a real nice guy."

Another man emails Ted sometimes three times a week. "He goes to IMDB.com, finds a movie I'm in, rents it, and then writes to say he saw me in one film or another and comments on the acting, the action, the direction, whatever interests him. Some women do the same thing."

Once at a convention in New York, Ted and Jeri were at his table when they noticed a crowd gathering down the row from them and realized the noise was increasing. Finally, three men appeared pulling a flat platform with wheels. On the platform was a life size statue of Ted made of plaster of Paris.

"I couldn't believe it," Ted said. "It was six feet four and must have weighed 300 pounds. They rolled it up to my table and people started coming from all over the place. They had me standing with this thing while they took what seemed like hundreds of pictures. The men said it took them nine months to build it and they started over four times because it wasn't exactly right. When I stood next to it you couldn't tell which was the real me."

At another convention in Baltimore the show's producer approached Ted who had a line of people at his table. "Can I break in here for a moment?" he asked.

Ted nodded at the line of people and said "I've got all these people here waiting."

The producer turned to those in line and said "please stand tight for a minute. I think you'll enjoy this."

The producer beckoned to a man who appeared to be about 45 years old who came forward with his wife and two children. He introduced himself and the producer asked him to take off his shirt. He did so and turned around.

264

"His entire back from his neck down was tattooed with a large picture of me, just my head and shoulder," Ted said. "He told me it had taken months to get it right."

"You never know what you're going see or who you'll meet," he said.

ONE OF THE FIRST conventions Ted attended was in New York. He and Jeri were at his table when a man they didn't know came behind the table, pulled up a chair and began visiting. Ted had no idea who the man was, what he wanted, or if he should even be in the room. Across the aisle, two young women stared at the man and were visibly upset. Finally, after a few minutes, one of the women approached the table, stared at the man and said: "You dirty bastard, where's my money?"

"You don't have any money coming," he said.

The woman stormed away but within minutes was back with a security official who took the man away. The women told Ted the man had been their agent but that he took the money they earned and promised it to them "after the show." They hadn't seen him again until just then.

The security people called Ted and asked him to meet with them. They told him the man was notorious for cheating people. "Don't have anything to do with him," they said. Ted promised he wouldn't.

That unfortunate incident did, however, lead to a contract with a fine agent for Ted. One of the security people at the convention suggested that he knew two agents who were in attendance and who were "top of the line." He asked if he could send them to visit with Ted who agreed.

Several days later, back in Los Angeles, Ted signed a contract with the two – Sean Clark and Bill Longley. Before long, however, the duo parted ways and Ted continued with Clark who remains his agent. Another agent he worked with in the motion picture business was Bob Brandies.

ONE OF THE difficulties faced by a man of Ted's size and background as a fearless stuntman and frequent heavy in movies is that he is often confronted by individuals who seem to want to prove they are tougher than him.

At a signing convention in New Jersey not too long ago it happened again.

"I'd been open ten or fifteen minutes," he said, "when two guys walked up. They were both well over six feet tall, maybe in their late 20s."

They spent a few minutes looking at pictures. Then they began asking questions. "You a stuntman? Who'd you do stunts for? What else did you do?"

Ted tried to be friendly, answered their questions, and they visited a few minutes.

Then: "Sounds like you were one of those Hollywood tough guys. You don't look that tough to me."

"I can't help what I look like," Ted said. "I'm up in years now but I got around pretty good in my younger days."

"You think you're tough, huh?"

"Let me tell you something," Ted replied. "People who know me leave me alone and you're starting to bother me." He stood up, took off his sports coat and said "if the two of you are looking for an argument you've found it. Now just how much farther do you want to take this?"

Both of the men began to back off. "No, we're not looking for trouble," one said.

"Then you better get away from me right now," Ted said. They left.

At the table next to Ted was Lou Ferrigno, who had starred in the TV series *The Incredible Hulk* from 1996 to 1998. In that series a nuclear scientist is afflicted with the tendency to change into a powerful green monster under stress. Ferrigno, a very large man himself who is a likely target for young toughs, asked if Ted knew who the men were.

"I have no idea," he said, "but they pushed me to the limit and I'd had all I could take from them."

Ferrigno shook his head. "They were young and you might have had quite a time with them."

Ted put on his coat and sat back down at his table. "There are times when age doesn't make all that much difference," he said.

Later that morning Ted had a disagreement with Ferrigno himself.

Ferrigno is a popular attraction at these signings and he soon had a crowd of people in front of his table. There were so many that they blocked access to Ted's table for his own fans. After 20 minutes Ted called to him and suggested that Ferrigno ask his people to make some space for Ted's. The man was indignant and said he didn't have time to deal with that and that it wasn't his business anyway.

Finally, Ted's new agent, Sean Clark, showed up with a roll of yellow tape which he laid out between the two tables. Ferrigno's fans politely moved over. However, after a restroom break, Ted returned to his table and found the tape was gone.

"I came unglued," he said. He walked to Ferrigno's table and confronted him. "Lou," he said, "I've tried to be nice and I'm going to ask you one more time. If things don't change you're not gonna like what I'm gonna do."

"Are you threatening me?" Ferrigno asked.

"I'm just telling you what I'll do," Ted said.

Ferrigno angrily shut down his table and left. Soon a crew of men showed up and moved his table and photos to another location.

Quickly, the show's producer was at Ted's table. "Mr. White," he said. "Did you threaten Mr. Ferrigno?"

"I did," Ted told him. "I will not be bullied." He explained how he had tried to be reasonable but that had not worked and the yellow tape had been removed.

Agent Sean Clark showed up at that time and asked "where's Lou?"

"We had to move him," the producer said. "Ted threatened to whip him."

Both men began to laugh. "You threatened to beat up Lou Ferrigno and scared him away?" Clark asked.

The producer chimed in, also laughing. "If Lou hadn't come to me himself and acted like he was frightened of you I might not have believed it either."

CERTAIN MOVIES HAVE a terrific impact on people who often believe that what are seeing is, in fact, reality. "That was certainly true of the man who stood across the aisle and wouldn't come near me while his wife held up pictures for him to see," Ted said.

He said the minute he and other stars walk into the hotel people start asking him for autographs. "I can't do that, though," he said. "The producers absolutely forbid it. They want those fans to pay to attend the show."

Ted was even hounded by the driver of a limousine who picked him up at the airport and wanted free pictures.

Still, he revels in the fact that thousands of movie-goers from across the country remember him in his various roles and want to have even just a bit of personal connection to him. "These conventions are usually a lot of fun," he said. "I make some money but they are very tiring. I do get to meet some interesting people, though."

35

The Best...and the Worst

WHEN TED BROKE into the business American motion pictures were in a period that might be called a late adolescent stage. Even though several Europeans had experimented with film as early as the late 1800s the resulting presentations were little more than novelty, even carnival, acts.

It wasn't until 1903 that Thomas Edison and his main director, Edwin S. Porter, produced the first movie Western, *The Great Train Robbery*. This film – barely 11 minutes long – is said to be the first movie that had a narrative story to tell. In fact, most films at the time were only one reel, or about ten to fifteen minutes long.

Early in the century Europeans and Australians began producing films as long as 80 minutes but it wasn't until D. W. Griffith's epics *The Birth of a Nation* (1915) and *Intolerance* (1916) that American filmmakers began to explore the full possibilities of their fledgling industry.

With the advent of sound Hollywood began its climb toward universal appeal and global dominance with classic movie stars such as Gable, Hepburn, Bogart and even child star Shirley Temple.

By the 1950s, when Ted got his first big break with *Onionhead*, movies were maturing. Moviegoers expected solid acting and directing, believable action and, now and then, even a "message." However, screenwriter William Goldman (*Butch Cassidy and the Sundance Kid* -- 1969) famously wrote that he didn't want to preach in films. He said he was a believer in the old movie adage "if you want to write a message, use Western Union."

Ted and other stuntmen at the time were jumping out of windows and off roofs onto a stack of cardboard boxes, using the "Running W" for horsefalls and injuring animals and making do with what now seem like archaic tools of the trade as they experimented with new (for then) ways of making stunts look real and as though they were done by the stars themselves. There were no computer graphics, no green screen backgrounds. It was all as "real" as they could make it and audiences loved what they did.

In the latter part of the twentieth century and into the twentyfirst, when Ted was working on films such as *Silverado* and the *Fast and Furious* movies, moviemaking was drastically different from "the old days."

The production of a film has always involved large numbers of cast and crew. But Ted says the number of people on a set has grown dramatically over the years. "A normal crew can be between 120 and 140 people," he said. "Depending on the movie or the scene, it can be many more than that."

The cast and crew of The Wild, Wild West, *indicating the number of people involved in the production of a film*

Gerald Mast asks: "Who is the ultimate creator of a film? The director? The producer? The writer? The photographer? The editor?"

He says thousands of people may contribute to the final product. "If one is to discuss the film as a work of art rather than as entertainment, as business, as societal mirror, or as manufacturer of the . . . new royalty, one must discuss the minds who know how to create great films and how those minds work."

"There are the stars, stuntmen and extras," Ted White said, "but the crew consists of a wide variety of people, depending on the film itself." Among them are the director and his or her first and second assistants, numerous trainees, script clerks, dialogue directors, carpenters and grips.

In addition, and more recently, the crew includes "green men" who put in tees, bushes, grass, flowers – whatever the director wants to help flesh out a scene.

There are also standby painters. "Not long ago if it was green you shot it," Ted said. "If it was brown you shot it. Now the director might say he wants a wall painted blue. The standby painters are called in and suddenly the wall is blue."

The wardrobe people begin work before the first film is shot. "They go to the location and find a dry cleaner who will agree to take the actors' costumes late in the evening and have them cleaned and ready for use before dawn the next day. They also often need two sets of costumes in case one set gets wet or dirty during a day's filming.

Likewise, the prop department begins work weeks before filming, gathering everything from furniture for dressing a set to guns and horses for Westerns to automobiles and trucks for films like *Fast and Furious*.

"There are companies in Los Angeles that have cars from the early days to the latest models," Ted said. "If a prop man needs 30 cars for a scene the next day the companies have them. If we're filming a wreck you need two identical cars in case reshooting is required."

He said everything has to work and look brand new. In the movie *Sunset*, for example, Tom Mix's car was a Duesenberg which was easy to come by in LA. When filming *Batman* with Jack Nicholson there were five Batmobiles, Ted said. "They cost a fortune and they were the most uncomfortable cars in the world."

While there are thousands of films produced and released annually from Hollywood and elsewhere throughout the world, Ted says it has become more and more difficult each year to get a film made. Everyone is hoping to produce the next blockbuster, he said. The cost of producing a film has risen rapidly in the past several years and those providing the funding for a movie are always hoping for a quick payback.

Production costs have always been a determining factor in the decision of whether to make a specific film or not and producers and directors are constantly eyeing the bottom line of a budget and trying not to exceed it. However, certain films have more leeway than others when it comes to finding and spending money.

Consider *Cleopatra*, a 1963 film directed by Joseph L. Mankiewicz and starring Elizabeth Taylor, Richard Burton, Rex Harrison, Roddy McDowall, and Martin Landau.

Adjusted for inflation *Cleopatra* is one of the most expensive films ever made. It was the highest grossing film of 1963, earning $26 million in the U.S., but it cost $44 million to produce (the equivalent of about $325 million in today's dollars). Therefore, it became the only film ever to be the highest grossing film of a year yet to run at a loss. The film did win four Academy Awards and was nominated for five more, including Best Picture (ultimately losing to *Tom Jones*).

Ted was called to Europe to put together the gigantic battle sequence at sea. However, when he got on the set Elizabeth Taylor went to the hospital with pneumonia. Told they wouldn't be able to work on the film for five to six weeks while she recuperated, Ted had to return to the U.S. to fulfill other commitments.

Similarly, *Cowboys and Aliens*, a 2011 "science fiction Western" film, cost more than $160 million to produce and grossed just slightly more than that. It was considered a financial disappointment. The film was directed by Jon Favreau and starred Daniel Craig, Harrison Ford and Olivia Wilde.

Reports say that the producers tried to create a "serious" Western despite the movie's relatively comic premise. With a fungus growing on their wounds, the aliens were attempting to represent frontiersmen dealing with adversity in a strange location.

Ted says his friend (stuntman and second unit director) Terry Leonard turned down one of the *Fast and Furious* films to do *Cowboys and Aliens*.

"Terry got the call to come do one of the *Fast and Furious* films the day after he been offered *Cowboys and Aliens*," Ted said. "He turned it down and I told him he was making a big mistake. I said that was a franchise. I told him they would keep making those things and that he was the man to do them. Terry lost a good job."

One of the more recent Westerns, *The Lone Ranger* was released in 2013 with a reported budget of $250 million. This film, directed by Gore

Verbinski, starred Arnie Hammer in the title role and Johnny Depp as Tonto.

Ted had appeared in the 1981 version, *The Legend of the Lone Ranger* playing the father of the man who would ultimately don the mask and become the fabled Lone Ranger.

The Lone Ranger has been a popular film topic over many decades. There have been at least five feature films based on him, along with a television series and films made for TV.

DURING THE PRODUCTION of a film Ted says the cast and crew can usually tell if the movie is going to be a good one or not. "It largely depends on the experience of the cast and crew and, of course, the director," Ted said. "A director can easily foul up a movie by making life miserable for everyone on the set and by not taking advice."

When working as the stunt coordinator on the three-part made-for-TV movie *Dazzle* in 1995 Ted discovered early on that the director Richard Colla didn't know how to handle scenes involving horses. "I found myself cringing at some of the directions he was giving the actors," Ted said. The film starred Lisa Hartman, Cliff Robertson and James Farentino and was written by Judith Krantz from her novel of the same name.

Ted went to the first assistant director and told him the director was wrong in the way he was shooting a particular scene. "I have no say in the matter," the assistant replied.

"The director was a hard man to talk to so I let it pass," Ted said. The scene was done the way the director wanted and "everybody on the set knew it was wrong."

Later, when writer Judith Krantz and her husband Steve Krantz, the executive producer, saw the resulting unedited film they agreed it should not have been shot as it was. They asked Ted if he knew it was being done wrong. Ted told them he had tried to make suggestions but was ignored. "In the future you take charge," he executive producer told him.

In another scene Linda Evans, another of the film's stars, is to be walking across a street when she is hit by a large truck. Ted was able to convince the director that, rather than having the truck come at her at high speed and risk actually hitting her, the scene should start with a shot through the windshield showing Evans throwing her hands up as the truck is about to hit her. Then, with the camera recording the action in high speed, the truck backs up. When the film is reversed it appears to be coming at her.

"When the director saw the film, which worked beautifully, he never said a word to me," Ted said.

Making pictures is a memorable, enjoyable experience ninety-nine percent of the time, Ted said. "But now and then you get on a film that you can tell isn't going to be good." Still, he adheres to the adage that "if you start something, you need to finish it."

"You can't simply walk away," he said. "You can try to override bad decisions if that's what you're being paid to do. But it all depends on the director and the producers. You can only do so much."

"OFTEN THE WORST part of movie-making is working with a director who doesn't really know what he or she is doing," Ted said. "You watch them guessing at how to set up a shot or putting in dialogue that doesn't work and you know it's not right but in most cases you can't do anything about it.

"The cast and crew can tell if the director knows his business the minute he first sets up the camera and tells the actors what to do. It can be a sinking feeling."

He said most directors are accomplished but "now and then you get one who drinks or is on drugs. That's when people can get hurt and when some actors will refuse to say a line as the director wants. Then you go through a long session with the director, the actors and the dialogue director. When that kind of thing is obvious and continual you don't really want to go to work every morning. You wonder what can happen today to screw things up."

Ted said another unpleasant part of movie-making is the time you spend sitting around waiting for the time when you're asked to do something. "But that's the nature of the business either on a good film or a bad one. Even if I'm not scheduled to be on screen until four o'clock that afternoon I still have to be there at six in the morning. I'm still getting paid but I sit there with many others – the greensman, the standby painters, the prop crew, wardrobe. All of us are sitting there waiting. When it's your turn you've got to be ready, make-up applied, dialogue learned, ready to hit the mark. It may take three or four minutes and then you're done for the day."

In contrast, Ted says there is real joy in being a part of the production of a film that everyone believes will be a good one.

"To me, one of the great experiences in making a picture is watching it unfold and being fortunate enough to be involved from the beginning to the end," he said. "It's a great pleasure to be a part of something like that, knowing that millions of people will see the movie and that you are contributing to its success."

He pointed to *Silverado* (1985) as an example. "Even though the weather was miserable, cold and windy, I looked forward to every day of it. It was an exciting part of my life."

Naturally, Ted recalls some films with great joy but has bad recollections of others.

"My favorite movie involvement was on *Hatari*," he said. "That was one of the great experiences of my life. Working with Howard Hawks, John Wayne and all the others was truly one of the most fulfilling parts of my life in the motion picture business."

However, one of the worst experiences for Ted was working on *The Misfits*. "I didn't appreciate the director," he said, "and the difficulties Marilyn Monroe caused were disturbing to the entire cast." He felt that working with Clark Gable was a good experience but the rest of the production process was not enjoyable.

*Ted ponders his next stunt while playing an FBI agent
for a TV show being shot in Florida*

36

Bigger Than Life:
Ted White and the Movies

"MY FIRST IMPRESSION of Ted White was that he was bigger than life," says Terry Leonard, himself one of the greats in the fraternity of stuntmen and second unit directors. "I thought he had a great gift of gab but I learned pretty quickly that everything he said was true. We worked and played together for all these years. The only thing I didn't do was play golf. I think golf courses are a waste of good farmland."

Another fellow stuntman, Dean Smith, called Ted "one of the great men in the motion picture business." He said the man was "a rock, a great teacher and a wonderful friend."

Similar accolades come from others – longtime friends, fellow stuntmen and women, directors, film crew members, even those who worked briefly with him on only one movie project or another.

Ted White came to the business in its relatively early years and matured with it well into the 21st century. As American movies got better and better, so Ted White improved his own skills. He reinvented himself time and time again to take advantage of opportunities and to make himself an individual who could be counted on to handle many of the roles required in making movies.

He was there when Westerns were the rage and action was the byword. He was there when tough guys were needed to make the good guys look better. He was there when fast cars took the place of fast horses and when vehicle crashes replaced horsefalls. And he was there when lawfirms needed visual evidence that clients were hurt due to negligence or sloppiness that was not their doing.

Ted White has helped keep the magic alive – magic that makes movies so important to so many people.

If, as the late movie critic Roger Ebert says, we live in a box of space and time, "movies are windows in its walls." He said movies allow us to enter other minds "not simply in the sense of identifying with the characters, although that is an important part of it, but by seeing the world as another person sees it."

Ted White and others like him helped take audiences, for a brief time, somewhere else, sometime else, and become interested in, and concerned about, lives that are someone else's. "Of all the arts," Ebert wrote, "movies are the most powerful aid to empathy, and good ones make us into better people."

Screenwriter Syd Field agrees and says that "movies have become so much a part of our lives that sometimes we forget how much they influence behavior, or our ways of thinking."

Ted can attest to the truth of that statement.

His role as Jason in *Friday the 13th: The Final Chapter*, for example, lives on as near reality in the minds of many of the film's viewers. Some, like the man who wouldn't come near him for an autograph, are still, after all these years, nearly traumatized by Ted's role and can't escape the lingering images of him as a "slasher."

Others revere him for his role as the hunter in *Starman*. Some bring him photos of his single appearance on *The Andy Griffith Show* or want him to autograph a photo of him with their favorite star.

And why not? Ted White, though not a household name, has made the films he appeared in better because of the skills he brought to bear and he has made the stars with whom he worked look better and more heroic than most of them probably should have looked.

"I feel like I've had the best days in the business," Ted said. "I've come up with the likes of Wayne, Gable, Rock Hudson, Fess Parker, Victor Mature, Marlene Dietrich, Betty Grable – most of the big names. In my 50-odd years I had the best of it. Yes, I'd say those were the best days of the motion picture business."

Ted is justifiably proud of his work. And he feels he has been lucky along the way.

"There are probably millions of guys who would like to be fighting

278

Jeff Bridges in *Starman* or with him in *Tron* or *Cutter's Way* or *Against all Odds*," he said. "And just as many would like to have worked with Wayne and Gable. To say you're not lucky is not right. You are. Other guys may also be lucky but you may be taller by an inch and that may have gotten you a good part. You may have a face that looks more like what they want than the other guy. Luck plays a big part."

Wife Jeri agrees that Ted has been "lucky" but likes the old saying: "the harder I work, the luckier I get." She said he always worked hard to hone his skills and better himself as a versatile member of the motion picture business. In addition, he cared for his friends.

"He'd get a call from a studio because they wanted a certain size of man or a specific type to double someone. When he got a call like that he'd call three or four of his friends as ask if they got the same call. If not, he'd tell them to check on it. I'd asked him why he called them when they were his competition. He'd say that if he didn't get the job he wanted one of his friends to have it. He made a lot of good friends with that kind of attitude. He would never backstab or try to cut somebody out of a job."

Terry Leonard says Ted looked after his friends.

"I did a big high fall in Los Angeles that was the highest in the world before airbags were invented," he said. We used cardboard boxes and in that eight-story fall I tore my back muscles so badly that I could hardly move. I was almost living in a whirlpool. But Ted called me to come help on a movie. I told him I was stove up but you don't argue with him when he puts the bullrush on you."

Terry barely made it to the studio and Ted made sure he was able to do something in the film and that he got paid.

"He's a very sociable guy," says son Ted Jr. "He's a people person. If he likes you he'll do anything in the world for you. If not, he'll probably tell you so. My dad has a great desire to be of benefit to people he likes."

"I've known Ted since I first got in the business," Terry Leonard said. "He was one of the first guys I met when I came to town, along with Chuck Roberson who doubled Wayne for a number of years. Roberson introduced me to Dean Smith, an Olympian and stuntman, Jack Williams, the most famous falling horse guy in the movies at the time, and Ted White. We became instant friends. All of us worked together a lot and had some great times."

Leonard said he would never forget how Ted stepped up and helped out on the movie *Used Cars*. "My first assistant director showed up drunk when we had a scene to film that used 125 cars. I told Ted he had that job and we ran the whole deal." Because of Ted's insistence on learning all aspects of the business he was able to take on that job without hesitation.

"When Ted passes they ought to lower all the flags in L.A. to halfmast because he's the real deal," he said. "He was kind of like a father figure to me but now he's more like a brother."

Ted's son Michael has seen all sides of his father. "He's got a real gentle side but he won't take any crap from anyone," he said. "He's still very much the same. A great guy with a great sense of humor. And he's an amazing story teller. He would tell me and my brother that he had a great idea for a movie and then start outlining it for us. Twenty or thirty minutes later we'd be completely entertained and then realize he was making it up on the spot."

In fact, Ted has written several screenplays including one set during the Olympics in Russia. He also wrote a script for Steve McQueen. MGM bought the script but McQueen died before it was made. A third script was about a cowboy taking a herd of cattle to Alaska during the days of sailing ships.

Ted approached screenwriting as he did other aspects of his profession.

"I have always been amazed at how analytical he can be," Jeri said. "He has a great way of envisioning something and figuring out how to make it work, such as planning a stunt."

She said he has always been interested in, and good at, building things. "Even in that he won't compromise," she said. "He could do it in an easier manner but that wouldn't work for him. It has to be right. He's that way in his profession. He's good at calculating things. If you want to jump from here to there the question might be how to make a ramp work. He used to drop sandbags. Now he figures it out on a computer."

Son Michael says his father can choreograph a movie fight scene in his mind and then lay it out step by step for the participants. "He can see all the details of a film fight before it ever happens," he said.

Throughout his career, Ted has been concerned with safety factors, for himself and for those with whom he has worked. "I'm grateful that he's taken such good care of himself," Michael said. "Even though he has battered and bruised his body, he's managed to be smart about how he took care of himself. Everything he has done comes from a perspective of safety. That attitude has kept him around for us."

However, there are times when accidents make injury impossible to avoid.

In one of the first stunts Ted did when doubling John Wayne in *Rio Bravo*, for example, he broke his shoulder tumbling down some stairs during the first take because a bootheel caught on a step. No one knew of his injury and he repeated the fall for a second take. When assistant director Paul Helmick asked him why he didn't speak up, Ted said he had come there to work and he wouldn't quit until the job was done.

Helmick was an assistant director on *Hatari* when Ted's Jeep was wrecked by a charging rhino and was again surprised with Ted wanted to try the shot again.

"It's hard to look yourself in the mirror in the mornings if you know you haven't done everything you could to make something work," he said. "If you're going to take the money, you have to do the job."

Even though he is basically retired from film making, especially in terms of stuntwork, Ted recently received a call to visit a studio and help them figure out how to most successfully do a complicated stunt.

He was pleased to receive the call and was glad to help. It's a way of keeping in touch with the movie community. And, he says, it's nice to know they remember him and respect his experience and knowledge.

"Do I miss it? In many ways," he said. "Mostly I miss the camaraderie with the people. Not just stuntmen but the actors, the crew, the producers, every one of them. They are all just genuine people coming together to do a job, to make a movie and hoping it turns out to be a good one."

Ted said he even misses being on the set at 5 a.m., "standing in line with the rest of the men and women for breakfast. It's just that feeling of being with them, being a part of something that you know is going to be creative. It's an exciting time. Every morning you want to go to work. It's a new thing, a new experience every time. You know this is something that people around the world will watch and that many of them will say 'I know that guy'."

Would he change anything? Ted says he wouldn't. "I've had too many beautiful experiences. I've also had some sad ones where I've seen people killed or maimed, but that's part of life. It's not a part you enjoy, or that you expect will happen, but it does. The good times far outnumber the bad, though, and while I've made some mistakes I can't think of much I'd change even if I could."

Jeri calls him "one of the last of a breed who lived the kind of life he's lived." She says Ted is "very manly" and that modern-day stuntmen are totally different. "Ted and his friends relied on themselves more than today's counterparts do. Now they rely on digital technology. Leading men are quite different now from those of the past – the Gables, Coopers, Waynes, Garners and many others."

Terry Leonard agrees. "There was a lot more to be learned when Ted broke into the business," he said. "There weren't so many visual effects. We did the real thing. There are lots of great athletes in the picture business today but they're not required to do many of the things we had to do."

"My dad," says Michael, "was the giant who made the celebrity look like one."

He says he has raised his children the same way he was raised by his father. "I can't be any more proud of my kids," he said. "My biggest blessing in life is watching my children flower and become creative beings. It's how I was raised by my dad."

Ted Jr. says one of the main things about his father was that "right or wrong, whatever he believed in, he stood behind it one hundred percent."

Ted is a patriot, Ted Jr. says. "That's a rarity in Hollywood. But he never talked to me about his time in the Marines. He said he would but as yet he hasn't. I respect him for that. If he wants to talk about it, he will."

Ted Jr. said when you see his father on the screen you are seeing the real man. "He was always 'Ted'," he said, "no matter what role he was playing, he played himself."

Screenwriter William Goldman believes truly skilled actors are rare. "A few," he says, "are blessed with brilliance. And of those, fewer still have even a shot at greatness." However, he says, "every century or so, we are blessed with a tiny handful, and as impossible as their task may be, *staying* great is that much harder."

TED WHITE HAS ENDURED, grown and "stayed great" for more than half a century. He has become bigger than life. He has made stars themselves greater than the sum of their parts.

He may be the most famous movie star you've never heard of.

But now you have.

At the end of the film *Sunset* the final frame freezes and the following text appears: "And this is how it really happened. Give or take a lie or two."

In Ted White's case, "this is how it really happened." Period.

Cast a Giant Shadow

EPILOGUE

FOR MANY OF US, movies are mileposts marking important stages in our life journey. They help us remember where we were, what we were like and who we thought we were as we took steps into our futures.

Some of us who are at a certain age find that the films of Ted White (and others, of course) provide "aha!" moments as we think back, and back, and back.

For a young boy starting elementary school in the high plains area of Russell, Kansas, Saturday matinees with friends at the downtown Mecca Theatre made him want to grow up to be a cowboy – or at least a Ted White who could play one in the movies.

There were Roy Rogers and Gene Autry, of course, and even the fact that Trigger and Champion could outrun cars didn't bother us. We liked Johnny Mack Brown and Rex Allen and "Hoppy" and Monte Hale and Tim Holt and Bob Steele (he had a great dark horse with a flowing white mane and tail) and Jimmy Wakely and Charles Starrett (the Durango Kid) and Whip Wilson and almost all the rest of them.

We liked "Wild Bill" Elliot as Red Ryder but who would have thought that "Little Beaver" would grow up to be Robert Blake and turn into a murderer in *In Cold Blood?*

We didn't particularly care for Sunset Carson whose outfit was a bit too fancy – even more than Roy's or Gene's. We thought Lash LaRue was Humphrey Bogart dressed in black cowboy clothes. And, doggone it, we thought Clayton Moore should have loosened up a bit in his role as the Lone Ranger.

But we went to all their movies and came away satisfied. We got to walk to the theatre by ourselves, sometimes having to drag our little brothers or sisters along. It was Saturday. It was movie day. Cowboys.

One evening before we were old enough to drive, a friend and I rode our bikes to a small town seven miles from home to attend a movie where we

285

planned to meet a couple of girls we liked (mine would later become my wife). Our parents thought we were "camping out."

But it rained and stormed that night and my father drove out to find us. He finally located us, resting comfortable and dry, in a nearby barn. If he was upset over having to fight his way through rutted and muddy gravel roads he didn't really show it.

I'll never forget the movie. It was, appropriately, *Trouble Along the Way* starring John Wayne.

Remember? Something like that happened to you, too.

In high school, I got to take the car (a Studebaker) out by myself for one of the first times – a milepost. My future wife and I drove to that same theatre to see *The Maze* in 3-D.

Much later, after a week of initiation into the Sigma Chi fraternity at Kansas State University, several of us exercised our newfound freedom and went to a movie. It was *The Brothers Karamazov*. "The Brothers K," as we referred to it, marked a day of achievement, of the end of something and the beginning of a new life. We were growing up. It was important. I'll bet the others remember the film for the same reason.

A couple of years later, while we were working summer jobs in Tulsa, Oklahoma, fraternity brother Don Rhoades and I saw several films. Among them was *The Horse Soldiers* which featured Ted White and a couple of other stars. How was I to know Ted would feature so strongly in my life in later years? Those two summers in Tulsa, the first time I had been so much on my own for so long, included others films. I remember them well, I remember the theatres, they were important. Among those movies were more that featured Ted White – *Exodus, The Alamo, Spartacus*.

How the West Was Won in Cinemascope in a Wichita, Kansas theatre with the largest screen we'd ever seen. Pre-children. The two of us. Dinner and a fantastic movie. What a life. A time when we thought we had it all. And, by golly, we did.

Soon it was *Hatari* (there was Ted White again) and a stereo that was an enormous piece of furniture where we listened to the soundtrack. Remember "Baby Elephant Walk?"

Post-kids, we went skiing in Aspen and saw *Downhill Racer* with friends Bill and Jeanne Hatcher, Norman and Phyllis Powers and Bob and Joyce Winter. The next day, though we weren't skiing as fast as Robert

Redford (or his double), it surely seemed like it. I had a birthday while we were there. A milepost in a life.

I think I've seen almost all of Ted White's films. If I haven't, I've heard so much about them it seems as though I have.

On a business trip to Hays, Kansas, my business partner Dave Stormont and I saw *Silverado*. I thought the bad guy in the eye patch who got shot off the roof deserved it. Ted White did a good job making me believe in his character. At the end of the film Kevin Costner shouts "We'll be back!" I'm still waiting. We picked up good business on that trip. It was a milepost. The movie is part of that experience.

There are others. *Rio Bravo, Cat Ballou, Blazing Saddles*. My Lord, so many. My son Greg and I seeing the first *Star Wars* together in Lawrence, Kansas. Taking my daughter Suzy (who begged me) to her first R-rated film. I don't remember what it was although I do recall that it was no doubt the language that earned the rating. Probably nothing she hadn't heard before. But I was glad to be there with her and to be able to talk about it afterward.

Thank you, Ted White. And thank you to all your friends and co-workers who, over the years, have created experiences that live vividly in my memory and that are like signal fires atop a nearby hill calling me back. Back to comfortable (and not-so-comfortable) theatre seats while I savored Monument Valley, the Serengeti Plain in Africa, Spartacus' march to Italy's seacoast, Batman's Gotham City, the Texas plains, the Nevada desert.

"We buy our tickets and hope for diversion," said Roger Ebert, "and usually we get it."

To many of us, movies are more than a brief diversion from the minutiae of everyday life. They are a respite, a postponement of whatever travail is to come next. And long afterward the good ones linger in our minds, not only as a mechanism of momentary escape, but also as a signpost, a marker along life's road, a pin in a map, a photo in an album. "I remember that," we say. "I know where we were, how we felt, what we did after the film. It was a significant time for us."

"Movies are a form of contemporary myth," wrote Syd Field, "and our heroes set out on their adventures in front of a tremendous audience. Technology, contemporary spirituality, and the enormity of today's audience have changed the American screenplay and the way American screenwriters are telling their stories."

287

Movies may indeed be changing. But like John Wayne, who morphed from the lackadaisical Singin' Sandy of B-Westerns to the determined Ethan Edwards of *The Searchers* – like Clint Eastwood who grew from the young Rowdy Yates in TV's *Rawhide* to the aging and reluctant killer William Munny in *Unforgiven* – Ted White has helped the movies change and improve while remaining relevant and important cultural entities in a world that needs to believe in heroes.

As I write this, Americans are struggling to deal with a rash of what have been considered terrorists attacks in the U.S. No doubt movies will be made depicting these atrocities or others. Will they help us remember? Of course. Will they teach us anything? I hope so. Will someone like Ted White help make one or more of the films significant mileposts in the life of an individual in Kansas or Idaho or London or Calcutta? I think we can count on it.

We need people like Ted White, men who are bigger than life and who are willing to take on the task of bringing enjoyment to the rest of us. Ted White and his movie brethren, both men and women, make us believe. They take us away, for a while, and give us hope.

Ted White has cast a giant shadow over the motion picture business and left his mark on hundreds of films and television productions.

Terry Leonard summed up Ted's career with the following: "As Paul Newman said in the film *The Life and Times of Judge Roy Bean*, 'if the story ain't true, it ought'a be'."

FADE OUT

TED WHITE'S FILMOGRAPHY
(Partial)

1950s

    Return of Jesse James -- 50
    Lone Star – 52
    Long Long Trailer – 53
    Friendly Persuasion – 56
    Giant – 56
    Man in a Grey Flannel Suit – 56
    The Big Country – 58
    Born Reckless – 58
    Man of the West – 58
    The Naked and the Dead – 58
    Onion Head – 58
    The Perfect Furlough – 58
    Horse Soldiers – 59
    Pillow Talk – 59
    Rio Bravo - 59
    A Stranger in My Arms – 59
    These Thousand Hills – 59
    The Young Land – 59

1960s

    The Alamo – 60
    Exodus -60
    Portrait in Black – 60
    Spartacus – 60
    Guns of Navarone – 61
    The Misfits – 61
    Escape from Zahrain – 62

Hatari – 62
Cleopatra – 63
Man's Favorite Sport – 64
Cat Ballou – 65
Cincinnati Kid – 65
Ship of Fools – 65
Von Ryan's Express – 65
Smoky – 66
What did you do in the war, Daddy? – 66
Will Penny – 67
Point Blank – 67
Planet   of the Apes - 68

1970s

Going Ape – 70
They Call Me Mr. Tibbs – 70
French Connection – 71
Prime Cut – 72
The Don is Dead – 73
Jarrett – 73
The Seven Ups – 73
Soylent Green – 73
Bingo – 74
Blazing Saddles – 74
Dirty Mary Crazy Larry – 74
Rollerball – 75
The Wind and the Lion – 75
King Kong – 76
Herbie Goes to Monte Carlo -- 77
Black Oak Conspiracy – 77
McArthur – 77
Comes a Horseman – 78
Convoy – 78
The Manitou – 78

1980s

      Bronco Billy – 80

      Night of the Juggler - 80

      O, god! Book II – 80

      Somewhere in Time - 80

      Up the Academy – 80

      Urban Cowboy - 80

      Used Cars – 80

      Cutter's Way – 81

      Demonoid: Messenger of Death – 81

      Escape from New York – 81

      History of the World: Part I - 81

      Legend of the Lone Ranger – 81

      The Comeback Trail – 82

      Mother Lode – 82

      Right is Wrong – 82

      Tron – 82

      Blue Thunder – 83

      A Killer in the Family – 83

      Against All Odds – 84

      The Wild Life – 84

      Cloak and Dagger – 84

      Friday the 13th: The Final Chapter – 84

      Reckless – 84

      Romancing the Stone – 84

      Starman – 84

      Flesh and Blood – 85

      The Spawning – 85

      Silverado -- 85

      Room with a View -- 85

      The Mission - 86

      Power – 86

      Quiet Cool – 86

      Ruthless People – 86

      Short Circuit – 86

      Death Wish 4: The Crackdown – 87

The Hidden – 87
Hot Pursuit – 87
Double Take -- 88
Riding Fast – 88
Shakedown – 88
Sunset – 88
84C MoPic – 89
Batman (with Jack Nicholson) - 89
Major League – 89
Roadhouse – 89

1990s

Deadly Stranger – 90
Downtown – 90
Conagher – 91
Far and Away -- 92
Blood In, Blood Out -- 93
The Hidden II – 93
Robin Hood: Men in Tights – 93
Bound by Honor -- 93
City Slickers II: The Legend of Curly's Gold - 94
Mighty Joe Young – 98
Follow Your Heart – 99

2000s

Gone in 60 Seconds - 2000
Fast and Furious –20 01
Double Take -- 2001
Four Feathers   --2002

TV SERIES
———

Highway Patrol – 1955-59
Cheyenne – 1955-63
Soldiers of Fortune – 1955-57
Sheriff of Cochise – 1956-58
Boots and Saddles – 1957
Man Without a Gun – 1957-59
Sugarfoot – 1957-61
Maverick – 1957-62
Perry Mason – 1957-66
Tales of Wells Fargo – 1957-62
Wagon Train –1957-65
Cimarron City – 1958-60
Lawman – 1958-62
Wanted: Dead or Alive – 1958-61
Adventures in Paradise – 1959-62
The Alaskans – 1959-60
Rawhide – 1959
Andy Griffith Show – 1960-68
Tallahassee 7000 – 1961
Daniel Boone – 1964-70
The Big Valley – 1965-69
Batman – 1966-68
Mission Impossible – 1966-73
Marcus Welby, M.D. –1969-76
McMillan and Wife – 1971-77
Kung Fu – 1972-75
Search – 1972-73
Streets of San Francisco – 1972-77
Kojak – 1973-78
Kolchak: The Night Stalker – 1974-75
The Rockford Files – 1974-80
The Six Million Dollar Man – 1974-78
City of Angels – 1976

Seventh Avenue—1977
Centennial (Mini-series) – 1978
Concrete Cowboy (Pilot) -- 1979
Knots Landing – 1979-93
Magnum: PI – 1980-88
The Fall Guy – 1981-86
Matt Houston – 1982-85
Hardcastle and McCormick – 1983-86
Murder She Wrote – 1984-1996
Spencer: For Hire – 1985-88
X Files – 1993-2003

OTHERS

Sands of Iwo Jima – 1949
Groucho Marx
Three Stooges
Tonight Show with Johnny Carson
Behold Hawaii (IMAX) – 1963

BIBLIOGRAPHY
INFORMATION SOURCES

INTERVIEWS

More than 50 hours of recorded interviews with Ted White

Recorded interview with Ted Alex Bayouth

Recorded interview with Jeri Bayouth

Recorded interview with Michael Bayouth

Recorded interview with Terry Leonard

Recorded interview with Dean Smith

Numerous unrecorded conversations with Ted White

BOOKS and PERIODICALS

Becky Bradley, *American Cultural History: 1950-1959*; Lone Star College, Kingwood Library, 1998.

Greer K. Chesher, *Moviemaking*; Moab, Utah, Canyonlands Natural History Association, 2003.

Kirk Douglas, *I Am Spartacus*; New York, Open Road Integrated Media, 2012.

Roger Ebert, *The Great Movies*, New York, Broadway Books, 2002.

Joel Engel, ed., *Oscar-Winning Screenwriters on Screenwriting*, New York, Hyperion, 2002.

Dwayne Epstein, *Lee Marvin: Point Blank*, Tucson, AZ, Schaffner Press, 2013.

Syd Field, ed., *Four Screenplays*, New York, Bantam Dell Doubleday Publishing, 1994.

James Garner and John Winokur, *The Garner Files: A Memoir*, New York, Simon & Schuster Paperbacks, 2012.

Holly George-Warren, *How Hollywood Invented the Wild West*, Pleasantville, New York, The Reader's Digest Association, Inc., 2002.

William Goldman, *Adventures in the Screen Trade*, New York, Warner Books, Inc., 1983.

William Goldman, *Hype and Glory*, New York, Villard Books, 1990.

Douglas Gomery, *Movie History: A Survey*, Belmont, CA, Wadsworth Publishing Company, 1991.

John R. Hamilton, John Calvin Batchelor, *Thunder in the Dust: Great Shots from the Western Movies*, London, Aurum Press, Ltd., 1997.

Phil Hardy, ed., *The Overlook Film Encyclopedia: The Western*, Woodstock, NY, The Overlook Press, 1991.

Janet Maslin, "Silverado: A Western," *The New York Times*, July 10, 1985.

Gerald Mast, "A Short History of the Movies," The Bobbs-Merrill Company, Inc., Indianapolis, 1976

Jack Nachbar, ed., *Focus on The Western*; Englewood Cliffs, N.J., Prentice-Hall, 1974.

Randy Roberts and Jemes S. Olson, *John Wayne: American*; Lincoln, Neb., University of Nebraska Press, 1995.

Robert Sklar, *Movie-Made America: A Cultural History of American Movies*; New York, Vintage Books, 1994

Neil Summers, *The Unsung Heroes*; Vienna, West *Virginia*, The Old West Shop Publishing, 1996.

Terry Teachout, "The Purest of Pleasures: Rio Bravo," *American Cowboy*, January 2009.

ONLINE SOURCES
(The following Internet sites were consulted)

www.amctv.com
www.bigmoviezone.com
www.b-westerns.com
http://cinemaroll.com
www.cln.org
htty://countrystudies.us
www.crazyaboutTV.com
www.desertusa.com
www.emmytvlegends.org
http://en.wikipedia.org
www. English.Illinois.edu
www.entertainment.howstuffworks.com
www.experts123.com
www.ezinearticles.com
www.fandango.com
www.fiftiesweb.com
www.filmbug.com
www.filmsite.org

www.fridaythe13thfranchise.com
http://fridaythe13th.wikia.com
http://horror.about.com
http://hypertextbook.com/facts/2007/TamaraTamazashvili.shtml
www.imax.com
http://www.imax.com/content/corporate-information
www.imdb.com
https://itunes.apple.com
www.loti.com
http://www.militaryvetshop.com/History/4thMarDiv.html
www.moviefone.com
http://movieline.com
www.movies.yahoo.com
www.newworldencylopedia.org
http://www.patriotfiles.com/index.php?name=Sections&req=viewa
article&artid=2968&page=1
www.pbs.org
http://www.pictureshowman.com/timeline_1950_1960.cfm
www.playbill.com
http://pinterest.com
http://quickstart.clari.net
http://rogerebert.suntimes.com
http://screenwritingfromiowa.wordpress.com/2011/09/07john-
fords-secret-formula/
www.scribd.com
www.seeing-stars.com
http://silverspurawards.eventbrite.com/
http://semper-fi.us/
www.spacedaily.com
www.studymode.com
www.stuntmen.com
www.taurusworldstuntawards.com/index.php?id=33
www.tcm.com
http://thoughteconomics.blogspot.com
www.time.com
http://trove.nla.gov.au
www.tv.com

http://www.vietnamproject.ttu.edu/dd786/fourth.html

www.voanews.com

www.westernclippings.com

www.wikipedia.com

Cast a Giant Shadow

ABOUT THE AUTHOR

In his career Larry K. Meredith has been a newspaperman, a salesman, an advertising and sales promotion writer for a Fortune 500 company, a university administrator and teacher, has owned his own marketing and video production company and has served as the Executive Director of a library district and the Director of the Publishing Certificate program at Western State Colorado University. . He has written hundreds of published essays and newspaper and magazine articles and is the author of the historical novel "This Cursed Valley." He and his wife Alley divide their time between Gunnison and Redstone, Colorado.

Cast a Giant Shadow

CPSIA information can be obtained
at www.ICGtesting.com
Printed in the USA
LVOW07s0040181017
552831LV00023B/814/P